HEROES
and
HUSTLERS,
HARD HATS
and
HOLY MEN

By the same author
Double Vision

HEROES
and
HUSTLERS,
HARD HATS
and
HOLY MEN

INSIDE THE
NEW ISRAEL

ZE'EV CHAFETS

WILLIAM MORROW AND COMPANY, INC.
NEW YORK

For Miri, Michali and Shmuelik

Library of Congress Cataloging-in-Publication Data

Chafets, Ze'ev.
  Heroes and hustlers, hard hats and holy men.

  1. National characteristics, Israeli.   2. Israel—
Social life and customs.   3. Chafetz, Ze'ev.   I. Title.
DS102.95.C43   1986   956.94   85-29680
ISBN 0-688-04337-2

Printed in the United States of America

First Edition

1 2 3 4 5 6 7 8 9 10

BOOK DESIGN BY PATRICE FODERO

Contents

Contents

Author's Note

Books like this one almost invariably begin with a disclaimer. Writing about one's own country is a necessarily frustrating exercise, one that leaves any author feeling humble and a bit apologetic. At the start of *The Italians,* Luigi Barzini put the problem this way: "It is notoriously easier to write about things and people one does not know very well. One has fewer doubts. But to write about one's own country was a tortured enterprise. I knew too much. I saw too many trees. I sometimes could prove one thing or its contrary, with equal ease. I was embarrassed by the exceptions. . . ." To Barzini's confession I can only add—me, too.

In addition to this general difficulty, however, writing about Israel presents special problems. Originally I had intended to render a formal portrait of the country and its people, but I soon realized that it would be impossible. Like a fidgety child, Israel refuses to sit still long enough, and just as important, I found myself fidgeting along with it. What has emerged, therefore, is not a photographic likeness of Israel, but an impressionistic sketch, one that I hope captures the spirit of the country.

The task of writing about Israel is also complicated by the enormous disparity between the country's image, and reality. Outsiders customarily perceive Israel in grandiose terms as the Holy Land, or the mysterious reincarnation of an ancient nation; as an embattled and heroic David, or an overbearing,

7

militaristic Goliath. Admirers and critics alike tend to see and judge Israel in moral, even metaphysical ways that are not usually applied to normal societies.

Yet there is another Israel, a nation of 4 million people who are engaged in routine daily pursuits. They may inhabit a uniquely evocative geography and live in the shadow of great, even inexplicable events, but they are not, themselves, larger than life. Israel is their home, a place to live and work, have fun and raise families—in short, a country like any other.

Heroes and Hustlers, Hard Hats and Holy Men: Inside the New Israel attempts to depict both these Israels, and the tensions between them that shape the country and its people. The early Zionist settlers are a part of the story but so is Shaul Evron, the modern-day pioneer who brought Wild Turkey to Tel Aviv. Menachem Begin, the Jewish Ghostbuster, is here, but so are clubhouse politicians who cut deals in proverbial smoke-filled rooms; Danny Sanderson, the King of Israeli rock 'n' roll; Tikvah, a Hebrew hooker with a rabbinical family tree; Leora and Shimshi Cohen, middle-class revolutionaries from suburban Jerusalem; and dozens of others, famous and obscure, heroic and mundane, who make up Israel today.

This book does not attempt to be a comprehensive history or systematic study of Israel. It has no chapters entitled "The Kibbutz," "The National Economy" or "The Arab Community." These and other such weighty subjects are important, and there are numerous books that deal with them. *Heroes and Hustlers, Hard Hats and Holy Men: Inside the New Israel* has a different purpose—to examine, from a personal perspective, the complexities and complexes of an adopted country which, after twenty years, I still find endlessly fascinating.

One last disclaimer. Unlike most people who write about Israel, I have resisted the temptation to offer The Chafets Plan for Peace in the Middle East. The Arab-Israel conflict is central to Israel's daily life, but I am concerned with it here primarily as it affects individual Israelis, and not with the broader issues of international diplomacy or the merits of mutual grievances. Someday I may inflict my own Middle Eastern polemic on the public, but this is not it.

One technical note: Many of the conversations cited in this book are, in fact, reconstructions from memory. They are, I believe, accurate in substance, although they may differ slightly from the original.

During the course of writing I have received a great deal of help and encouragement. I am indebted to Harry Wall, Dan Syme, Eli Ben-Elissar, Deborah Harris and Leora Nir for reading all or parts of the manuscript and making valuable suggestions. Naturally, I alone am responsible for the views expressed in the final product.

I also want to thank my editor and friend, Bruce Lee. Very simply, without him this book would have not been written.

Introduction:
Ordinary People in Unusual Circumstances

El Al flight 001 leaves New York every night except Friday, nonstop for Israel. Nowadays it lands at Ben Gurion International Airport, but when I first took it, back in August 1967, David Ben Gurion was still very much alive and the airport was known simply as Lod International. Of all the changes that have taken place in Israel since then, that one is probably the easiest to explain.

I was twenty years old when I boarded flight 001, on the way to my junior year of college abroad, at the Hebrew University. Air travel still had a certain magic then, and I found it easy to fantasize while on planes—at thirty thousand feet I could turn even a visit to relatives in Chicago into an urgent diplomatic mission or secret undercover assignment. Now, headed for Israel for the first time, I buckled myself in and proceeded to stage a private twelve-hour film festival.

These movies, all starring me of course, on location in the Holy Land, were unhindered by any real notion of the country I was bound for. In Pontiac, Michigan, where I was born and raised, we belonged to a Stevensonian Reform temple whose primary religious doctrines consisted of "Be a good person," and "Don't forget to say hello to Aunt Mae after services." My knowledge of Israel came primarily from a few Bible stories, *Exodus* (the movie, not the book), casual conversations with Israeli exchange students at the University of Michigan and, of course, images from the recently televised

11

Six Day War. All this amounted to a fairly thin notion of Israel, but it did provide the material for some pretty exciting cerebral cinema.

I closed my eyes and pictured myself wandering through the Galilee, dressed in a flowing white robe. At Michigan I had taken two semesters of Hebrew in preparation for my junior year in Jerusalem. Our textbook had been developed by the American State Department for teaching the language to diplomats, and for some inexplicable reason the first lesson had contained this exchange: *"Eyfo ha' Brooklyn Bar?"* ("Where is the Brooklyn Ice Cream Parlor?"), to which the proper answer was: *"Ha' Brooklyn Bar b'rechov Allenby"* ("The Brooklyn Ice Cream Parlor is on Allenby Street"). Now, here in the Galilee was Joshua at the head of his vast army. Staff in hand he approached me, his most trusted scout. We gave each other the Hebrew handshake—a cross between the Roman centurion grip and "five"—as he fixed me with a piercing stare. *"Eyfo ha' Brooklyn Bar?"* he demanded. *"B'rechov Allenby,"* I answered with easy confidence.

As the plane flew eastward I ran a whole series of such scenes in my head. Me as a pioneer, dressed in simple khaki, working the barren desert; as a bearded young rabbi sitting in a Jerusalem synagogue, surrounded by admiring pupils as I expounded on the Talmud; as a battle-hardened commando charging into Jerusalem to liberate the city to the strains of Ferrante and Teicher's theme from *Exodus*. (I cut Pat Boone out of the soundtrack; after his version of "Tutti Frutti" I had never been able to take him seriously.)

It is not surprising that after twelve hours of daydreaming, interrupted only twice by the first kosher meals I had ever eaten on purpose, I was more than a little psyched up when El Al 001 landed in Israel. As I descended from the plane I barely noticed the brilliant Mediterranean blue of the sky, or the blast of humid August heat. Instead I heard the sound of trumpets and a deep, Ed McMahon-type baritone voice intoning: "He's home. Two thousand years of exile, and the Kid is home at last." When I reached the bottom rung I bent down, closed my eyes for one last dramatic moment and kissed the ground, as I imagined my ancestors must have done when they returned from the Babylonian captivity. Unlike the homeland of my ancestors, however, the ground I kissed was a steaming tarmac that left airplane grease on my knees, palms and the tip of my nose. Several of the ground crew found this hilariously funny, and I walked into the first Jewish airline terminal since the days of the Maccabees feeling more than a little foolish. That experience, like much of what happened in the next few months, taught me a valuable lesson: It's great to be home, but you've still got to keep your eyes open.

Not that I really considered Israel "home." Despite my emotional arrival, I had no intention of settling permanently. I considered myself an American, and it never occurred to me on that day in early August 1967 that I might be anything else. My airborne fantasies were just that, and nothing more. I had never even seen a desert, much less farmed one, never held a weapon in my hands, didn't know the Talmud from the telephone book. I was in Israel on what would later come to be known as a roots trip, but despite my mother's dark premonition that I would never come back from "Asia," as she put it with geographical precision, remaining for more than a year simply wasn't part of the plan.

I came to Jerusalem with romantic and one-dimensional ideas about the country, but they weren't too different from those of most people in the summer of 1967. Israel then seemed to be a shining city on a hill, an almost mythological place inhabited by larger-than-life heroes. Stereotypes flowed from Israel's uniquely evocative geography, its inexplicable rebirth after two millennia, its come-from-behind military triumphs. The Six Day War, with its scriptural battlefields, dashing sabra generals and David-and-Goliath symbolism, burnished this image, making Israel seem, from a distance, more like an epic poem than a real country.

Even from up close it proved to be an exceptional place, especially during that first summer after the war. People sang in the streets; motorists called greetings to passing soldiers; pictures of the nation's leaders hung in every shop. There was a sense of unity and purpose, a recognition that this was a moment of high drama and achievement. The Israelis believed their own legend that summer, saw themselves as others saw them. There was a palpable sense of making not just history, but ancient history; of somehow rewriting a badly written page in the annals of the Jewish people.

During my first few months in Israel I was surprised to find that much of what I had imagined about the people was apparently true. I actually saw poster-perfect Israeli soldiers, tassel-haired blonds who ambled through the streets in boisterous groups, self-confident and unapproachable as varsity football jocks in Ann Arbor. There really were sunburned farmers dressed in blue work shirts and khaki shorts, grizzled pioneers who had defeated malaria, Arab marauders and nature itself to carve fields and villages out of swamp and desert. I saw hollow-cheeked Holocaust survivors with blue tattoos on their arms; bearded, black-robed Chassidic Jews who lived in the narrow alleys of Mea Shearim, a self-imposed ghetto not far from the ancient walls of the old city; hawk-faced Bedouin who wandered the streets of Jerusalem with camels in tow, on the lookout for tourists who wanted their picture taken with a genuine son of the desert. In time I discovered that even the potbellied merchants on Jaffa Street were exotic; the most unprepossessing of them seemed to have fantastic tales about their youthful exploits in the underground, fighting the British and the Arabs on the road to independence. I looked in vain for people without drama in their lives, ordinary people like the ones I had known in Michigan, but there didn't appear to be any. Somehow, everyone seemed special.

The Biblical sites and scenery I had dreamed about were all there, too. I traveled to the Ayalon Valley, rolling and green, where Joshua had once made the sun stand still and which, perversely, reminded me of a well-kept golf course; to the Sea of Galilee, small and calm as a pond, where Jesus had walked on the water and people now water-skied; to the ancient city of Jericho, an oasis set like brilliant red-and-green feathers in the bleak moonscape of the Judaean desert. Coming from Michigan, where visitors are taken to the Detroit Historical Museum to see a genuine replica of a street circa 1890, it was sometimes impossible for me to imagine that I was actually in the presence of The Real Thing, and not a gigantic Biblical theme park.

My midwestern upbringing also left me unprepared for the geography of Israel. I grew up with the feeling of limitless land, land for thousands of miles in every direction. Now, for the first time, I found myself conscious of the pinch of borders. Soon after I arrived I bought a Lambretta, and I was both pleased and disconcerted to find that, even at a leisurely pace, I could drive anywhere and back in a single day. Israelis were constantly telling me about how large the country seemed after the territorial acquisitions of the Six Day War—"Before then, Israel was only seven miles wide," they bragged, and dragged me to hills with a cross-country view to prove it—but to me everything seemed amazingly small, and from time to time I felt a tinge of something like claustrophobia. Sometimes at night I would turn on my transistor and spin the dial, hearing Arabic music and incomprehensible jabbering from neighboring countries. I imagined that they were saying ugly things about the Jews, and it gave me a chill to realize that I had inherited blood enemies who were no farther than a short car-ride away.

There were Arabs in Jerusalem, too, still dazed by the Israeli victory and the hordes of tourists who followed in its wake. One day I visited the Arab market in the old city with an Israeli student who offered to show me where he had fought only a couple of months before. After wandering for an hour or two, we bought some oranges at an open-air stall and sat down to eat them under the awning of a souvenir shop.

As we lounged in the shade, talking, I idly peeled an orange, tossing the skin on the ground. Suddenly an enraged Arab shopkeeper emerged from his store and demanded that I pick up the peels. At first I was embarrassed to have littered so thoughtlessly, and I gathered up the refuse as he watched. Then, in a flash, it dawned on me: This was *my* country, *my* capital city. I tossed the peels back on the street and told the shopkeeper to pick them up himself. He looked at me narrowly, turned on his heel and walked back inside.

My Israeli friend had watched the scene, and I turned to him for approval. Instead he bent over and began picking up the peels himself. "What are you doing that for?" I asked him.

"Because you're a shmuck," he said.

15

The next day I went back to the shop to apologize to the Arab merchant. I explained to him that I was new to the country and had gotten carried away. He accepted my apology without visible emotion, and then tried to sell me some trinkets. I bought a brass Bedouin tea set, paying his first price, which even then I knew was way too high. "Jewish guilt," I thought as I walked out of the store, disgusted with myself for the second time in two days.

During those first few months in Jerusalem I found that I knew very little about Arabs—and not very much more about Jews. On my first weekend in Israel I went hungry because no one had informed me that restaurants and stores would be closed on the sabbath. On Yom Kippur eve I took my Lambretta out for a spin and was stoned by a group of furious orthodox Jews for disturbing the sanctity of the holy day. And on more than one occasion I astonished Israelis with my ignorance of basic facts of Jewish life and customs. In the States I had been considered pretty Jewish by my friends—Jewish enough, for example, to want to spend a year in Israel—but in Israel I suddenly found myself little more than a tourist in what I increasingly wanted to see as my own country.

This realization sent me into a burst of Jewish catch-up. I enrolled in half a dozen courses in Jewish history and philosophy at the Hebrew University, and augmented them with special Talmud studies at a local yeshiva. I became fascinated with the *Fiddler on the Roof* atmosphere of Mea Shearim, where even little children wore white stockings and earlocks and spoke in Yiddish. (I tried to learn the language myself and was bemused to find that in the standard text, early vocabulary words include *Cossack, pogrom,* and *cholera.*)

I was determined that nothing in the Jewish experience be foreign to me. I studied Hebrew with a fanatic concentration and insisted on speaking it, despite my fractured syntax and limited vocabulary. I visited kibbutzim where I picked peaches and ideological arguments—long, tedious discussions of Zionist doctrine that everyone but me seemed to have resolved a generation before. I went to the beach in Tel Aviv to mingle with the Jewish sunbathers, climbed Masada, memorized the words to popular songs, celebrated holidays I had never heard of. And as time went by I became convinced that I wanted to remain and become an Israeli. Whatever that was.

In that first summer I spent countless hours just wandering around Jerusalem, talking to anyone who would talk back. One day I was walking in Kiriat Yovel, a neighborhood not far from the dorm where I lived, when I saw a strange little house draped with dozens of blue-and-white Israeli flags. Even in that season of high patriotism the decoration seemed excessive, and I stopped in front of the house to stare. As I did, the door opened and a little old man appeared on the porch. He was dressed in khaki shorts, from which knobby, gnarled legs protruded, and an old-fashioned tank-top undershirt, and he had a halo of white wispy hair that reminded me of pictures of Ben Gurion. "I was just looking at your house," I said in English. "Come in and have tea," he answered, as if he had been waiting for me all afternoon.

The inside of the small house was unadorned by flags, although there was a picture of Moshe Dayan against a sky-blue background on one of the walls. There were also a number of old photographs in gilt frames, but these were the only decorations in the otherwise spartan living room/dining room/kitchen area where we sat. I introduced myself as an American student, and he responded in accented English learned during the British mandate. We sat at his table, which was covered with a yellowing doily-type tablecloth, and he explained about the flags and about his life in Israel.

Today, eighteen years later, the only thing I can't remember about our conversation is the old man's name. He had come to Palestine from Russia shortly after World War I, and had what I later learned was the standard biography for his generation: kibbutz, a stint with the Mandatory Police, service with the Haganah militia in the War of Independence. His son was killed in that war, he said, and pointed without evident emotion to one of the gilt-framed photographs on the table.

The old man talked about his daughter on a kibbutz in the Galilee, and another daughter in Jerusalem. He had moved to the city, he said, to be near her and his grandchildren. One, a nineteen-year-old, has taken part in the capture of Jerusalem, an event that had inspired him to drape his little house with flags. There was a picture of the grandson, a kid about my age wearing glasses and a beret. "Now he is an officer," the old man said with pride.

We sat at the table for hours. The old man told me stories from the twenties and thirties—about the struggle to revive the Hebrew language, the effort to smuggle illegal immigrants into the country, the hardships of life on the frontier. He obviously relished the opportunity to reminisce, and every time he slowed up I pumped him for more. It was awesome to me that this little old Jewish man, who looked like my grandfather, had done so much, had actually helped change the course of history.

When it was time to go I thanked him. "I'm going to stay here and become an Israeli too," I said. It was a thought I had had since arriving in Jerusalem, but this was the first time I had said it out loud.

"Very good," he said. "We need young people."

"I only hope I've got what it takes to make it here," I said, fishing for approval but meaning it too. "Everybody in this country seems to be some sort of hero."

The old man smiled. "I know," he said. "When I first came here the pioneers of the second *aliyah* seemed like heroes to me. And now, after all these years, my grandson is a paratrooper, another kind of hero. But believe me, young man, we are not really heroes. We are just ordinary people living in unusual circumstances."

In the years since that conversation Israel has gone from a high-spirited adolescent to a brooding, introspective young adult, changing and maturing in ways that would have been hard to imagine in the summer of 1967. And, during that time, I have indeed become an Israeli. Gradually Hebrew has replaced English as my first language. I have served in the army, worked in politics, government, journalism and even show business (as the co-author of the first doo-wop song in two thousand years, a Hebrew version of the Dell Vikings' "Come Go with Me"). I have sired two Jerusalem-born children, been through a divorce and two marriages, paid off

18

a mortgage. Along with other Israelis I have lived through five elections, four-digit inflation, three wars, one peace—and almost seven thousand days in the only country in the world where Jews are on their own. Today, Israel seems less heroic than it did when I first arrived, but then again, as the old man said, perhaps it always was.

PART I

HEROES

1

Horatio Alger vs.
Dick the Bruiser

Chaim Laskov was the original Israeli Horatio Alger hero, the most inspirational rags-to-riches story of his generation. Not that Laskov ever made any money to speak of: He and his peers—at least the best and the brightest of them—weren't concerned with material possessions. They were idealists, the sons of Zionist pioneers, and they exemplified the pioneering values: modesty, self-sacrifice, simplicity and courage. For them, virtue was its own reward.

Laskov was brought to Palestine as an infant, shortly after the end of World War I. His parents were Russian Jews who joined the postwar wave of immigration, known as the Third Aliyah, whose members included a number of Israel's future leaders, such as Golda Meir. The Laskovs settled in Haifa, in a run-down neighborhood by the Mediterranean seashore. In 1929, during the Arab riots that shook the Jewish community in Palestine, Laskov senior was murdered, and ten-year-old Chaim became the man of the family.

Poverty was common among the Jews of Palestine in those days, but few were as poor as the Laskovs. Chaim was forced to go to work to support his family while at the same time continuing his education. He was a brilliant student whose scholastic achievements won him a scholarship to Haifa's prestigious Reali gymnasium. Laskov walked to school with his shoes slung over his shoulder to save the precious leather. As often as not he had to skip lunch. Barefoot and sometimes hungry, he became a teen-age legend in Haifa—an outstanding pupil, a favorite of his teachers and a model for his classmates.

Above all, Chaim Laskov had "values." He was a fervent patriot, a Zionist true believer. When the romantic British captain Orde Wingate formed his famous night raiders to combat Arab marauders in the mid-thirties, young Chaim volunteered and became one of Wingate's prize disciples. At the start of World War II he joined the British Army in order to fight Hitler—and to gain needed military experience for the coming struggle for independence. Laskov served in Italy and each month he saved his army salary; some he sent home to his family, some to the Reali school to repay his scholarship.

Laskov left the British Army as a major and returned to pre-state Palestine, where his military training made him extremely valuable. In the War of Independence he was assigned to command a brigade. He quickly became known as one of the most competent Israeli military leaders, an officer more respected than loved but a man who could get the job done. He became a favorite of the Old Man, David Ben Gurion, who saw in the young warrior all the qualities that the early Zionist visionaries had hoped to instill in their children. Following the war, Ben Gurion persuaded Chaim Laskov to stay on and help build the nation's army.

Laskov's rise was rapid. Within a few years he became a general, went to Oxford for special studies, then returned to Israel to be appointed chief of staff at the age of thirty-eight. He held the job for three years, and when he retired he was still a young man with unlimited opportunities. But Chaim Laskov wasn't interested in making money or living the good life. He had been raised for duty and sacrifice, for public service. He asked for a chance to continue making a contribution to the state, and Ben Gurion agreed, appointing him director general of the newly created Port Authority.

It was in that job that Laskov first encountered Yehoshua Peretz, leader of the Ashdod port's dock workers. Peretz was something out of Laskov's worst nightmare—a burly, prematurely balding twenty-two-year-old stevedore with a flair for self-promotion and an eye for the main chance. Like Laskov, Peretz was a self-made man who had grown up fast.

At the age of twelve he had left his native Morocco and come to Israel alone; as a boy he had known hunger and poverty and loneliness. But that was where the similarities ended. Laskov, a national hero, dressed in the simple khaki of the pioneers; Peretz wore flashy clothes and sported a pinky ring. Laskov knew the Bible almost by heart and could quote great swatches of the classics from memory; Peretz could barely read without moving his lips. Laskov had spent his entire life in the forefront of the military struggle for Jewish independence and security; Peretz served in the army as a cook, although he later bragged that he had been a paratrooper. Laskov lived an exemplary private life, as befitted a son of the puritanical founding fathers; Peretz, who liked to refer to himself last name first, as "Peretz, Yehoshua," as if calling his name off some imaginary honor roll, had two women and didn't care who knew it. At the port of Ashdod, Horatio Alger met Dick the Bruiser.

In 1969, shortly after coming to power in the stevedore's union, Peretz formulated a list of demands and threatened to shut down the port if they weren't met. Laskov asked for a meeting with the young labor leader. Peretz, Yehoshua put on an extra dab of French after-shave, kissed his women good-bye and went off to negotiate.

Laskov's approach was, as usual, direct. What was it exactly that Peretz and his men wanted? Peretz was equally direct—more money and better working conditions. Laskov shook his head and in a fatherly way began to explain the pioneering verities to the younger man. Money, after all, wasn't everything, not even the main thing. And anyway, the workers weren't poor, certainly not as poor as he had been as a boy. Did any of *their* children go to school barefoot? Were any of *them* forced to skip lunch? What did they know of real poverty? As for softer working conditions, certainly they must realize that the whole point of Zionism was to transform and purify Jews through hard physical toil. Work should be regarded as a privilege, not a hardship.

Peretz was unconvinced. He wanted money, not lectures. Laskov grew more emotional. How could the workers even think of striking? he demanded. The port was essential to the national economy, to the well-being and security of the hard-won Jewish state. Peretz and his men had the honor of being stevedores in a Hebrew port in the first independent Jewish nation in two thousand years—and with that honor came responsibility. Laskov was certain that Peretz and his men wouldn't make a mockery of their duty by acting selfishly.

Peretz listened to Laskov impassively, carefully. Then he walked out of the director's office and called a wildcat strike that paralyzed Israeli shipping and sent the country into an uproar. Peretz was a master of manipulating the media, a favorite of reporters, who were fascinated and appalled by the brash upstart. "I'm a labor leader," he told them, "not a rabbinical student. I went in there to talk about money and he made a joke of the whole thing by making a speech about the Macabees." Unspoken was the determination that nobody makes a fool out of Peretz, Yehoshua.

From then on, the port of Ashdod was shot through with dissension and labor disputes. Every move by the director general was thwarted by Peretz, every declaration mocked. Laskov never knew what hit him, what he had done wrong. He hadn't lied to the union leader, certainly hadn't intended to insult him. He had simply spoken to him in the only language he knew, the language of the Zionist pioneers. He had shared with the young man his own vision of the state they were building together, each in his own way. Peretz had shown a lack of idealism and commitment, not to mention "values," by demanding something as unworthy as money.

The dispute simmered for two years, and in the end it was Chaim Laskov—former chief of staff, darling of the founding fathers, the Israeli Horatio Alger—who was forced to resign. Some said it was his own fault for failing to understand Peretz's "mentality"—a common euphemism in those days for what the establishment saw as the primitive ideas and attitudes of the newly arrived Oriental Jews from North Africa and the Middle East. Many pointed to his departure as a victory for the Orientals over the European elite. Others saw it as a personal failure, caused by Laskov's lack of flexibility and diplomacy.

But there was more at issue than a personality clash, or even ethnic tensions. The early Labor Zionist founders had two contradictory and still unresolved dreams. On the one hand they intended to create a socialist utopia, an elite society that would become a moral "Light Unto the Nations." But at the same time they hoped that in this society Jews could become "normal"—*am k'chol ha'amim,* "a nation like any other." Laskov, the idealist, was the son of the first; Peretz, nobody's good example, was the representative of the second. Laskov lived in a Biblical land of heroic expectations, Peretz in a small town in a little Mediterranean country. Laskov felt responsibility for steering the Jewish ship through the stormy seas of history; Peretz wanted only to serve in the crew, putting in his eight hours and then lying on deck for some sun, occasionally tossing a line over the side to catch a few tuna. The conflict between the two approaches was inherent in the Zionist enterprise—and at the port of Ashdod, in the years after the Six Day War, it erupted in a way that has been visible ever since.

The conflict in Ashdod was a signal, a sign that the heroic goals of the pioneers were no longer the universally accepted norms of Israeli society, an early challenge to the assumptions of the founding fathers and their sabra sons. It was, however, by no means a decisive defeat. Israel, after all, was the creation of the pioneer establishment, and that establishment held the country in a tight grip. In the years immediately after the Six Day War there were still giants in the land, men and women who had broken the mold of a hundred ghetto generations, rebelled against the homelessness and helplessness of the Jewish condition and set forth to change the world. The Israel I came to in 1967 was the measure of their success and the basis for their moral authority, an authority that was accepted as the natural order of things by the majority of their fellow citizens. It was they who set the tone for the new nation, their values and attitudes and styles that defined the very essence of Israeliness.

In 1971 Israeli journalist Amos Elon published *The Israelis: Founders and Sons.* The book, which was widely read at home and extravagantly praised abroad, purported to present, in the author's words, "the spirit of the place . . . and what we loosely call the character of a people." At the time, the book was controversial primarily because of its analysis of Israeli attitudes toward the Palestinian Arabs, and even today it offers a good summary of the left's critique of Israeli policy in the conflict with the Arab world. But when it was published, even Elon's detractors paid little attention to what the book did not include. Missing from *The Israelis* were the majority of the Israelis themselves. Elon hardly mentioned Israel's Oriental Jews, roughly 50 percent of the population in 1971. He barely noticed the country's orthodox communities. Menachem Begin's name did not even appear in the index, and the pre-state underground Irgun movement that Begin had led was mentioned only twice. There was no discussion of new immigrant groups, of anyone, in fact, except Israel's "WASPS"—White-Ashkenazi-Sabras with "Protekzia."

In light of the social changes that have taken place in Israel since 1971 it is easy to dismiss Elon's book as an exercise in snobbery—the equivalent of a book on "The Americans" that ignores everyone who arrived after 1776. But the truth is that when it was published, Elon's view seemed so natural that even I—serving at the time in the army—accepted my exclusion from the charmed circle of Israelis as inevitable. It was understood that the country was made up of the "Real Israelis"—and the others.

In a sense this distinction flowed naturally out of the disdain and clannishness that founders always feel toward newcomers. But there was more to it than that. Technically, becoming an Israeli meant acquiring citizenship and residing in the country; but in fact, as defined in those days, it entailed accepting an entire system of values, attitudes and norms—specifically those of the pioneers who had founded the country and established its institutions, styles and ground rules.

These pioneers were still very much in evidence when I first arrived in Israel, men and women in their sixties who presided over the country with a stern paternalism. Superficially they looked like old Jews I had known in America, little white-haired people with Yiddish accents, but this was a comparison that they themselves surely would have rejected. For the ironic fact is that the pioneers who first carved a Jewish state out of the desolate landscape of Palestine were people with a harsh and unbending contempt for "Jewishness" as they understood it.

28

One of the many things I knew nothing about when I first came to Israel was Zionist ideology. For me, the entire matter was straightforward. There were Jews, they had needed a country, and Zionism had provided one. For some reason it had never occurred to me that Israel was an ideological creation, and that the doctrines of Labor Zionism—themselves largely the product of Eastern European thinking—profoundly affected perception and behavior in Israel.

With an ever-diminishing enthusiasm I read the Zionist tracts of the nineteenth and early twentieth centuries. I had the usual American impatience with ideology and I found much of the literature foreign, even bizarre. There were Marxist analyses, full of incomprehensible jargon; political programs that mixed pragmatic calls-to-action with mystical nature worship; heated rebuttals to long-forgotten arguments. More than once it occurred to me that reading this stuff was in itself a form of initiation, like being forced to memorize the names of every past president of a fraternity. Still, as I plowed through it I began to detect some common threads that made certain aspects of present-day Israel more comprehensible.

I learned, for example, that at the heart of Labor Zionist thinking from the beginning had been a basic assumption about the nature of "the Jewish problem." Early political Zionists like Herzl and Pinsker saw anti-Semitism as a Gentile disease and reasoned that a Jewish state would be its only cure. But it was left to their disciples, the young revolutionaries of Eastern Europe who came to Palestine as settlers in the first years of the twentieth century, to add a socialist-naturalist dimension to the dream. They hated not only what the Gentile world had done to the Jews, but what they believed it had caused the Jews to do to themselves. They looked in their mirrors and saw an image not too different from that of the anti-Semitic caricatures—the image of rootless, parasitical and debased people, unable to provide for themselves or to defend their families. They were utopian socialists as well as nationalists, these young revolutionaries, and they saw the solution to the Jewish problem not merely in the attainment of a state but in the transformation of the Jewish character and the purification of the Jewish soul.

The central vehicle for this transformation was to be hard,

productive labor. The prophet of this doctrine was a Russian Jewish mystic named Aaron David Gordon, a frail, Tolstoyesque figure who came to Palestine in 1904, in his mid-forties, to seek redemption through physical toil.

Gordon was much older than most of his fellow pioneers and he became their guru. "The Jewish people has been completely cut off from nature and imprisoned within city walls these two thousand years," he wrote. "We have become accustomed to every form of life, except to a life of labor—of labor done at our own behest and for its own sake." This, Gordon preached, was the central impediment to Jewish spiritual health. "A parasitical people is not a living people," he taught. "Our people can be brought to life only if each one of us recreates himself through labor and a life close to nature."

Gordon's message was embraced by the young socialist pioneers who settled in Palestine. They adopted the cause of redemption through toil with a kind of religious zeal that their ancestors had invested in the study of the holy books. They were, for the most part, rigidly secular in their outlook, hostile to traditional orthodox Judaism, which they saw as an outgrowth of the stultifying conditions of the ghetto. But despite their atheism they were intensely spiritual. They baptized themselves in sweat and sought to become, in the truest sense, born-again Jews.

One aspect of this transformation became the pioneers' close identification with the pre-diaspora history and Hebrew culture of the Bible. At an early stage of the Zionist Movement, some activists who saw the attainment of a state as paramount had proposed achieving it outside of the land of Israel. But the pioneers wouldn't hear of it—they wanted not only a state but a Hebrew state, one that would permit a return to the national roots that Gordon and the other ideologues described. Their Biblical ancestors had been people who "lived close to nature," and here, on the same soil, twenty centuries later, they would resume that way of life as if the intervening millennia had been nothing but a brief interlude. Few of the early pioneers knew Hebrew when they arrived in Palestine. It would have been easier simply to use Yiddish, the language most of them spoke best. But Yiddish belonged to the dark alleys of Europe, and so they forced themselves to recapture Hebrew. It became the fashion to discard ghetto names for new Hebrew ones. The pioneers took to calling themselves Ben-Tsvi (son of a deer) and Avigur (father of a cub) and Allon (oak tree), until the membership rolls of the average kibbutz sounded like a convention of Indian chiefs. It was an effect they cultivated, a primitive return to the ancient land and the ancient ways.

The early pioneers set out to create institutions that would express and fuse their Biblical nostalgia and collectivist ideology. Within a generation, under conditions of extreme hardship, they managed to invent the kibbutz, to set up a central labor organization, to erect the infrastructure of a welfare state—schools, hospitals and clinics, even sports organizations—to create the rudiments of an army, and to establish a viable political system in which the Israel Workers Party (Mapai), led by David Ben Gurion, became the perennial power. These were breathtaking achievements for a handful of young people with no practical experience, but they were accomplished at enormous personal sacrifice. Pioneering was grim, serious work, and the pioneers developed a style of austerity and humorless ideological orthodoxy. They went about their tasks with a kind of frenzied patience, *dunam* after *dunam*, noun after unfamiliar Hebrew verb. They judged each other by the stern code of productivity—to be called "a good worker" was the highest accolade. *Ha'avodah hi hayenu*—"work is our life"—was a common slogan, and it became second nature for these former yeshiva students and Russian radicals. Even today, in their eighties and nineties, the surviving pioneers' compulsion for productivity and their contempt for frivolity endure. Not long ago a group of them was brought to an old-age home in the Galilee town of Afula. Within a week they organized themselves into a work brigade, tore up the director's flower beds and replanted them with vegetables.

From the very beginning of the modern Zionist enterprise it was these pioneers who dominated the scene in Palestine, setting its political priorities, its styles and attitudes. But there were other Jews who came to the country as well. Some were romantics drawn to the drama of the return to the ancestral homeland. Others were victims of persecution who sought a

31

new start in the fledgling Jewish society of Palestine. They were Zionists, but not necessarily socialists, and they were unmoved by the flinty Hebrew Calvinism of the pioneers. The devoutly orthodox among them gravitated to the ancient holy cities of the Land of Israel: Jerusalem, Hebron, Safed and Tiberias. Others, neither orthodox nor pioneers, sought another alternative.

In 1909 a small group of men founded Tel Aviv on the sand dunes of the Mediterranean shore, next to the ancient port city of Jaffa. Tel Aviv was the first Hebrew city to be built in two thousand years, and, like everything else in those days, it had a serious purpose: to serve as a kind of capital for the outlying settlements. But as Tel Aviv grew and expanded in the twenties and early thirties, it took on a relative urbanity and even a hesitant gaiety that many of the pioneers found reactionary and decadent. They felt contempt for the shopkeepers and other members of the bourgeoisie who provided services, regarding them narrowly as examples of the nonproductive class that the Zionist experiment intended to render obsolete. The pioneers decried the coffeehouses and literary discussions of Tel Aviv, its Purim festival with its floats and beauty queens, the casino that hung out over the lip of the Mediterranean shoreline like a dandy's moustache. For them, Tel Aviv represented all that was wrong with the Jewish soul, bright neon poised against the hard flame that burned in their stark collective settlements.

The competition between the attractions of the city and the harsh austerity of the countryside came to a crashing end with the start of World War II. Within a single decade 6 million Jews were murdered in Europe, the British were forced out of Palestine, and the Jews fought and won their first war in two millennia. The dream of a Jewish state had come true, but there were almost insurmountable challenges still to be faced. Hundreds of thousands of refugees from Europe and the Middle East flooded into the country and had to be absorbed. National institutions and organs of government had to be created.

It was the most eventful decade in modern Jewish history, a time in which every ounce of the pioneers' determination and fanaticism was needed, a period when the very notion of personal gain, self-expression or undue frivolity seemed unworthy to the point of sacrilege. Tel Aviv became, in those days, what it had been meant to be from the start—the provisional capital of the Hebrew workers' state, a functional and drab administrative and service center for the new nation.

From the very outset, the pioneers, now in their fifties and sixties, were in total control of the new state. The vehicle for this control was Mapai, the Israel Workers Party led by David Ben Gurion. The tasks they faced in establishing and governing the new nation would have been formidable in any case, but they were made especially daunting by the ambition of the Mapai leaders to transform the immigrants into New Jewish Men and Women.

During the pre-state period, the 650,000 Jews in Palestine had constituted an elite community. Through a process of self-selection they were mostly people who had chosen Zionism. Many were pioneers but even the urban middle class was well aware of, and heavily influenced by, the doctrines and styles of Labor Zionism. But the new immigrants from Europe and the Arab world were a different proposition. The Europeans were shattered by the effects of the war. Few of them were Zionists in any but the broadest sense, and many had no notion of the pioneer ideology that held sway in Israel. They came simply because they had no place else to go. The Oriental immigrants came out of fear of their Arab neighbors, or because of religious sentiment. The vast majority of them were emotional, not ideological, Zionists.

Faced with this mass of uninitiated newcomers, the born-again Mapai leaders set about an audacious undertaking: to transform them—or at least their children—into Real Israelis. The entire country became a laboratory for turning diaspora dross into Israeli gold, with the pioneer veterans and their sabra sons serving as the alchemists. This was achieved through a system of centralized government control unparalleled outside the communist world.

The authorities in Jerusalem effectively decided everything from manners and morals to the price of fish in the market. The government controlled more than 90 percent of the land and built cities, towns and villages according to its master plan. It constructed most of the country's housing and arbitrarily assigned people to apartments. The government was Israel's largest employer (and the Histadrut Labor Federation, also controlled by Mapai, the second largest), which meant that the party leaders could determine pretty much who would work, at what and where. In addition, Mapai controlled the Jewish Agency, thus presiding over fund-raising activities abroad and Israel's relations with the diaspora.

The Ministry of Education set up and supervised the national curriculum, which turned the doctrine of Labor Zionism into a kind of official national ideology. The emphasis in school was on good citizenship, patriotism and the acquisition of practical skills useful in state-building. The educational system was thoroughly elitist, with only a minority of pupils going on to academic high schools while the majority studied a trade or dropped out altogether sometime after the eighth grade.

Central control extended beyond economic, educational and social policy, however. The government assumed responsibility for the national ambience as well. Public committees were established to approve or censor films, plays and other forms of entertainment. In 1965, a proposal to bring the Beatles to Israel was vetoed by such a committee in language reminiscent of the anti-Little Richard diatribes of the Memphis city council in the mid-fifties.

The government also controlled the airwaves, running the national radio out of the Prime Minister's Office. It provided a rich fare of classical music, patriotic songs, interviews with government officials, Zionist speeches and morale-boosting talk shows consisting mostly of sabra heroes of the War of Independence nostalgically recalling their exploits while the rest of the country, presumably, listened admiringly.

When I got to Israel, the basic elements of this system were already in place. I had never encountered anything remotely like this kind of government control. I was astonished, for example, to find that Israel had no television. For me, the absence of TV was disorienting, as if some vital natural element was missing, and I found the reason for it somewhat chilling. The government, it seemed, considered television a bad influence and, until 1968, simply refused to allow it. Even when television was finally introduced, the Mapai leaders saw to it that its broadcast day would end at 11:00 P.M., to make sure that workers didn't stay up till all hours of the night.

Many of the pioneer fathers were cultured, sophisticated people, but they had little interest in instilling such characteristics in the younger generation. A favorite parable told of a mathematician (or concert pianist or professor) who had abandoned his sterile pursuits in order to become a farmer, or to do physical labor. This was the Zionist Ideal. Israeliness well into the sixties was synonymous with parochialism and self-denial. An interest in frivolous things—gracious architecture, fine food, flowery manners or simply having a good time for its own sake—was treated with sour disdain.

The puritan ethic was everywhere. Teen-agers were expected to join a youth movement, where they were introduced to the values and verities of the pioneer ethos. In the Scouts, for example, girls were periodically checked to make sure that their skirts weren't getting too tight (at least forty centimeters—the width of two standard-sized floor tiles—was the minimum stretch). Boy-girl parties were discouraged, dancing (except for folk dancing) was frowned upon, and the young people who sat in the coffeehouses of Tel Aviv's Dizengoff Street were denounced by oldtimers as nihilistic idlers, members of an "espresso generation" awash in a sea of caffeinated debauchery.

In the fifties and sixties the needs of nation-building took precedence over personal preferences, sometimes in ways that seemed rather cruel. This was brought home to me for the first time by a physics student named Yisrael who lived next door to me in the student dorms at the Hebrew University. Yisrael was a sabra, born in Beersheba, both the product and the exponent of the Labor Zionist doctrines that had shaped his generation. As we became friendly he took me under his wing, often explaining the intricacies of Israeli society. We must have had a dozen conversations during my first months in the country, but the one I remember best was when he informed me that I was excellent "human material."

This phrase, as Yisrael explained it, stood for a system of human quality control, in which each group of Jews was assigned a collective value. Romanians were "healthy but untrustworthy," Yemenites "hard-working but primitive" and so on. These evaluations were apparently self-evident (and, as I later learned, almost universally accepted among the sabra elite) and, as presented by Yisrael, they seemed as absolute as the elements on the periodic table. He was prepared to concede that there might be variations and exceptions within each group, but these were essentially irrelevant; what mattered was that the various communities could be classified, and that each constituted a type of human clay that could be molded with lesser or greater difficulty into building blocks for the new country.

There were, of course, objective limitations to this process, especially for those who, like me, were members of what Yisrael referred to as "the generation of the desert." Like "human material," it was a phrase I didn't know, but Yisrael, who hadn't been inside a synagogue since his bar mitzvah, explained that it was taken from an old rabbinic story.

"The rabbis asked each other why Moses led the children of Egypt through the desert for forty years instead of taking them directly to the promised land," he said. "After all, Moses must have known how to reach the Land of Israel. But if you remember the Bible, as soon as the Hebrews left Egypt they started to moan and groan about life in the desert. 'Maybe we were slaves, but at least we had food and a place to sleep'—that kind of thing. Well, according to the rabbis, Moses realized that the people still had a slave mentality, that they weren't ready yet for freedom. And so he led them through the desert for forty years, until they died off and a new generation, born in freedom, emerged. It's the same now," he concluded grandly, "and the immigrants are the generation of the desert."

At the time, I had already decided to remain in Israel, and this story struck me as more than a little depressing. Fresh off the plane from America in its mid-sixties explosion of ego and individualism, I found it almost impossible to regard myself as material with a predetermined value to be used by some master builder; or to imagine that, at twenty, my primary function would be to sire some free Hebrews. But strangely, it never occurred to me to doubt that Yisrael's view was the correct one. In those days, Israel was in the grip of High Certitude.

America was a society of essay questions, or at least multiple choice, but Israel after the Six Day War was strictly "true or false." During the next few years I heard the phrases *human material* and *generation of the desert* again and again, and in time I came to realize that they were at the very heart of the sabra elite's approach to outsiders.

Yisrael was one of the kindest people I have ever met, and he saw that the doctrines he explained to me were a problem. "I know that it seems unfair," he told me, "but that's how it is. And you're lucky, *habibi*. Americans are the very best material. If anyone can become one of us, you can."

It is a measure of the prestige and authority of the establishment that this approach was, for many years, virtually unquestioned. Nor was it meant unkindly. The Zionist fathers acted with generosity in throwing open the gates of the country at a time when self-interest might well have dictated a period of consolidation without the burden of absorbing almost a million destitute immigrants. And clearly, this influx, coupled with the burdens of state-building, had required a firm hand—someone had to teach the newcomers Hebrew, provide them with housing and jobs in an extremely meager economy, and educate them for life in a socialist democracy. It had fallen to the veteran leadership to do these things, and if they had acted with paternalistic condescension, their motives had been essentially benevolent.

Certainly this is the way the nation's leaders saw themselves. They had made enormous personal sacrifices to achieve a state. They were socialists, trained to view society in collective terms, and Zionists with a sense of responsibility toward Jews everywhere. Naturally they expected the immigrants who arrived after 1948 to make some sacrifices as well, to work at shedding the psychological baggage they had brought from the diaspora. In return they would be rewarded, as the pioneers themselves had been, by becoming, or watching their children become, New Jewish Men and Women.

Besides, the success of the pioneer establishment was undeniable. Simply put, these people knew what they were doing; their way worked. This seemed especially true in the years after the Six Day War. The white-maned revolutionaries produced a generation of Hebrew warriors, personified by the golden Moshe Dayan, and in 1967 this generation had won an almost mythical victory over Israel's enemies. Who could doubt in those self-confident times that the country was on the right course, that individual sacrifices were being repaid in self-respect, security and economic well-being?

And yet, at the very apogee of their success, at the moment of the highest High Certitude, subterranean forces of resistance and change began to bubble. The post-Six Day War period opened new vistas, stirred dormant ambitions and resentments. It would be a generation at least before the Arab world could mount another military challenge—Dayan himself had said so—and people began to think about themselves and their personal goals. The confrontation between Yehoshua Peretz and Chaim Laskov at the port of Ashdod was only the tip of an iceberg. The heroic era of the pioneers began drawing to an end after 1967. Quietly, gradually, Israel began entering a new phase. From an elite society it was becoming a real country—*am k'chol ha'amim,* "a nation like any other." Like most changes of this kind, it needed a catalyst; and that catalyst arrived, with sudden and shocking force, on Yom Kippur day, 1973.

2

A New Kind of Hero

When the Yom Kippur War broke out, the country was figuratively asleep, and I literally was. At about 2:00 P.M. I was blasted out of a dream by the air-raid siren next to our apartment building. On any other day I might have thought it was a test; but on Yom Kippur, when even the traffic lights are turned off and the radio is silenced out of respect for the sanctity of the holy day, it was clear that nobody was conducting a drill.

Within a minute of the siren blast the telephone began to ring. Friends called to hear what I knew and to pass along their own scanty information. Meanwhile I sent my wife and daughter downstairs to the air-raid shelter. Neighbors were already sweeping it out and stocking it with preserves and jerry cans full of drinking water. In the midst of all this activity, men were giving last-minute instructions to their wives before collecting their gear and reporting to their reserve units. Despite the shock of the invasion, no one seemed unduly worried. Everyone assumed that the Arabs were in for the beating of their lives, and people wondered aloud at their irrationality in taking on Israel.

I was as confident as everyone else that this war would be a repeat of the smashing victory of 1967. By this time I had been in Israel for six years, and I had thoroughly absorbed the conventional wisdom of the Era of High Certitude. Less than a year earlier I had completed my national military service, and I had yet to be assigned to a reserve unit, but I had no intention of being left out of the action. I called my former commander and told him I was on my way, got my uniform out of the closet, and headed for my old base, only about forty minutes from home.

There wasn't much to do when I got there. Although the base was in the middle of the West Bank, the area was quiet, and the closest border—with Jordan—remained peaceful. We spent most of our time speculating about what had gotten into the Arabs and what the Israeli army would do to them.

It was a strange feeling, being in the army during wartime. I thought back on the first time, more than three years earlier, that I had put on an Israeli uniform. I had looked forward to joining the army ever since I had decided to stay in the country; military service was the one irreducible condition for becoming, if not a Real Israeli, then at least a member of the community in good standing. Besides, I had the idea that the mere act of serving in the army would transform me, somehow link me up with the heroes of the Six Day War and Israel's other military triumphs.

That first day in basic training we were issued musty kit bags stuffed like sausages with essential gear, and green fatigues which, in my case, were a size too small. I was twenty-three and married, older than the other recruits, who were all in their late teens, but I was just as excited as they when, after changing into our uniforms, we emerged from our tents and blinked at each other shyly in the August glare. A tough-looking master sergeant with a handlebar moustache hollered us into formation, just like in the movies, and then stood, hands on hips, regarding us for a long moment.

"Attention!" he yelled, and we straightened our backs. "Do you know what you look like?" he screamed. No one answered, of course, so he told us. "Shleppers! You look like a collection of shleppers! But we're going to turn you shleppers into Israeli soldiers. . . ." As the tirade continued, I struggled to keep a straight face. "Shlepper" was what my grandmother used to call me when I came in with dirt on my clothes as a kid. And here was this brutish platoon leader, right out of Central Casting, flannel-mouthing us in Yiddish. What could be cuter, I thought, and suddenly, despite the uniform and the unfamiliar setting, I felt very secure. I wasn't in *the* army; I was in *my* army—and for the first time since coming to Israel I felt as though I really belonged.

Still, basic training proved to be less uplifting than I had imagined. For one thing, my Hebrew was still shaky, a fact the instructors exploited as a pedagogic device. During training they would shout, "Chafets, do you understand?" and when I answered in the affirmative they would turn to the platoon and say, "If Chafets understands, everybody understands." They took a special pleasure in this because I was the only college graduate in the group—in fact, probably the only one on the base.

I reacted to my dummy status with small acts of rebellion that got me more than my share of KP—long dishwashing sessions with a bearded religious officer peering over my shoulder to make sure I didn't mix up the milk and meat dishes. During these details I met Israelis from strata of society I hadn't had much to do with at the Hebrew University.

One day in the kitchen a group of us got to talking about our hometowns. One soldier was from Haifa, as I recall it, and another from Tel Aviv. The guy next to me said that he was from Jerusalem, and I said that I was, too. He slapped my back with a soapy hand in a gesture of civic solidarity. "You can't even compare Haifa or Tel Aviv to Jerusalem!" he crowed. "Jerusalem is the greatest city in the world—isn't that right?" I nodded in affirmation, warmed by the thought that even a greaser like him wasn't indifferent to the meaning of living in the City of David. I was about to say something about the special spiritual quality of the city but my neighbor wasn't finished. "Jerusalem is number one," he said. "One Jerusalemite can stomp three or four Tel Avivis—am I right or not! Jerusalem guys are the toughest guys there are!" I tried to look tough myself, but it was an aspect of life in the holy city that I had never considered before.

Not all my romantic notions were smashed in the army. I could still choke up just standing on parade with the flag waving in the breeze, or watching the orthodox soldiers put on prayer shawls and form a group for morning services in the field. But there were plenty of times when the thrill of being in the Jewish Army was blunted by the drudgery of being in

41

the army, period. I especially hated the morning runs that were scheduled for 5:00 A.M., and after the first few days I could only psych myself up for them by playing announcer. All during basic training I slogged through those runs dressed in an Israeli uniform and carrying an Israeli weapon and muttering under my breath: "He's at the five, he's at the ten, he's breaking into the open. . . ."

The war of attrition that had been going on then against Egypt across the Suez Canal ended while we were in basic training. No one knew how long the cease-fire would last, and we were sent down to the canal to build fortifications against the event of renewed fighting. Naturally we were excited to be heading into what had been, and might well again become, a battle zone, and our platoon rode into the Sinai singing and chattering happily. It wasn't until we approached the canal that it occurred to me that we were going someplace dangerous.

"Nothing to worry about, though!" I told myself. "If anything happens, the army will be there to take care of it!" Suddenly I realized that we *were* the army. I looked at the other kids on the bus, none of whom impressed me as the supermen of the Six Day War victory albums, and wondered for the first time if we had been that good, or if the Arabs had been that bad.

At the canal I got my first glimpse of Egyptian soldiers. The waterway is only about a hundred yards wide, and they were clearly visible on the other side. On the first morning we were there, I climbed up on a sandbank and watched a small group, dressed in sand-colored uniforms, working on their own fortifications. It was my first view of The Enemy, and I was trying to absorb it when one of them turned on a radio and I heard the strains of Mitch Ryder and the Detroit Wheels singing "Devil in a Blue Dress." One of the Egyptians began dancing around and when he looked across the canal he saw me and waved. I waved back, put down my rifle and did a couple of Temptations moves for his benefit. "Moshe Dayan's mother is a whore," he yelled in Arabic, but I wasn't offended. I had made contact with the Other Side, and besides, the music made me homesick for Michigan.

Now, three years later, with a war raging, I tried to picture the scene at the canal. I wondered if the Mitch Ryder fan was still over there. It didn't occur to me at the time that he might be on our side of the waterway.

It wasn't until several days later that the country realized that the Syrian and Egyptian forces had succeeded in breaching our lines. On the first day of the war the chief of staff appeared on television and confidently told the public that the Israeli Army would "break the bones" of the Arab invaders. It was only a few days later that Prime Minister Golda Meir dispatched General Aharon Yariv, former head of military intelligence and a man of outstanding credibility, to a televised news conference in which he made it clear that there would be no repeat of the 1967 romp.

Yariv's appearance on television shocked the country, but the most symbolic and memorable TV interview of the war was with a simple soldier named Benny Massas.

Massas was sitting on a hill, smoking a cigarette, when the correspondent from Israel television found him. He wore a wool stocking cap and his uniform was filthy. In the background was the towering snowcapped peak of Mount Hermon, on the Golan Heights.

With his stocking cap and his three-day growth of beard, Benny Massas looked like what he had been only a few days earlier, before he had been called into the reserves—a fisherman from the Galilee town of Tiberias. Now he was an infantryman who had just fought in one of the bloodiest battles of the war—the recapture of the Mount Hermon fortress from the Syrian Army—and the TV man wanted to know how he felt.

Benny looked up at the extended microphone with a blank expression. "How do I feel? Tired, *habibi*, tired."

"Do you know what you and your friends have accomplished here?"

Benny paused for a long moment. "Yeah, we took the hill."

The correspondent seemed at a loss for the next question. "What did they tell you about your mission?" he finally asked.

"They told us it was important. They said that it was the

eyes of the country up here." Massas's attitude made it clear
that he had taken their word for it, but that it didn't matter
much. He had fought a battle. Some of his friends were dead,
others wounded. You could see it all in his face.

It was a small scene from the nightmare, the worst war that
Israel had fought for a generation, but there was something
about it that captured the attention and the imagination of the
entire country. Overnight, Benny Massas became media famous, and his phrase—"the eyes of the country"—was re-
peated from one end of Israel to the other. Fifty years before,
not far from Mount Hermon, the great Jewish hero Yoseph
Trumpeldor had fallen in battle defending the settlement of
Tel Hai. Trumpeldor's last words, since taught to every Israeli
schoolchild, had been: "It's good to die for our country."
Those had been the right words then; but half a century had
passed and Benny Massas, the son of immigrants, the fisherman from Galilee, had the phrase for the seventies—a statement of fact, not a battle cry. He was an infantryman, a
grunt. To him Trumpeldor was a street name. They had told
him that the battle was important, and he had fought his way
up the hill. He was tired. There was nothing more to say.

The war was not supposed to have happened in the first
place. Moshe Dayan and the generals had assured the country
that it would not, and in the Era of High Certitude, that was
enough, the right answer on the true-or-false quiz. Now
Dayan—the sabra's sabra, symbol of the heroic Israel—visited the Syrian front. He was appalled by what he saw, and
uncertain if the still only partially mobilized army could hold
the advancing Arab forces. Dayan reached Prime Minister
Golda Meir and informed her of the situation. "The Third
Temple is in danger" was his grandiose phrase.

Dayan was not the only one to lose his poise during the
war. With the fighting still going on, general officers who had
emerged from the Six Day War as the greatest warriors since
King David suddenly began squabbling among themselves,
looking for scapegoats. The commander of the Egyptian front
was unceremoniously relieved in the midst of the fighting.
Former Army Chief of Staff Chaim Bar Lev was blamed by
Ariel Sharon for having built a worthless defense line along
the canal. One of Sharon's fellow divisional commanders ac-

cused him of failing to provide promised reserve troops and thus costing Israeli lives. The head of military intelligence was roundly condemned. The Yom Kippur War put an end to the myth of the infallible Israeli general and dealt a blow to the prestige of military figures that continues today.

The politicians seemed just as confused as the military. Golda Meir, the quintessential Zionist earth mother, appeared as a dispirited and ineffective old lady. She and her colleagues in the Cabinet were unable to rally the country or to provide it with any sense of leadership.

In the vacuum created by the squabbling and the confusion, Yom Kippur became the war of the little guys. No general—with the controversial exception of Ariel Sharon—emerged as a hero. The heroes were the privates and sergeants and junior officers—most of them civilian reservists—who stopped the Arab advance on the Syrian and Egyptian fronts. When the fighting ended and people had a chance to look around, they realized that they had been alone, and that the fathers and mothers and glorious big brothers of the pioneer elite had failed, for the first time, to provide any inspiration or leadership.

The reaction to this discovery was emotional and highly charged. The government set up a commission of inquiry which placed blame on the general staff of the army. The chief of staff and the head of military intelligence resigned in disgrace. But the public was unappeased. Protesters, many of them veterans of the war, stood outside the Prime Minister's Office day after day, demanding Golda's resignation. Pickets bearing signs inscribed MURDERER dogged Moshe Dayan. These had been more than political leaders; they had been demigods, symbols of the New Jew. But the Yom Kippur War broke the spell of two generations of pioneer heroes in two weeks.

Golda Meir and her colleagues held on for a few months, but the war made it impossible for them to continue. In the spring of 1974 she announced her retirement, taking Moshe Dayan with her into political oblivion. By this time the country was in a deep postwar funk. Three thousand soldiers had died—an enormous number for a nation of less than four million—and the almost manic self-confidence of the post-Six

Day War period was replaced by self-doubt, pessimism and fear. The Arabs had demonstrated a military competence that no one had dreamed of; and worse, a political and economic unity that enabled them to pull off an oil scare in the West. Israel's economy was a shambles, with carless days and darkened store windows to save energy and, for the first time, serious inflation. Meanwhile, billions of dollars were pouring into Arab coffers. For the first time since 1967, people began to feel that time might not be on Israel's side.

When Golda resigned, Itzhak Rabin was selected by the Labor Party's central committee to replace her. The choice was widely heralded as a historic one—the first Israeli-born premier, the changing of the guard and so on. Rabin, from a distance, seemed to have all the best qualities of the sabra elite: modesty, honesty, a heroic war record (including his service as chief of staff during the Six Day War) and a no-nonsense approach to problem solving. On closer inspection, however, he proved a disastrous choice. He was introspective and painfully shy, unable to get along with his fellow Cabinet ministers (especially Defense Minister Shimon Peres) and generally incapable of inspiring the country or providing solutions for its economic and social problems.

Doubts about Rabin surfaced even before his term began. Shortly before the Labor party was due to make its choice of a successor to Golda, Ezer Weizman, Rabin's second-in-command during the Six Day War, made public the fact that Rabin had suffered a breakdown on the eve of the 1967 conflict. According to Weizman, Rabin had fallen into a deep depression and had offered to turn command over to him. Rabin's version of the story was somewhat different, of course—he had been exhausted, taken a day off to rest, and then come back to the job. But there was more than a little truth to Weizman's story, and it had the effect of tarnishing the Prime Minister at the start of his incumbency.

Once Rabin took office, things got worse. Asher Yadlin, the son of one of the best-known pioneer families and a man with impeccable party credentials, was nominated by Rabin to serve as governor of the Bank of Israel—until it emerged that he had stolen millions, and he went to prison. Avraham Ofer, Israel's housing minister and another member in good standing of the elite, was implicated in a scandal and found dead by his own hand in his car on a lonely stretch of beach near Tel Aviv. For two generations the Labor Zionists had ruled on the basis of their moral authority; now, in the mid-seventies, it all seemed to be unraveling. The younger generation of sabra leaders appeared to be a collection of squabbling generals, incompetent administrators and venal clubhouse pols. The skepticism that followed the Yom Kippur War deepened, and people began publicly questioning many of the most cherished verities of the Era of High Certitude, including the natural right of the Labor party to govern. An election was coming up, and there was heresy in the air.

One night in early 1977, only a couple of months before the scheduled election, Maccabi Tel Aviv, Israel's basketball champions, beat the Russian team in the European Cup Series. The victory set off a wave of celebration in Israel. Tens of thousands of fans flooded the streets, pouring flat domestic champagne over each other and jumping into the fountain in front of the Tel Aviv city hall. While the celebration was in full swing, Prime Minister Rabin appeared on television to deliver a special message to the nation. A few days earlier *Ha'aretz,* Israel's leading morning newspaper, had revealed that the Rabins had an illegal American bank account. It was a relatively minor infraction, but Rabin, who had been in the American capital as Israel's ambassador during Watergate, understood the kind of heat he would have to take, especially after the Yadlin and Ofer affairs. He announced on TV that he was resigning as head of the Labor party's ticket in the upcoming election; his sucessor as head of the party would be his despised rival, Shimon Peres.

While Rabin was making his announcement, the basketball celebration raged through the streets. In the midst of all this excitement, a friend of mine went out to the airport to pick up an American cousin. On the drive back into town the two of them discussed the news of Rabin's resignation, and its probable impact on the political scene. When they reached Tel Aviv the American looked around at the thousands of revelers in astonishment. "Jesus," he said to his cousin, "I knew he was unpopular but I didn't think he was *that* unpopular."

He was, though. They all were in 1977. After the Yom Kippur War the government had tried to sell the public on the slogan "We're all responsible"—a novel notion in a country run by a tiny, central elite. For decades the people had abdicated any real responsibility, preferring to rely on the judgment and leadership of the pioneer establishment and their sons. But the war had let a genie out of the bottle. For decades the pioneers had seemed larger than life, and had fostered great expectations. In 1973 these expectations had been disappointed—and now, four years later, the pioneer would have to pay.

3

The Revolt of the Jews

One day, as the 1977 political campaign neared its conclusion,
I took a cab from my office in Likud headquarters on Tel
Aviv's King George Street over to the television studio in
nearby Givataim.* I got in the front seat, Israeli style, next to
the driver, a fiftyish man with a potbelly and a salt-and-pep-
per moustache, turned down the radio and asked what people
in politics always ask cab drivers in an election year. Who did
he think was going to win?

"Whaddya mean, who? We are, *habibi*. It's in the bag this
time."

"And who's 'we'?"

He looked at me for a long moment, as if I were a moron.
"The Likud, of course. Weizman. Those Labor turds don't
stand a chance against Weizman."

I was intrigued by the answer. Not the Likud part—that
year the cabbies were all voting Likud. But usually they
evoked the name of Menachem Begin, not Ezer Weizman. Of
course Begin was still in the hospital recovering from a massive heart attack, and Weizman, as campaign chief, was running the show and had been highly visible in recent weeks.
Still, it was unusual to hear his name mentioned in the cab-

---

*The Likud is an electoral bloc whose main components are the Herut
party, founded by Menachem Begin, and the Liberal party. Today's Labor
party is an outgrowth of Ben Gurion's Mapai.

bie's almost reverent tone. "What's so great about Ezer Weizman?" I demanded.

"Listen to this, *habibi,*" he chortled. "The other day I'm standing at a light, Dizengoff corner of King George, and I hear this horn. I look around to see who's the idiot that's honking, and right next to me I see this big car with Weizman sitting in front. He goes like this with his hand for me to roll down my window, and I roll it down and he says to me, 'Hey, how old are you?' 'Fifty one,' I tell him. He says, 'Can you still get a hard-on?' and I tell him, 'Of course I can still get a hard-on.' 'Okay,' he says, 'then on May seventeenth I want you to get a hard-on and take it to the polls with you and fuck the Labor party with it.' Ya, *habibi,*" the driver laughed. "'Fuck the Labor party with it.' I can't wait!"

In its own way the election of 1977 was as much a watershed as the Yom Kippur War. For thirty years the Labor party had ruled Israel, winning eight straight national elections in the process. But on May 17, 1977, the country went to the polls and did just what Ezer Weizman had suggested. On that day, elections in Israel became, for the first time, not a ceremony of ratification but the vehicle for change.

It was a time of great drama, not only for the country but for me personally. I was in politics that year as director of the information department of the Liberal party, one of the two major partners in the Likud. If the heroic age of the pioneers died in 1973, it was officially buried four years later: and I was, in a manner of speaking, one of the gravediggers.

My association with the Liberal party had begun two years earlier, in 1975. Since the Yom Kippur War I had been working as a writer for the Foreign Ministry, churning out brochures and position papers with only modest success. One day my editor, an octogenarian former Oxford don, informed me that my work seemed to be improving. "You write English almost as though it were your mother tongue" was how he put it. It was the kind of compliment calculated to make anyone start thinking about a new job, and so when I saw an ad in the paper that read, "Public Institution in Tel Aviv seeks experienced information officer," I clipped it out and put it on my desk. The ad gave no address, just a post office box number.

After a day or two, in a what-the-hell mood, I sent off a copy of my curriculum vitae to the mysterious P.O.B.

A week or so later I got a call from the Liberal party asking me to come in for an interview. To say I knew almost nothing about the party would be an understatement. I was aware that it was an outgrowth of the General Zionist Movement, whose supporters were mostly middle-class nonsocialists from Central Europe. I knew that it was aligned with Menachem Begin's Herut party, and was one of the two main components of the Likud. But I would have been hard-pressed to name a single politician associated with the Liberals, and I had no idea what, if any, policies they favored. Clearly the job of information director for such an obscure party would be a considerable challenge, and when they offered it, I accepted. Mostly I was curious to see how politics in Israel operated from the inside, to get a firsthand look at what made the system run. At the time I had no notion of ever being associated with a winner—in 1975 the idea that Labor might lose an election seemed ridiculous.

On my first day at work I learned an important lesson— that parties in perennial opposition don't have much work to do. My boss, Liberal Secretary-General Avraham Sharir, gave me a cup of coffee and informed me that I would be the party's "think tank." What did that entail, exactly? I wondered. "Well, just go upstairs to the room we've assigned you and, ah, think."

"Okay" I told him. "I'll come down later and let you know what I've thought about."

"Fine" said Sharir. "You do that."

At first my thinking lacked a certain direction, but I soon became friendly with a colleague who, while as idle as I, seemed to have an excellent grasp of the essential principles of Liberal doctrine. "We are for free enterprise," he told me. "We strongly support compulsory labor arbitration. We believe in a separation of synagogue and state. Our foreign policy is anything Menachem Begin says it is. Our heroes are The Late Sapir and Bernstein of Blessed Memory. They were the founders of the party, I think, and their pictures are on the wall in the auditorium. That's a very important point

51

around here, getting their titles right. The Late Sapir and Bernstein of Blessed Memory, never the other way around. I think the titles were agreed on in advance in a coalition agreement."

Coalition agreements were, as I came to find out, a matter of supreme importance in the Liberal party, whose members were forever grouping themselves into warring factions and temporary alliances. They were a relentlessly middle-class group of men in their forties and fifties. Despite the Liberals' capitalist pretensions, the real action and the real money were in the Labor party; these people were mostly small businessmen, lawyers on the make, professors with eccentric views, Rotarians and Masons, and a handful of independent farmers. The Labor dynasty relieved them of the burden of governing, Begin's dominance saved them the necessity of devising any serious opposition strategy, and they were thus free to engage in politics for its own sake. They hatched complex plots, devised serpentine strategies and fought with a joyous venom I have never encountered anywhere else. Meetings of the Central Committee were especially acrimonious, as members howled and brayed over everything, from international monetary policy to the cost of heating the building, with a kind of undifferentiated contentiousness.

The leader of the party, and one of my all-time favorite Israeli politicians was Simcha Ehrlich, or Reb Simcha as he was affectionately known. He was a man who liked to keep things simple, a goal that sometimes required prodigies of Byzantine political intrigue, of which he was a master. Ehrlich was born in Poland and came to Palestine as a young man, but there was something Skeffingtonian about him, as if he had left home one day for a Boston political clubhouse and had somehow wound up in Tel Aviv by mistake. He was a little pug-faced man in his sixties, with slicked-back white hair and dark-framed glasses that couldn't completely conceal the cynical twinkle in his eyes. He rarely talked, and when he did it was in a tight-lipped monotone. He abhorred any idea bigger than a rumor. Among the ideologues who made up Israel's political leadership, Ehrlich was a rarity—an inside man who somehow had seized control of a major party.

Not long after coming to work for the Liberals I decided it

was time to put my American know-how to use. I went to Reb Simcha with a proposal that I was certain could revolutionize the party: a sensitivity training weekend for the members of the Central Committee. Ehrlich invited me to present the plan to the seven-man party executive.

When the meeting began I was careful to couch the notion in practical terms, but as I watched the puzzled faces of the men around the table it occurred to me that they might actually think I was insane. Finally one of them broke in. "What's the point of all this?" he demanded.

"Well, think of it this way: This kind of program can teach you how to run a more efficient meeting, to save time. Or, how to say no to someone without hurting his feelings . . ."

"Excuse me, Mr. Chafets (unlike most Israelis, the Liberals always called each other mister), but I have a question." It was Itzhak Berman, a sixtyish corporation lawyer. He was another favorite of mine, a shrewd, cynical man with a brutal wit who seemed to get immense fun out of politics. (Later, when the Likud came to power, Berman became minister of energy, and he subsequently resigned his post over a matter of principle during the war in Lebanon.) "I don't understand one thing. You say this course can teach you to say no to someone without offending him?"

"That's right," I said, delighted that I was finally getting through.

"Well, in that case I'm against it. After all, what's the point of *saying* no to someone if you don't want to offend him?" The others nodded in agreement, but only Reb Simcha got the joke.

After the sensitivity training fiasco I decided to resign and I went to see Ehrlich. "You have a promising career here," he told me. "Why throw it away?"

"Well, I've discovered that I don't get any satisfaction from my work."

Ehrlich stared at me for a long moment, chewing over a new concept. "Satisfaction, young man. You want satisfaction, get married. This is politics."

In the end I stayed on at the Liberal party, mostly out of inertia, and in the winter of 1977 new elections were called. For the Likud, with its intraparty rivalries, making up a campaign staff meant striking a delicate balance between officials of Herut, the Liberals and the smaller factions. I was selected to serve as coordinator of the information department (largely, I think, on the strength of my sensitivity training scheme, which convinced the rival Herutniks that I must be harmless) and moved over to the Herut headquarters, the ominously named "Fortress" on King George Street. Geographically it was only a few blocks away from the Liberal party offices but psychologically and politically the distance might have been measured in light-years.

Once, shortly after coming to work for the Liberals, I found myself discussing them with a friend of mine, a young professor of political science at the Hebrew University. I described their strange, relentlessly middle-class attitudes and practices, so different from the austere socialist ethos of the pioneer elite, or the nationalist rhetoric and populist policies of Herut. "The key to understanding Israeli parties," my friend told me, "is to remember that they all have their roots in the various prestate underground movements. For example the Labor party today is an outgrowth of the Haganah and the Palmach. And Herut is the logical extension of the Irgun."

"And what about the Liberals?" I wondered. Where did they fit in?

"They were in the underground, too," the professor laughed. "In the black market."

It was unfair in a way—a number of the Liberal leaders served with distinction in the armed forces during the War of Independence and afterward. But in a country of mythological expectations and red-hot ideological conflict, the Liberals, from the beginning, stood for the values of Israel Minor—the Israel of small capitalism, small pleasures and small ambitions. One of the first articles of their catechism was: "The state exists for the individual, not the individual for the state." I agreed wholeheartedly, but it had taken considerable character to stand up for such a selfish and prosaic notion during the decades of grandiose rhetoric and unstinting self-sacrifice, and the party had come in for more than its fair share of contempt and mockery during the Heroic Age.

Nowhere was that contempt more keenly felt than at Herut headquarters on King George Street. Herut, as my professor friend had pointed out, was an outgrowth of the pre-state Irgun, led from its inception as a political party by Menachem Begin. The party had an outlaw image that made it more than a little disreputable; and this image intensified over the years as the former underground forged an alliance with many of the country's have-nots. The Liberals were needed, or so the theory went, to provide Begin with some of their bland respectability, but they were not taken seriously as politicians or vote getters.

Begin and his followers payed lip service to the anti-socialist, middle-class doctrines of the Liberals, and many of Herut's leaders, including Begin himself, led ultra-bourgeois personal lives. But in temperament and outlook, the Herut leader was far closer to the pioneer visionaries than to the shopkeepers and white-collar workers of the Liberal orbit. Begin, too, was a revolutionary and a dreamer, a prophet of his own version of Israel Major. His disputes with the Labor camp had the flavor of doctrinal controversies among rival clerics; and often they were exacerbated precisely by that essential similarity. Certainly the Herutniks, like the Laborites, saw themselves as inheritors of a great tradition of activist Zionism whose tasks went far beyond the immediate gratification of the needs of Israel's citizens.

The partnership between the Liberals and Herut was, at bottom, an unequal one. Herut was a mass movement led by the charismatic Begin, the Liberals an insignificant blip on the nation's political screen. (One of the strangest things I learned about the party was that it actively discouraged membership, on the theory that new members might upset the internal balance of power. It was easier to join the local country club than to become a member of the Liberal Party in those days.) And so it was only natural that the Likud's 1977 campaign, like previous ones, was dominated by Herut—that is, by Menachem Begin.

Actually, Begin had very little to do with the campaign itself. He was in the hospital, recuperating from a massive heart attack, and he left most of the day-to-day politics to Ezer Weizman and the campaign staff. But Begin's spirit hung over everything. He was, at once, the party's greatest asset and its greatest liability.

It is difficult for anyone who didn't grow up in the Israel of the fifties to understand the depth of antipathy and emotion that Begin aroused in the Israeli establishment. At an early strategy session, several of the advertising executives assigned to the campaign claimed that selling Begin to the country would be the single most difficult aspect of the election. "People are scared stiff of him," one of them said.

I was skeptical, and said so. "He's an old man, sick in bed with a heart attack. And he's been around for thirty years now, in Parliament. Who in his right mind would be afraid of him?"

"I am, for one," piped up Menachem Zilberman, one of the agency's consultants. "When I was a little kid, my mother used to warn me that if I didn't finish my supper, Begin would come and get me." The room burst into laughter, but Zilberman was serious. "Listen, you don't forget something like that," he said.

In order to deal with the Begin problem, Weizman ordered a campaign aimed at humanizing the Likud leader. We papered the country with posters showing a benevolent picture of the Old Man with the caption MENACHEM BEGIN—DEMOCRAT AND FAMILY MAN. He was both, of course, but these adjectives hardly summed up one of the most complex figures of modern political history.

One night a few weeks before the election, several of us were leaving the television studio where we prepared the Likud's evening campaign broadcasts. It was well past midnight when we walked into the warm, humid Tel Aviv night, exhausted after another sixteen-hour day. Suddenly there was a rustling from the bushes next to the door, and a huge figure jumped out of the darkness. "Boo!" yelled the man who was, within two months, to become Israel's defense minister. Weizman had come to view the rushes for the next day's broadcast and, seeing us on the way out, couldn't resist a little fun.

Suddenly Weizman looked across the street, at a billboard plastered with Begin posters. "There he is. Menachem Begin the democrat, the family man. Here we are at one o'clock in the morning, killing ourselves to get him elected. How does he do it, anyway? His name should be Houdini, not Begin!"

Weizman didn't need to explain what "it" was. All of us had wondered, at one time or another, about the strange hold that the Old Man held over his party and over an increasingly large part of the Israeli public. In fact, I had heard almost the identical question asked on the first occasion that I had ever seen Menachem Begin in action.

Shortly after I had come to work for the Liberal party, the Likud inner circle held a meeting in the Knesset in Jerusalem to discuss whether or not to support a proposal to hold municipal and national elections jointly. Fifteen or so seasoned political leaders sat around a long, rectangular table. In the center was Begin, who, as leader of the Likud, chaired the meeting.

The issue on the agenda was important, if prosaic, and Begin began by posing the question in a neutral way that gave no indication of his own preference. Then he opened the floor for discussion, calling on Simcha Ehrlich, who was seated to his right.

One by one the assembled politicians analyzed the pros and cons of the proposal. Begin sat patiently and appeared to be following the discussion with attention; but when I looked closely I could see that his eyes, nearly hidden, as usual, by his thick horn-rims, were glazed over. The purse-lipped look of concentration on his face was, I realized, directed not to the political debate but to some inner monologue. When a speaker finished, Begin would focus just long enough to call on the next, then return to his private reverie.

Most of the men at the meeting were in their fifties or early sixties, and I was struck by the familiar, homey atmosphere of their deliberations. Dressed in suits, sipping tea, they resembled the board of directors of a large American synagogue called in to discuss a raise in the rabbi's salary or the cost of new books for the Sunday school. And yet, seated around the table were men with biographies. They had seen their families destroyed by the Nazis, fought the British in the underground, survived prison and exile. A couple had been war heroes. They had thrown off their own origins and reinvented themselves as revolutionaries, conspirators, guerrilla warriors. But here in the Knesset conference room they droned on about the municipal elections as if it had all been a dream, as though they were a collection of accountants and ophthalmalogists and garment manufacturers. It was as if, despite the exertions of youth, they had been genetically programmed to revert to what nature and two thousand years of life in the diaspora had intended them to be: middle-class Jewish grandfathers.

I looked again at Begin. Certainly no superficial observer would have guessed that he was any different from the others. Back in the forties, as commander of the Irgun underground hiding from the British, he had successfully disguised himself as a young rabbi, protected by the sheer ordinariness of his appearance. He had been a man of mystery then, who had arrived in Palestine late—1942—and was unknown to most of the Jews in the tightly knit *yishuv* pre-state community. People read his inflammatory rhetoric on illegal wall posters and listened to his stirring messages about Hebrew struggle and resistance on the broadcasts of the Irgun's illicit radio station, but hardly anyone actually knew what he looked like. Photographs taken at one of his first major public appearances after the departure of the British, at Tel Aviv's Rina Park, show a slender young man in a double-breasted suit, wire-rimmed spectacles, slicked-back hair and a moustache, a revolutionary leader who looked remarkably like Groucho Marx.

Now in his early sixties, Begin no longer resembled Groucho. He seemed like what he had been trained to be: a Polish-Jewish lawyer. Only imagination made it possible to see him as he had been perceived for a generation—as a dangerous man. Thirty years earlier he had been Public Enemy Number One to the British in Palestine, a fugitive with a price on his head; and he had been hated almost as much by the pioneer establishment as by the Mandatory authorities. When a ship, the *Altelena*, approached the shores of Israel with arms for Begin's Irgun troops, David Ben Gurion had ordered it sunk—with Begin on board. The incident had almost precipitated a civil war on the eve of independence. Begin had shown restraint and prevented his men from retaliating, but the bitterness remained.

After independence, Begin ran for the Knesset at the head of a ticket made up of Irgun loyalists, and he emerged as the principal parliamentary opposition to the Mapai-led government. But despite the fact that they often drank tea within a table of each other in the Knesset dining room, Ben Gurion refused to so much as mention the younger man's name in public, referring to him in parliamentary debates as "that man sitting next to Member of Knesset Bader." Begin was a pariah, the leader of a party deemed unfit to join a national coalition. "Anyone except Herut or the communists" had been the political slogan then. Begin had learned defiance in those years, and as an old man, nearing what appeared to be the end of his career, he still kept the fires of pride and resentment burning under his bourgeois exterior.

The meeting droned on, directed by Begin with a detached courtesy. The men around the table were in agreement—the municipal and national elections should be jointly held. Only the last speaker, a second-rate party hack, disagreed, arguing that they should be conducted separately—a view that seemed irrelevant in light of the consensus to the contrary. When he was finished, Begin cleared his throat. "Good, very good," he said in a voice barely louder than a whisper—a tone, I learned, that was customary in these meetings. "We've heard the arguments for and against the proposal, a worthwhile exchange of views. As chairman of the meeting, it is my duty to summarize. It appears to me that we can agree to adopt the suggestion made by our good friend"—he nodded in the direction of the last speaker—"that the elections be held separately. In my view that will serve the best interests of the country, and of the Likud. Is there any disagreement?"

There was silence around the table.

"Fine. I'm glad we have reached a general agreement on this matter. Now—"

"Wait a minute, just a minute," a voice from the end of the table interrupted. It belonged to a representative of the Greater Land of Israel Movement, a small party in the Likud bloc, and he was livid. "What do you mean, 'agreed,' Mr.

Begin? You've just heard everyone at the table say the elections should be held together, and now you simply decide the opposite. On what basis," he shouted, "on what basis do you make such a decision?"

Begin gazed at the man with a benign expression. "I understand," he half-whispered," that you feel an injustice is being done. This is a democracy, and we are free men. Let us vote and have a democratic resolution of the matter. Whoever favors holding the elections separately, please raise his hand." Slowly, one by one, the assembled politicians voted. Some lifted their arms above their heads, a couple rested an elbow on the table and casually waved a hand, a few sheepishly raised a single finger in assent. But all of them voted with Begin—except the Land of Israel man.

"How can you do this?" he shouted at his colleagues. "What in hell are you afraid of? You've all just voted against yourselves—don't you realize that?—against your own positions. What are you afraid of?" He spun, red-faced, in the direction of Begin, who had remained silent and composed throughout the diatribe. "How do you do it?" he demanded.

Begin looked at him blankly, as if he hadn't heard the question. "*Nu*, my friend, we seem to be in general agreement here. Your view is a minority opinion, but we are a democratic group, and we value the rights and dignity of the minority as we do those of the majority. Still, this is an important issue, and I would like to arrive at a unanimous decision. Let me ask you on behalf of our colleagues to reconsider your vote."

Begin peered at the man with ironic benevolence, and the two held each other's eyes for a moment while the rest of the assembled politicians watched. Then, slowly, almost involuntarily, the man from Greater Israel raised one finger. The room burst into calls of approval, and one or two of the pols patted him on the back, but he continued to regard Begin narrowly. "I still don't know how you do it," he muttered.

It was vintage Begin, a performance so good that most of the people in the room seemed to regard it as natural. And after a generation of undisputed leadership, first of the Irgun, then of the Herut party and, since 1973, of the Likud electoral bloc, Begin's dominance *was* natural, perhaps the one constant in the public careers of most of the men gathered in the room that day. They were not merely politicians, not just Likudniks—they were Beginites.

Menachem Begin himself was a born patriarch. In the underground he had been flattered and delighted when his followers began referring to him, still in his mid-thirties, as "the Old Man." The members of the Irgun called themselves "the fighting family"—Begin's family—and he shouldered the burdens of clan leadership willingly, demanding only loyalty and deference in return.

Which is precisely what he received. Incredibly, between 1949 and 1977, hundreds of thousands of Israelis supported Menachem Begin through eight straight electoral defeats. In those days, to be a Herutnik meant cutting yourself off from the patronage and *protekzia* that were the rewards of Mapai orthodoxy. Such orthodoxy was the key to success in the civil service, the army, the labor movement. It was often the condition for getting a bigger apartment, a better job, a business loan, a place in a prestigious school, a scholarship to study abroad. It was the condition for social status, political power and respectability. Herut, on the other hand, had nothing to offer—except Menachem Begin.

Under the circumstances it is amazing that so many people followed Begin into the political wilderness, but they did, and somehow, through the years their numbers grew. From time to time a challenger within the party emerged, but Begin put down attempts on his political life with an adroitness that bordered on sleight of hand. No one could touch him, no one could defeat him within the circumscribed world of his Movement, and this gave him the rarest gift a politician in a democracy can have—absolute control over a party fashioned in his own image.

Begin went into the 1977 election still in firm control of the Likud and of the veteran Irgun activists at its core; but even in Labor's enfeebled condition, that wouldn't have given him a broad enough base to win. Only a year or so before the election, Prime Minister Itzhak Rabin had contemptuously dismissed him as a museum piece, an old-time ideologue whose day had passed. Israel of the post-Yom Kippur period appeared to be a country no longer receptive to ideology; it wanted pragmatic answers, mundane approaches to everyday problems. On the face of it, Begin was precisely the wrong man for such a public mood.

But Begin proved the experts wrong. Despite the razzle-dazzle campaign put on by Weizman and the ad agency, Begin himself refused to change. In his television appearances toward the end of the campaign he looked frail and weak, but he talked with his usual fervor about the great issues that pre-occupied him. He made no effort to tailor his message to the supposed concerns of the public, just as he refused to bow to our requests that he wear makeup or a blue shirt for TV. He appeared, as he had always appeared, as himself, an old-world nationalist visionary full of flowery phrases. We could call him "family man" and "democrat" all we liked, but Begin preferred—and used—a different term to describe himself. He was, and he wanted to be seen as, "an old Jew."

On the evening of May 17, 1977, I went to Likud headquarters, along with several hundred other campaign workers, to wait for the results of the election. At exactly 11:00 P.M. television anchorman Haim Yavin came on screen with one of the most electrifying announcements of his career. Based on exit polls taken throughout the day, Labor had suffered an astonishing defeat. The Likud would form the next government, and Menachem Begin would be Israel's sixth Prime Minister.

The hall erupted into a pandemonium of victory whoops and back-pounding. I grabbed the man standing next to me—a grizzled veteran of the party's political wars who had helped show me the ropes when I first came to the Herut headquarters—and began dancing him around in a circle. "We won, we won," I shouted. He caught me by the shoulders, pulling back. I could see that tears were running down his cheeks; his face was flushed with what I thought was excitement. Suddenly he started shaking me violently and yelling. "What do you mean 'we,' you little shit? You've been here for three months. I've been waiting all my life for this." He pushed me away and fell into the arms of a old Irgun comrade.

If some of the Likud stalwarts were poor winners, the old

guard emerged as even worse losers. That night on television Itzhak Ben Aharon, former Labor party member of Knesset (MK), ex-head of the Histadrut Labor Federation and a man who personified the pioneer elite, was asked about the Likud's victory and its implications for the country. The old socialist glared at the interviewer. "The results are a mistake," he snapped.

"But Mr. Ben Aharon," said the reporter, obviously taken aback by the vehemence of the reply, "this is a democracy, and the people have spoken."

Ben Aharon, who looks like an aging Jewish chipmunk, fixed the camera with a vengeful eye. "The people are wrong," he declared, obviously unwilling to accept the judgment of his inferiors.

Ben Aharon's reaction was natural enough. He was not merely a politician out of a job or the representative of a party that had suffered a political defeat. The pioneers had come to the land of Israel to create a new kind of Jew, and they had succeeded to a remarkable extent. And now the people had rejected their values and goals, turned their backs on the golden opportunity to continue to "build and be rebuilt"—and had elected Begin, the symbol of all that was wrong with the diaspora. This was more than a political defeat; it was an act of mass heresy. Who were these "people" who had spoken? Cafe idlers and beach bums, fat-assed businessmen out for the quick buck, pimply disco dancers, orthodox holy rollers, half-literate Moroccan riffraff—all those who had resisted the opportunity to be reborn and had opted instead for the frivolities of materialism, the sentimentality of religious mumbo jumbo, the nostalgic clinging to outmoded cultures. These weren't Real Israelis. They were, by God, Jews!

I stayed late at party headquarters that night, and the sun was already rising as I walked down King George Street toward my car. The results were in, and the country had gone to bed. Only a milk truck unloading containers in front of a grocery store at the end of the block disturbed the early morning silence. A revolution had taken place only a few hours before, but there were no banners or barricades, no burning buildings, nothing except the clang of metal milk crates on the pavement of the deserted street. On the surface everything seemed to be the same as it had been, but I knew that couldn't be—not if the Likud had won an election. Suddenly the enormity of what had happened hit me. Reb Simcha, a man who still counted in Yiddish and who believed that the state existed for the good of its people, would become finance minister. The Defense Ministry was about to get Weizmanized. And Menachem Begin, the Black Pope of Zionism, was the new Prime Minister.

"Well," I thought to myself, as I got into my car, "I wonder what's going to happen now."

4

Mr. Begin and His Generals

Menachem Begin's victory surprised everyone but him. He was a man of iron self-confidence—he would have had to be to lose eight straight elections and keep coming back for more—and for a generation he had been certain that his day would come, "by the ballot, not the bullet," as he often said in his pedantic way.

The sources of Begin's self-assurance are obscure, but by all accounts he was never much troubled by introspective doubts, even as a young man growing up in Poland. But by the time he was elected Prime Minister his confidence had hardened into a nearly absolute belief in his own instincts. After all, he had spent a lifetime believing in a series of highly improbable ideas—and watching them come true, one by one.

The first of these was, of course, the creation of the State of Israel itself. When Begin became a Zionist, in the twenties, the odds against an independent Jewish country emerging in his lifetime were huge—certainly a majority of his fellow Polish Jews would have bet against it. But Begin, according to those who knew him as a young man, never doubted for a moment that a Jewish nation would, indeed, come into being.

Begin started out as a Labor Zionist but, still in his teens, he was converted to the nationalist doctrines of Ze'ev Jabotinsky. Jabotinsky preached, and Begin believed, that European Jewry was headed for an unprecedented disaster. The great majority of Europe's Jews considered this nothing but alarmist nonsense; but Begin lived to see this conviction, too, become a tragic reality.

When Menachem Begin arrived in Palestine during World War II, the conventional Zionist wisdom was that diplomacy and pioneering activity would eventually end the British control of Palestine and that violence was counterproductive. Begin, on the other hand, believed that only an underground guerrilla war would drive the British out and set the stage for Jewish independence. Historians disagree on the impact of the "Hebrew revolt" which he led, but Begin himself was totally convinced that in this, too, his instincts had been correct: that it was the Irgun's struggle that precipitated the British withdrawal from Palestine.

Following the War of Independence, western Palestine was divided between Israel and Jordan, with the old city of Jerusalem, Hebron and the rest of Judaea and Samaria lost to the Arabs. For nineteen years, while the Israeli political establishment became reconciled to this state of affairs, Begin never ceased to believe that those territories should—and would—eventually come under Israeli control. This view was considered extremely eccentric—until it came to pass in the Six Day War.

And, of course, Begin had never stopped believing that he would someday be elected Prime Minister of Israel, even in the years when he was the most despised man in the country. Time after time he had gone to the people, and time after time he had been rejected. Only a year or two before the 1977 election, not even his most loyal supporters (and not even those of us on his campaign staff) would have bet on his chances of winning what appeared to be his last campaign.

With a track record like this, it is not surprising that Begin came to office with an extremely clear program and an unshakable conviction that it could be achieved. He intended to consolidate Israel's hold over Judaea and Samaria, and at the same time, to make peace with the Arabs. These goals appeared contradictory, but Begin was certain they could be accomplished. He had, after all, seen stranger things happen.

In order to pursue his policies, Begin realized that he would first need to expand his political base. The coalition of outsiders that had brought him to power—old-line Revisionists, the Oriental working class, young people and disaffected Labor voters, along with religious parties that, in 1977, abandoned their historic alliance with Mapai—gave him a bare majority. It was enough to set up a government, but not enough actually to govern. Everything worth controlling was in the hands of the Labor establishment, which greeted the victory of Begin's coalition with all the enthusiasm of Bostonian Whigs at Andy Jackson's inauguration ball.

Following Begin's election I found myself on the receiving end of some of this antipathy. A day or two after the victory, Eliahu Ben-Elissar, Begin's spokesman with whom I had worked during the campaign, was appointed director general of the Prime Minister's Office. He, in turn, offered me the job of director of the Government Press Office.

I was not exactly overqualified for the post. I was still only twenty-nine, and I had been in Israel less than ten years. I had mastered Hebrew since the "if Chafets understands, everybody understands" days of basic training, and I had worked in information for the Foreign Ministry and the Liberal party. I could also speak English, and I read *Time* magazine nearly every week. There were some who thought that these were rather slim credentials for the job, which is one of the senior positions in the Israeli civil service, and I found it difficult to argue with them. On the other hand, the Likud wasn't overstocked with people who *were* qualified to serve as liaison to the international press. Besides, I reasoned, if you don't reward your friends and confound your opponents after a winning election, then what's a democracy for?

During my first week on the job I attended a cocktail party in Tel Aviv where I met a number of foreign correspondents. One, an Israeli who worked for several British and South African newspapers, asked me about my plans for the Press Office. I blandly told him that I intended to read as much of the material being filed as possible, in order to keep myself informed—a goal so obvious that I forgot I had mentioned it to him, until a couple of weeks later. What reminded me was a parliamentary query, tabled by MK Shulamit Aloni, leader of the opposition Citizens Rights party, and addressed to the Prime Minister. The query stated that MK Aloni had been informed that the new director of the Government Press Office was planning to use the Shin Bet—the Israeli secret service—to spy on foreign correspondents, and asked for the Prime Minister's response.

Naturally I was somewhat taken aback. I didn't even know the Shin Bet's telephone number and I couldn't imagine where Ms. Aloni could have come up with such a bizarre notion—until I learned that the correspondent was also a functionary in the Citizens Rights party. His calculation was simple: Chafets works for Begin, and Begin is a fascist, ergo . . .

There were more than a few such incidents during my first months at the Press Office, but eventually things calmed down. The Likud offered too many real targets for people to be concerned with me, and gradually I became friendly with a number of establishment journalists and politicians. There was a predictable moment in these relationships when the Israeli WASP would confer the ultimate accolade. "What are you doing with *them?*" he would ask. "You don't belong with Begin. You're one of us." There was a delicious irony in this, of course: Finally, after a decade in the country, I was insider material.

It was, naturally, far too late for Begin himself to win any such acceptance from the national elite, and this posed a serious problem. But to rule effectively he needed the cooperation, or at least the acquiescence, of the establishment, and he set out to build some bridges in that direction. Basic to this plan were two men: Moshe Dayan and Yigael Yadin.

A couple of days after the 1977 election, Begin was rushed to the hospital with what appeared to be a relapse of his heart condition. From his sickbed he made a startling announcement: that he had chosen Moshe Dayan as his foreign minister. The appointment came, literally, out of left field—Dayan had just been elected to the Knesset on the Labor party slate. This, however, bothered neither Dayan nor Begin. Both were practical men, and each had something the other wanted. Begin's colleagues were upset, of course; at least half a dozen Likud politicians by actual count were, at the time of Dayan's appointment, convinced that they would be perfect for the job. But no one dared challenge the Old Man's judgment, and the would-be foreign ministers began looking for other cabinet positions for which they would be perfect. On the Labor side of the aisle, Dayan's old colleagues went into great paroxysms of indignation, calling him a traitor and an opportunist, but Dayan scarcely seemed to notice. He felt that he had been badly treated by his party after the 1973 war; and besides, Moshe Dayan was a man who didn't have to account to a bunch of politicians.

In the biographies that Knesset members fill out before each session, Menachem Begin always listed his occupation as "attorney and journalist," and Moshe Dayan called himself a farmer. These may have been strictly true, but were hardly representative of what the two men had actually been doing since adolescence. A more realistic listing would have shown Begin's profession to be "leader"—and Moshe Dayan's to be "national hero."

Dayan, more than any single Israeli before or since, personified the New Jew that the pioneers had tried to create and the sabras hoped to become. He was born in a Galilee kibbutz and raised in the farming village of Nahalal—the Israeli equivalent of growing up on Plymouth Rock. His father, Shmuel, was a pioneer and Mapai member of Knesset and a colleague of Ben Gurion's, and Moshe Dayan himself was a quintessential Israeli insider. When he became foreign minister, his cousin Yigal Horowitz was minister of commerce and industry; another cousin was a Labor MK; and his former brother-in-law, Ezer Weizman, was minister of defense.

But despite Dayan's impeccable establishment credentials, there was something of the maverick about him. He was a man who flouted rules, raiding archeological sites around the country for his private collection. He radiated sexuality, and carried out a number of highly publicized affairs with married women. As chief of staff he had reportedly said that no soldier who didn't spend a little time in a military jail for insubordination was really worth his salt. Dayan discovered and protected Ariel Sharon, just as Dayan himself was protected by Ben Gurion, who saw him as a modern day Joshua. Hero of two wars, darling of the press and the public, Dayan was endlessly fascinating to his fellow countrymen, one of the few politicians actually to possess that elusive quality, charisma.

And then came the 1973 war, a war that Defense Minister Dayan failed to anticipate or to prepare for. Overnight he went from hero to villain, from a likely Prime Minister to an electoral liability. People had identified with Dayan, made him the symbol of Israel's greatness, and his failure in the Yom Kippur War somehow diminished the entire public, left it feeling cheated and fearful. And, of course, that carried a political price: Dayan was dumped from the party's first string and replaced as defense minister by his long time junior partner, Shimon Peres. Always a lone wolf, he became a forbidding figure in those years. In the Knesset dining hall, where politicians mix and mingle and party leaders sit surrounded by entourages, he always occupied a corner table in the rear. No one plopped down to gossip or join him in a cup of tea, and even the waiters tried to keep their distance. He looked like a man about to explode with frustration and bitterness, and although the explosion never came, it was clear that his own party no longer had any use for him.

But Menachem Begin did. Dayan diminished was still Dayan, and Begin saw that making him foreign minister would give his government an aura of legitimacy and continuity that might otherwise be impossible to attain. Begin was like a man who, buying out an old family industry, keeps on the former proprietor as an act of goodwill and a link to resentful and suspicious employees and townspeople.

And so it fell to Menachem Begin to rehabilitate the protégé of his archenemy, David Ben Gurion, and to give him one last great role. In return, he got what he wanted: a firm bridge to the sabra establishment. Some Herutniks feared that Dayan as foreign minister might exert undue influence on Begin, cause him to moderate or alter his basic views—and it is more than possible that such a thought crossed Dayan's mind as well. But Begin, who enjoyed being underestimated, was not concerned. For one thing, Dayan was a hardliner whose views on most aspects of foreign policy were not far from his own. More to the point, Dayan had no political base, no alternative to the Old Man. Whatever influence he would have would be a gift, to be granted or withdrawn at the Prime Minister's pleasure.

After securing Moshe Dayan, Begin commenced his courtship of Professor Yigael Yadin, the classiest and most elusive figure in Israeli public life. The Jerusalem-born son of a well-known archeologist, Yadin first came to national prominence while still in his twenties. He was a military prodigy, a boy general who ran the army during the War of Independence and, at thirty-two, became Israel's second chief of staff.

Despite his meteoric career, Yadin did not want to be a military man. He fought with Ben Gurion over proposed cuts in the defense budget and quit the army to return to his first love, archeology. His work on the Dead Sea Scrolls earned him a Ph.D. from the Hebrew University, and his flair for the dramatic won him an international reputation. Yadin was the perfect intellectual-warrior hero, an idealist who had turned his back on the power and glory of a military career for the purity of the academic life; but even in academia he remained a man of action, an excavator and organizer of explorations into the ancient secrets of the Land of Israel.

During the long years of his civilian activity, the myth of Yadin, the Israeli Cincinnatus, grew, and he became a sort of public resource, a national ace in the hole. It was comforting to know that Yadin, the purest and wisest of his generation, was there if he was ever really needed. The fact that he was indifferent to honors, to titles and to power only made him more attractive, and in every period of crisis or transition, enthusiastic admirers put Yadin's name forward, only to have the great man decline to run.

But Yadin was only human, and he finally came around. After the general collapse of national morale that followed the Yom Kippur War, he allowed his supporters to convince him that it was his duty to step in and save the situation. A few months before the 1977 election, Yadin announced the formation of the Democratic Party for Change (Dosh). It was a good-government party, founded on the principles of economic liberalism, foreign policy moderation, administrative efficiency and electoral reform, and it attracted the dissatisfied idealists of the sabra upper-middle class, eggheads, do-gooders, and longtime Yadin enthusiasts. Not surprisingly, it also drew more than its fair share of narrow-eyed professional pols who knew a good horse when they saw one. Yadin, a political naïf, decided that his list of candidates for the Knesset would be determined by open, democratic balloting among party members. A fellow professor came up with a voting system that was supposed to be the most representative and democratic ever devised by the human mind; unfortunately, it was also the most complicated. Predictably, the professional politicians figured it out faster than the reformers, and when the caucus votes were counted, the Democratic Party for Change presented a list of candidates that included some pretty familiar faces.

In the general election that followed, Yadin's party polled fifteen seats in the parliament—a very strong showing for a new slate and almost, but not quite, enough to give him the balance of power. Dosh pulled almost all its votes from the Labor party, and Begin came up with just enough to put together a governing coalition without Yadin's help. But the new Prime Minister wanted the archeologist in his government, not only to broaden his coalition but to put him to work as an ambassador of goodwill for the Begin program. Some of Yadin's followers strongly opposed making any deal with the Likud; it would, they said, be selling out their principles, and after all, Dosh had been created as a venture in political principle. This view was heatedly contested by the clubhouse wing of the party, which explained to Professor Yadin that joining the government was the most principled thing he could do. After all, he had come back to public life in order to make a difference, and he couldn't do that as a member of the opposition. He would, they assured him, be able to change things from the inside. Begin would be no match for him; he would become Yadin's puppet, a figurehead Prime Minister to be used to accomplish Dosh's goals.

And so the former chief of staff joined the government with the exalted title of Deputy Prime Minister, and suddenly Menachem Begin, the eternal outsider, found himself flanked at Cabinet meetings by the two most glorious of the glamorous sabra sons, General Dayan and General Yadin. In public he treated them with elaborate courtesy. They were, after all, his treasures, Roman princes fallen into the hands of a Barbarian king, and he was careful to do nothing that might diminish their value.

Besides, Begin had a genuine admiration for war heroes.

72

Despite his image as an underground leader, he was the most civilian of men. In his Irgun days he had been a political strategist and propagandist, not a military figure, and one of his greatest disappointments was that he had never actually participated in any of the group's operations. Begin was drawn to dashing macho types, and he sometimes displayed a boyish desire to imitate them. During the latter part of his first administration, when he assumed the duties of defense minister, Begin spent Thursdays among the generals at the Defense Ministry in Tel Aviv. During these sessions the dandyish Prime Minister would appear with an open collar instead of his customary tie and jacket, and one or two of his less reverent aides began referring to this as his "Clint Eastwood outfit."

Begin never let his sincere admiration for the military achievements of Dayan and Yadin overpower his political instincts, however, and he kept both men on a short leash. Dayan, with his great experience, sharp intellect and total political dependence was the more useful, particularly after the peace negotiations with Egypt got under way. Yadin, on the other hand, was a man with a party, at least when he arrived in the government. It took Begin about fifteen minutes to realize that the professor-general might know a lot about archeology or military tactics, but that he was completely innocent of even an elementary knowledge of politics. So Begin did what any red-blooded Prime Minister would have done: He picked his pocket. He played on the reawakened vanity of the Deputy Prime Minister, exploited his loyalty and basic decency, maneuvered him into a series of party-splintering decisions and, at the end of his first administration, rewarded him with some warm words and a firm handshake. Yadin had come into the government in 1977 at the head of a fifteen-man Knesset faction; he retired as the leader of a four-man group.

Moshe Dayan stayed on until the Camp David accords were concluded, and then was pushed aside. Now that the focus was turning to the Palestinian issue, Begin was no longer interested in Dayan's services. The Prime Minister offered the job of chief autonomy negotiator to Interior Minister Yosef Burg, and Dayan, who had considerably more political street smarts than Yadin, understood that he was out. Unlike Yadin, he didn't retire after leaving Begin, but he should have. In the 1981 election he ran at the head of his own Knesset slate and got just two seats; he died a bitter and disappointed man only a few months later.

Yadin and Dayan had both been useful, but they were aging superstars brought in for a season, not real Begin team players. Since the fifties the army had been the political farm club of the Labor party, a place where generals like Dayan, Itzhak Rabin, Chaim Bar Lev and Motta Gur had won their reputations and popularity before stepping directly into senior party jobs. In those days, Herutniks didn't get far in the army; and when the Likud came to power it had only two bona fide military heroes of its own: Ezer Weizman and Ariel Sharon.

Superficially Weizman and Sharon had a good deal in common. They belonged to the same generation of sabras whose baptism of fire came in the War of Independence. Both were headstrong, flamboyant commanders, known for their ability to inspire subordinates and exasperate superiors. Neither had an especially high regard for the views of others.

Although both Weizman and Sharon were hawks, neither was a genuine Beginite. Weizman's roots were in the Zionist aristocracy—his uncle Chaim was Israel's first President—while Sharon was the son of a pioneer Labor Zionist family. The world of Menachem Begin was a strange place, and both of them chafed at the discipline and constraints it imposed.

Weizman came to Herut first. In 1969, when he left the army, Begin brought him directly into the party leadership, appointing him a Cabinet minister in the post-1967 government of national unity. Begin and Weizman made an improbable team. Although the party leader was only eleven years older than the general, he often seemed more like his grandfather. Begin was serious-minded, even lugubrious; Weizman irrepressible and sometimes juvenile. During the first year or two of their association, Begin gallantly referred to Weizman as *mon general,* while Weizman reciprocated with the offhand contempt of a golden-boy quarterback for the captain of the debating team.

In 1970 the government of national unity broke up and Herut went back into opposition. Weizman attempted to exploit this development to challenge Begin's leadership, but the Old Man put down the revolt with his customary efficiency. Ezer Weizman was effectively read out of the party, and in the process Begin labeled him "a charming, naughty child"—an appelation that stuck.

Menachem Begin allowed the apparently chastened general to rejoin Herut in time for the 1977 election, and put him in charge of the campaign committee. But the tensions between the two men were never really resolved; their temperamental differences were simply too great. When I joined the Likud's campaign committee, in early 1977, I got a chance to see for myself what it was that made Weizman so attractive—and so exasperating to Menachem Begin.

Every morning at eight Weizman held a staff meeting, ostensibly to discuss strategy and developments, but actually to serve as a forum for his nonstop stream-of-consciousness monologues. At these sessions the ex-air-force chief, whom everyone called Ay-zer, would pop open a bottle of beer, drape his lanky body over a chair and hold forth, a man with an apparently insatiable need for attention. Unlike the private musings of most public figures, however, Ay-zer's monologues were well worth listening to, hilarious, ribald, often bizarre, sometimes touching—and always completely uninhibited. He would say anything that occurred to him, but always with such style that his audience—the twenty or so politicians who gathered each morning for the meetings—found him fascinating. Weizman radiated star quality, and among the political operatives who gathered in his office each morning he was as conspicuous as Michael Jackson at an Indianapolis Elks Club mixer.

Unlike most of his contemporaries Ezer Weizman did not grow up in the puritanical atmosphere of the pioneers. His father was wealthy (the family owned one of the first private automobiles in Palestine), and as a boy he went with his parents on vacations to Beirut, where he acquired an early appreciation of good food and drink and sophisticated entertainment. During World War II, Weizman served as a young pilot in the RAF, an experience that left him with the devil-may-care attitude and flamboyant self-confidence that have been his trademarks ever since. Later, as commander of the

Israeli Air Force, he instilled a camaraderie and sense of style that were highly unusual for Israel. He was a charismatic leader much imitated by little Weizmans, a trend setter, an unabashed egoist who ran the air force as if it were his personal preserve.

Weizman was a man of mercurial moods, none of which he kept to himself. He sometimes spoke of his own mouth in the third person, as if it were an organ somehow detached from the rest of him and independent of his best judgment. Often he offended people by saying whatever popped into his head. On one unforgettable occasion, at one of the morning meetings, a woman activist took the floor to complain about the paucity of female candidates on the Likud Knesset list. It was a sore point, and she was right—only a couple of women were among those slated for safe seats—but she was also annoyingly shrill in denouncing the party's sexism. As Weizman listened to her I tried to imagine what his reply would be. The percentage answer would be a soothing admission of the problem and a promise to do something about it in the future. I had been around enough politicians to expect the obvious.

Instead, when the lady finished her harangue, Weizman flashed her a killer smile. "Well, you're right about the number of women on the list, my dear," he told her. "But just remember one thing—we've got a lot of male candidates with female characteristics."

Yet it was impossible to stay mad at Weizman. He had a nickname for everyone and a way of creating instant intimacy. In a melancholy mood he could speak in a choked voice about his son, Shauli, who had been wounded at the Suez Canal during the war of attrition. Or, suddenly up, he would regale us with the romantic exploits of his youth. Weizman in one of these moods had the capacity to draw you in totally, to make you a part of some charmed inner circle. Unlike his forbidding brother-in-law Moshe Dayan, Weizman was that rarest of politicians, a warm, spontaneous and funny human being.

And yet it was precisely this unpredictable charm that caused others to wonder if Weizman was serious and substantial enough for national leadership. He himself must have been afflicted with some of the same doubts. The day after the Likud's victory, the senior campaign staff gathered in his office in a mood of great jubilation. Suddenly the door flew open and a furious Weizman came charging into the room. "What are you all so happy about?" he shouted. "Don't any of you realize what a responsibility we have now, the work that all of us are going to have to do to make this the kind of country we want? This is no time for laughter and jokes! Let's get down to business here." It was a bizarre tirade from Israel's leading disciple of political sunshine, and I couldn't help thinking that it had the tone of self-hypnosis, like a compulsive eater's when he berates himself to keep from falling off a diet.

Despite these doubts, however, Weizman was appointed minister of defense in Begin's first Cabinet. The Likud's other general, Sharon, abandoned the party temporarily in 1977, running instead on his own, independent slate, and leaving Weizman as the only bona fide military expert in Herut. That, coupled with his campaign leadership, made Ezer the only logical candidate for the post.

Weizman's first months in the Defense Ministry were uneventful, but in November 1977, President Anwar Sadat of Egypt made his astonishing trip to Israel—and changed Ezer Weizman's political life. When the visit was announced, Weizman was in the hospital, recovering from injuries he had received in a car accident a few days earlier. The doctors advised him against getting out of bed, but he had no intention of missing the greatest diplomatic event in Israeli history.

The Sadat initiative, despite its obvious potential, caused considerable trepidation among Israel's political and military leaders. Nothing like it had happened before, and it confused nearly everyone. Begin and Dayan were wary of a trick and welcomed the Egyptian President with a positive caution. The Labor party leaders were stunned and resentful that Sadat had chosen the hard-line Begin as a negotiating partner. Almost alone among Israel's major political leaders, Weizman grasped the greatness of the moment and the possibilities it offered. When Chief of Staff Motta Gur, fearful of a ruse, ordered the army on alert, the defense minister nearly exploded. And when Sadat arrived at Jerusalem's King David Hotel, Weizman was there to greet him.

Weizman got to the hotel late, and Sadat was already in

conversation with Begin and several of his advisers. In evident pain, the Israeli defense minister hobbled toward the Egyptian President. Ten years earlier, he had devised the plan that enabled Israel to destroy the Egyptian Air Force on the ground and humiliate Sadat's country. Sadat watched him with curiosity as Weizman suddenly stopped and, in what appeared to be a spontaneous gesture, raised his cane to his shoulder like a rifle and drew to attention. "Mr. President," said the Israeli defense minister, "I salute you." Sadat, recognizing a fellow actor—and a fellow visionary—was obviously moved; Begin, observing the scene, was less so.

The breakthrough with Egypt was the beginning of an evolution in Weizman's thinking that brought him, within a few years, from the right wing of the Likud to the left wing of the Labor alignment. Temperamentally he is the rarest of all Israeli politicians—a genuine optimist, unaffected by the demons of recent Jewish history. The notion that Israel might break out of its isolation and win acceptance in the Middle East fired his imagination, and as time went on he grew almost frantic in his impatience with the cautious maneuvering of some of his fellow Cabinet ministers. Naturally, since he was Weizman, that impatience became a matter of public knowledge. On one memorable occasion he violently ripped a peace placard off the wall of a meeting room in the Prime Minister's Office, snarling that the government didn't really want peace. Throughout the negotiations with Egypt, Weizman loudly and repeatedly admonished his colleagues for their timidity and ghetto mentalities, which he contrasted with his own liberated attitudes.

Weizman was one of the few Israeli leaders to understand Anwar Sadat. Unfortunately for him, he completely misread Menachem Begin. He was important to the Prime Minister—as an effective liaison with Egypt, a popular vote getter at home and a link with the Zionist aristocracy. But no one could survive in Begin's world without accepting his authority, and this was something the nephew of Chaim Weizmann and former commander of the air force simply could not bring himself to do. Begin goaded him, played him off against rivals, dismissed his ideas and generally gave him the treatment. Weizman responded with a growing lack of civility. During one of the Prime Minister's periodic health slumps, when Begin took to dozing off during Cabinet meetings and going home from the office early, Weizman began referring to him as "the late Menachem Begin."

Begin countered by stepping up the pressure and by totally removing Weizman from the negotiations on Palestinian autonomy. He was hoping to turn the impetuous pilot into a political kamikaze, and he did. Generally fed up, Weizman quit his post as defense minister and sent the Prime Minister a blistering letter—which of course became public—full of bitter criticism of his policies.

This was just what Begin had been waiting for. He used Weizman's letter as the grounds for suspending his party membership, and suddenly the architect of the 1977 victory—and the man most likely to succeed Begin as leader of the Likud—found himself without a party. He sat out the 1981 elections, and during the next couple of years he made a good deal of money importing Japanese cars, always waiting for a chance to get back into politics.

As long as Begin was in control of the Likud, Weizman was persona non grata. But in the fall of 1983, Begin mysteriously quit and was replaced by Foreign Minister Yitzhak Shamir. Not long afterward Shamir's minister of finance resigned, and Weizman put out feelers for the job. Back in the campaign of 1977, Shamir had made some television spots for the Likud that Weizman, as campaign chairman, had thrown out. "He's too ugly to be on television," Weizman had reportedly said. "Hell, he's got more hair on his eyebrows than I've got on my balls." Naturally the remark got back to Shamir. When the time came to appoint a finance minister, Shamir let Weizman dangle for a day or two and then chose someone else.

In the 1984 elections Weizman ran on his own ticket, as his former brother-in-law Moshe Dayan had done three years earlier. Like Dayan, he made a disappointing showing, receiving only three seats in the parliament. Weizman ran on the politics of sunshine, insisting that the time had come for Israelis to put aside their fears and anxieties and look toward a brighter future. Most voters found this unconvincing and although an Ezer Weizman rally was still the best political show in town, winning the charm vote wasn't enough. Still, the vagaries of the Israeli electoral system came to his rescue. Neither the Likud nor Labor won enough seats in the 1984 election to form an effective government, and the two parties were forced to join forces in a government of national unity. In this situation Weizman's three seats became important, and he traded them for membership in the Labor alignment, becoming a minister without portfolio in the government led by his old friend—and the man he had helped to defeat in 1977—Shimon Peres.

Menachem Begin began his first term with four war heroes in his cabinet; but when he was sworn in for his second, in 1981, only one—Ariel Sharon—was left. More than a year earlier, when Ezer Weizman resigned from the Defense Ministry, Sharon had wanted the job. Begin had demurred then, saying that as defense minister, Sharon might ring the Prime Minister's Office with tanks, a remark that he later claimed was in jest. But in the campaign of 1981, Sharon performed masterfully, leading tens of thousands of voters on tours of the West Bank to visit the settlements whose construction he had supervised during Begin's first administration. After the Likud's reelection, Begin overcame his reluctance and rewarded Sharon with the Defense portfolio.

A few months before that election, the Likud held a conference at Jerusalem's Binyanai Ha'uma convention center. On the dais the leaders of the party came to attention to sing the anthem of the Irgun underground. Sharon stood near the center of the group, moving his lips, faking it. "Look at that fat Mapainik," a friend of mine whispered. "He doesn't even know the words." Indeed, during his twenty-five-year army career, Sharon was a member of Mapai, and although as a military officer he was forbidden to take part in political activities, he was closely associated with David Ben Gurion and Ben Gurion's protégé Moshe Dayan. In July of 1973 he retired from the army and, finding the Labor party overstocked with ex-generals, joined the Liberals, but it was never a comfortable match. Sharon's blustery military style frightened the party's leaders, and their cautious middle-class attitudes drove him to fits of frustrated rage. Simcha Ehrlich was especially good at this, using forty years of clubhouse expertise to torment the inexperienced Sharon.

During his first months with the Liberals, Sharon had one great political success: he was instrumental in putting together the Likud. The bloc was Sharon's brainchild, and he was elected to the Knesset in 1973 as one of its leading candidates. But life in the parliamentary opposition bored him, and Ehrlich and the others made him miserable with their interminable discussions and maneuvering. When Labor party Prime Minister Itzhak Rabin offered him a job as his adviser, Sharon resigned from the Knesset, left the Liberal party and went to work for the government.

Sharon's departure was greeted with satisfaction by the Liberal leaders, who assumed that they had seen the last of the fractious and disruptive general. In the 1977 Knesset campaign he formed his own party, Shlomzion, in an effort to exploit his presumed popularity as a hero of the Yom Kippur War. As party leader, Arik Sharon displayed an estimable flexibility, offering the number-two slot to super-dove Yossi Sarid, seeking alliances with several left-wing factions and hinting that he would have no problem making territorial concessions in the West Bank. But Sharon was less popular than he thought. His party won only two seats in the Knesset.

Following the election, Sharon, by now an ex-Mapai, ex-Liberal, ex-Shlomzion former adviser to Prime Minister Rabin, joined Herut—his fourth party in less than five years. Originally he wanted to be named chief of staff of the army, but Weizman vetoed the idea. Next, there was a suggestion that he be put in charge of the secret services, but Ehrlich and others quashed that proposal. Finally Begin decided to make Sharon minister of agriculture, with responsibility for the West Bank settlement program.

The idea had its detractors, especially among the old guard of the fighting family who considered Sharon an unreliable interloper. But Begin wanted him, and that was enough. The West Bank settlements were at the very heart of Begin's policy and he needed someone who knew how to get things done. And, for a generation, Israeli Prime Ministers had been turning to Ariel Sharon when they needed results.

Sharon's career as a troubleshooter began in the early

fifties, when Israel, unable to cope with Arab terrorist attacks through conventional means, decided to adopt a policy of active retaliation. Such a policy required an elite commando unit. Moshe Dayan, then chief of military operations, surveyed the field and chose Sharon to head Unit 101.

Under Sharon's leadership 101 became an instant legend. He handpicked his men, imbued them with a sense of elite camaraderie not too different from that of Ezer Weizman's pilots, and led them on a series of dangerous, highly effective raids behind enemy lines. The unit was supposed to be a secret, but word spreads in a country the size of Israel and very shortly Sharon's commandos turned into a kind of national varsity that every young hotshot dreamed of making.

The unit gloried in its irregular, all-for-one and one-for-all reputation. Not long after it was formed, one of its men was arrested by M.P.'s and taken to a military police station in the Galilee town of Tiberias. The soldier exchanged harsh words with his interrogators and they gave him a going over. When word got back to 101, the unit staged one of its most daring raids—on the Israeli military police station. In an operation that would have done credit to the Dirty Dozen, they surrounded the station, cut its telephone wires, and then invaded, beating some of the M.P.'s bloody and leaving them locked in their own cells. Sharon was not personally involved, but his spirit pervaded the operation and he stood up for his men. Ben Gurion and Dayan, delighted to have an effective commando force, were prepared to accept a little disorderly conduct as the price of aggressiveness, and the commander of 101 got a taste of the rewards of success.

Sharon went on to command a paratroop brigade in the 1956 Sinai Campaign, and led the armored charge in northern Sinai in 1967. Following the war, when Palestinian terrorism became a problem in the Gaza Strip, Prime Minister Golda Meir reached out for Sharon as Ben Gurion had in the past. She dispatched him to the Strip, where he acted with his customary directness and efficiency, killing or capturing virtually all the terrorists within a few months. (This lesson—that terrorism could be successfully combated by military means—was obviously a strong element in Sharon's thinking when he set out after the PLO in Lebanon, in June of 1982.)

Sharon's military career was checkered with charges of insubordination, excessive aggressiveness and an apparent inability to tell the truth. It was generally conceded that he was one of the best combat officers around, but his personality was far too abrasive and extreme for him to achieve his goal of becoming chief of staff. He was passed over for the appointment and left the army in a huff in the summer of 1973.

A few months later Arik Sharon was back in uniform, a reserve general commanding a division on the Egyptian front. Yom Kippur was Sharon's war. Many of the country's leading military men had gone to pieces in the first days of the fighting, but Arik kept his head and showed his customary competence and daring. He led the Israeli counterattack across the Suez Canal, becoming a national hero and, to some, a national savior.

Thus, when Menachem Begin came to office and decided to put Sharon in charge of his settlement program, he was following a long and honored tradition among Israeli Prime Ministers. Begin was a great leader but a terrible executive; his idea of a meeting was to gather people together, make a speech about his overall goals, and then leave them to figure out how the goals could be accomplished. Sharon knew—and Begin found that knowledge invaluable. Some people felt that Sharon's influence over Begin was a product of the Prime Minister's inordinate respect for military heroes. Others mentioned the fact that Sharon's family and Begin's had been friendly in the old country. Probably both had some impact on Begin's thinking. But above all, Begin wanted Sharon because Sharon was the finest executive available, a man who knew how to get big things done.

Arik, for his part, was extremely careful not to give Begin cause to doubt him. He had come a long way from the days when, as an inexperienced ex-general, he had tried to bully the regulars at the Liberal clubhouse. Even his enemies admit that Sharon knows how to read a map, and in the government, he showed that he had learned the rules of political topography in Beginland. The Ezer Weizman affair taught him the danger of antagonizing the Old Man. After all, none of them—Weizman, Sharon or any of the other Likud ministers—had an independent power base. The party belonged to

Begin, and that meant they were all playing by Begin's rules, first among which was "Honor thy father." Sharon was famous for his temper and ill-mannered impatience—at one Cabinet meeting he threatened to lay Deputy Prime Minister Yigael Yadin on the Cabinet table and strip him naked—but it was always "Yes, Mr. Begin" when the Prime Minister was involved. Arik was like Eddie Haskel in the old *Leave It to Beaver* show, full of flattery and angelic good behavior around the Old Man.

The "Beginization" of Ariel Sharon went beyond sycophancy, however; as time went by, Sharon became increasingly identified with Begin's "emotionalist" philosophy. As Weizman moved to the left, Sharon passed him going rightward. He no longer flirted with the doves, stopped hinting at a willingness to make territorial concessions to Jordan or meet with the PLO. Instead he became a spokesman for Begin's view of Israel as an embattled state surrounded not merely by Arab enemies but by the malevolent forces that have plagued the Jews for centuries.

Sharon, the burly, aggressive sabra general, made an unlikely victim—it was hard to believe that he could really share Begin's own diaspora fears and phobias. Many, especially in Herut, doubted the sincerity of his conversion and saw his adoption of Beginite rhetoric and symbolism as nothing more than political opportunism. Some of Begin's closest aides warned him that Sharon could not be trusted, and that he was perverting Begin's philosophy for his own uses.

Menachem Begin was no more blind to Sharon's considerable faults than his predecessors had been. But he had spent his career dominating and controlling powerful colleagues, and he had no reason to believe that Sharon would be any different. In the meantime, the Prime Minister was delighted by Arik's apparent conversion. The fact that a man of Sharon's force and sabra credentials accepted Begin's Jewish Hobbesianism gave it a more practical, Israeli aura.

In the end, Menachem Begin's confidence in his ability to handle Arik Sharon was misplaced. As the only important military figure in Begin's second administration, the defense minister exerted an enormous influence over the Old Man, and he used it to maneuver the country into war in Lebanon.

It is probably still too early to assess fully the diplomatic and military effects of the war. Certainly it accomplished its short-term goal of weakening the PLO's infrastructure in Lebanon and, by extension, its political influence in the Arab world and beyond. Just as certainly, it failed to achieve the broader aim of installing a pro-Western, pro-Israeli government in Beirut. Historians will probably debate the logic and wisdom of the conflict for decades. But there is no doubt that it deeply divided Israeli society and brought an inglorious end to Menachem Begin's political career.

In its initial stage, the war was widely supported. Begin announced in the Knesset that its goal was to drive the PLO out of artillery range of Israel's northern settlements, a policy that Labor endorsed. But it soon became apparent that the campaign had a more ambitious intent; and it also became clear, sometime in August of 1982, that it was not succeeding. Israeli forces surrounded Beirut but proved unable to bring the war to a conclusion. Civilian casualties mounted in the Lebanese capital, Israeli losses grew, and the country became increasingly split between those who wanted more force and those who wanted a halt to the fighting.

For the first time in history a substantial number of Israelis opposed a war—and protested against it, in print and in public squares—while the fighting was still going on. Some of the protest was partisan. The argument that this was the first war in which Israel was not acting in self-defense, for example, ignored the 1956 Sinai Campaign, which David Ben Gurion launched as a preemptive measure against Egypt's military buildup. Similarly, those who sought to portray the shelling of Beirut as unprecedented seldom mentioned the equally fierce attacks on Egypt's cities along the Suez Canal in the late sixties.

Begin and Sharon were quick to point out these inconsistencies as proof that the criticism was politically motivated, and to a certain extent they were right. Lebanon was the first war in which the government had a left-wing opposition (in previous conflicts Begin had given Labor his enthusiastic support), and this certainly played a role in the general antiwar climate that developed. But this explanation ignored a deeper truth—that the Israel of 1982 was a different country from the Israel of 1956, or even 1970. The Yom Kippur War taught the public the danger of blindly trusting its military and political leadership.

Then, too, Begin underestimated the impact of Ariel Sharon on the country. Sharon as an instrument of policy was one thing; but a great many people were scared stiff by the notion that he was in control of policy and overall operational planning. Sharon's dominance became clear in the aftermath of the Christian massacre of Palestinians at the Sabra and Shatilla refugee camps near Beirut. The defense minister was informed of the slaughter almost immediately; Begin learned of it the next day, from a BBC newscast. It was obvious that the defense minister had simply ignored the Prime Minister, and that Sharon, and not Begin, was running the show in Lebanon.

It was this discovery, as much as moral indignation over the massacre or general opposition to the war, that brought hundreds of thousands of Israelis into the streets to protest. The war lost its momentum and became a long, painful process of extrication. Sharon was brought before the Kahan Commission and stripped of his job as defense minister. Begin hung on a little longer, but in the fall of 1983 he stunned the country by retiring and going into seclusion.

There was something chilling, almost unnatural, about Begin's decision. For decades he had sought to assume the burdens of the Jewish people, and established a uniquely personal relationship with the entire country. For his supporters he was a father figure, a man to whom they could always turn. Even his opponents saw him as something more than a mere politician; for them he was a kind of uncle, and if they hated his ideas and mocked his personality, he was nonetheless seen as a man of immovable family loyalty. Now, suddenly, Begin was no longer interested. He didn't just resign; he withdrew, displaying a totally uncharacteristic apathy toward the people he had cared about and the policies he had insistently championed for almost half a century.

There was tragedy in the impersonal way in which this most

personal of Israeli leaders brought his career to an end. And there was irony in the fact that Begin, who, like his predecessors Ben Gurion, Meir and Rabin, had concentrated almost entirely on foreign affairs and security matters, may well be remembered most for the psychological, social and economic changes that took place during his administration.

Indeed, as Prime Minister, Menachem Begin often seemed all but unaware of domestic developments. He was so remote I sometimes thought that if he had been dropped off in downtown Jerusalem he would have had a hard time finding his way home. Begin's natural habitat was behind his desk in the Prime Minister's Office, surrounded by maps and documents; the Knesset dining room, where he sipped tea and chatted with his entourage; Herut party headquarters on King George Street in Tel Aviv; the campaign trail, where tens of thousands of supporters gathered to hear his spellbinding Hebrew oratory; or a plane, headed for negotiations with other world leaders. Outside these arenas he seemed lost, a Prime Minister out of touch with the daily concerns and activities of his constituents. Like David Ben Gurion he was a creature of Israel Major, concerned primarily with the larger-than-life mission he conceived for his country, and for himself.

Yet, despite his preoccupations, the Begin years were a time of massive social change. Whole segments of the population moved from outsider status to full participation in society. Long-suppressed fears and ambitions began to surface and to have an impact on the national mood. A new, critical attitude developed: Never again would the nation allow itself docilely to accept the wisdom of its leaders, or to be led into a war it didn't fully understand. At the same time, a previously unknown emphasis on individualism and personal gratification began to appear. These were changes that Begin didn't plan, and often failed to grasp. He was the last of the founding fathers, a man who lived in dreams of the past and future; but, bewilderingly, he served as the Prime Minister of a people who were, more and more, living in, and for, the present.

5

Red Toenails and a Blue Tattoo

When my daughter, Michal, was six, in the spring of her first-grade year, I noticed a change coming over her. Suddenly she became afraid to go to bed in the dark; often she had a hard time falling asleep. A few times she cried out in the middle of the night and woke up with a headache. Obviously, something was bothering her.

Michali has always been a self-possessed little girl, and when I asked her what the problem was, at first she pretended she didn't know what I meant. I kept prodding her gently and suddenly it popped out of her. "Abba," she sobbed, "why does everybody want to kill us?"

"Michali, what do you mean? Who wants to kill us?"

"Us, the Jews. Everyone wants to kill the Jews. But why, Abba? What have we done wrong?"

I was stunned by the question, and by Michali's fear. One of the reasons I had decided to live in Israel was to bring up children free of the tics and neuroses of diaspora life. And now here was my sabra daughter shaking with insecurity. "Who told you that everyone wants to kill the Jews?" I almost shouted.

"Our teacher. She told us about Haman and Pharaoh the king of Egypt. And Hitler. Abba, he puts Jews in the oven and burns them up. And the Christians, too." Michali burst into tears. "Abba, is John one of those Christians?" John was a friend of mine who worked for the International Red Cross.

"Yes, baby, John's a Christian, but he doesn't want to hurt you. He loves you—you know that." I put my arms around her and rocked her back and forth. Now I understood what the problem was, where it had come from. Michali had been studying the Jewish holidays in school that year, really learning their meanings for the first time. In March her class had been taught the story of Purim, which celebrates the deliverance of the Jews of ancient Persia from the genocidal designs of Haman. In April they had learned about Passover, with its tales of slavery, the killing of the firstborn Jews and the flight across the desert. Then, in May, Holocaust Day; and shortly thereafter, Memorial Day, a solemn occasion that commemorates the more than twelve thousand Israeli soldiers who have fallen in battle. To a six-year-old, it all seemed to have happened at once, to be happening now. I told that to Michali.

"But, Abba, did all those things really happen?" she persisted.

"A long time ago, baby," I said, "before you were born."

"Why?"

There are moments in the life of any father when he finds himself unequipped to deal with a basic question. This was one of mine. In our Reform temple in Pontiac, I had been taught that Judaism was one of the Three Great American Denominations, along with Catholicism and Protestantism. Our home had been resolutely ecumenical and upbeat in the *Father Knows Best* style of the fifties. As a kid I attended Sunday School but the Jewish holidays meant almost nothing to me. The real holidays—the ones you studied in school and got a vacation for—were the American ones. I knew the story of Thanksgiving by heart, could sing every Easter song ever written and once, in the second grade, I had even played the part of Joseph in the school Christmas pageant. My father, the son of Russian immigrants, had been uneasy about that, but my mother, a third-generation midwesterner, dismissed the whole thing. "After all," she had said with a smile, "Joseph was Jewish. This is just type casting."

The brooding overtones of American Jewish literature were almost totally absent from my childhood. Sometimes on Sunday afternoons we would drive to Detroit to visit my father's family, a large clan of Yiddish-speaking peasants from Eastern Europe, and I would occasionally catch a whiff of their immigrants' melancholy, a hint of bitterness at ancient indignities, even an un-American sense of fear. Once, my father's father, who was a socialist with a little grocery store in the heart of Detroit's black ghetto, had a widely discussed dream: Governor Orville Faubus of Arkansas, dressed in a white sheet, was chasing him through the streets of his little village in Russia. I must have been ten years old at the time, and I remember thinking how funny it was that my grandfather would take a dream seriously.

I can never remember anyone in my family—or in our temple—discussing the Holocaust. Back in the fifties and early sixties there was a kind of taboo about the subject. Of course, as I grew older I learned about World War II, and that Jews had been killed in gas chambers. But the whole thing was a distant abstraction, something that had happened before I was born, on a continent I had never seen. It had nothing to do with me.

One Friday night when I was fifteen, I went to the movies with some friends. For some reason, the Huron Theater screened a documentary on World War II in addition to the regular feature; and in it, along with footage of Hitler ranting and raving on a balcony and German tanks rolling through Europe, were the first pictures I had ever seen of concentration camps and their survivors. Even now I can remember the stacks of bones, the emaciated inmates, the haunted-looking children.

On the way home after the movie, some of the guys started laughing about the film. We were tough kids, some black and some white, and ethnic put-downs were a part of our attitude. "Chafets, you see any of your relatives in that movie?" somebody asked.

"Naw, man, I didn't have any relatives in Europe. We're Americans."

"That's what you think. You better be careful, or somebody's gonna put your ass in an oven." Everybody laughed and I laughed too. I was the only Jew in the gang, and laughing was my usual tactic when the subject came up. It was easier that way, and I knew they were only kidding. But this time, in the midst of the laughter, I felt a sharp sense of shame. It suddenly struck me that those people in the movie *were* connected to me. It was a horrifying realization, and I remember looking at the other guys, kids I had grown up with and known all my life, and thinking: "Why, these are goyim."

"Hey, man, anybody tries to fuck with me and the Israeli Army'll start kicking ass." Another first, Israel. I doubt if I could have found it on a map of the world, and I had certainly never looked. All I knew about Israel was that it was a country in which children were supposedly starving and that it had an inexplicable passion for planting trees. Now, suddenly, it was going to stage a private air strike just for me.

Nothing special happened to me the next day. I didn't run away to join a kibbutz, or enroll in a Talmudic academy (there wasn't one in Pontiac, anyway) or even check out a book on the Holocaust from the library. But a seed had been planted. Looking back, I realize that that night marked the end of my Jewish innocence, that it was the moment I made the connection between myself and the fate of the Jews.

At first I hated that connection. It was foreign to me, to the facts and circumstances of my life. I was an American, one of the Big Three, not some pathetic target of hatred and contempt. I scrutinized my own experiences, searched every rejection and failure for traces of anti-Semitism. Had Harry Kelly, the basketball coach, benched me because I was Jewish? Were my lousy grades in algebra the result of prejudice? Even in my newly conscious state, I couldn't really believe it. The fact was that I had almost no personal experience of anti-Semitism beyond a little ethnic razzing in which I gave as good as I got. I had no rational reason for identifying with Jewish suffering—but I couldn't help it.

It took me five years to get from the Huron Theater to El Al flight 001. During those years, as I finished high school and went on to college, I felt myself becoming more and more Jewish. It was an involuntary, even unwelcome development; sometimes I felt like a victim of *The Invasion of the Body Snatchers*. But I couldn't deny that it was happening.

In those days I often thought of my uncle Pinchus. Pinchus was an ancient Hungarian Jew who spent his days in a mom-and-pop grocery store in Detroit, and his nights, from April until October, in his kitchen listening to the Detroit Tiger ball games on the radio. He would sit, a glass of tea in one hand, a small book of psalms in the other, and follow the team's progress through one dismal season after another. I found this peculiar since Pinchus barely knew English, had never to my knowledge actually *seen* a baseball game and didn't, I was quite sure, even know the rules. But it was his belief that the Tigers were Jews; the rest of the American League, goyim. Pinchus felt compelled to know how the Jews were making out; and crazy as it seemed to me, so, increasingly, did I.

One of the things I hoped to find when I finally got to Israel was a release from this compulsion, a return to the easy self-acceptance I had always felt until that night at the movies. I was sure that in Israel no one worried about persecution; after all, who was there to persecute Jews in a Jewish country? Israel meant normality, self-assurance, an end to the sense of being different and vulnerable.

That's what I expected to find in Israel, and at first I thought I had. In the weeks after the Six Day War, the country was in a state of euphoria. Jerusalem was overrun with American tourists, the August sun was bright and Israel seemed to be a nation of happy warriors.

And then came the holidays, Rosh Hashanah and Yom Kippur. It was the first time I had ever experienced Jewish holidays in a Jewish setting, and it came as a shock. A wave of melancholy washed over Jerusalem. I went to the Western Wall, where worshipers from a hundred diasporas wailed heartbroken prayers. During the memorial service on Yom Kippur, I saw people tear at their clothing in grief, or pound the massive stones of the Wall in frustrated anguish. I began to realize that Israel, despite its sabra élan and Mediterranean sunshine, is a nation of orphans and refugees, a place where people jostle and bray at each other all day long and then go home to cramped apartments to drink tea alongside gilt-framed photographs of the dead. The horrors of modern Jewish history hadn't been overcome here, and they were no abstraction; Israel, I began to understand, takes Jewish pain personally.

As the years have passed I came to understand the near universality of that pain, and the role it plays in the national

93

psyche. Each of the major groups in Israel—immigrants from the Arab world, immigrants from Europe and veteran Israelis—has experienced major trauma in its collective lifetime. It is this common experience, more than any other single thing, that unites Israeli society.

Many of the Middle Eastern Jews of Israel came willingly, but a great many others came out of fear of Arab violence. Almost all of them were forced to leave their countries illegally, abandoning all their property and valuables. The Europeans, of course, were victims of the Nazis, and more recently of the Communists.

For veteran Israelis, the great trauma was the War of Independence. On the day Israel became a state, there were roughly 650,000 Jews in Palestine. They were forced to repel an invasion of Arab armies from the south, the east and the north. The War of Independence was primitive by modern standards, fought mostly at close range with small arms. Six thousand Israelis died in that war—almost 1 percent of the entire population, and roughly as many as have died in all Israel's wars since then. In the intimate *yishuv,* the pre-state Jewish community, hardly a single family was untouched.

Nor are the traumas of the various communities wholly distinct. A good many immigrants arrived in time to fight and die in the War of Independence. And most of the veteran Israeli settlers lost relatives in the mass murder of European Jewry. Israel, for all its bravado, came into being with a population of scarred and frightened people.

This mood was compounded by the fact that the catastrophes of the 1940s were not, except for their size, unprecedented. The early Zionists, looking at Jewish history, had simply assumed that Jew-hatred was a universal condition.

In 1882, for example, a proto-Zionist physician named Leo Pinsker diagnosed anti-Semitism as a disease caused by the unique position of the Jews in the diaspora. "Among the living nations of the earth," he wrote, "the Jews occupy the position of a nation long since dead. With the loss of their fatherland, the Jews lost their independence and fell into a state of decay which is incompatible with the existence of a whole and vital organism." Thus, according to Pinsker, "The world saw in this people the frightening form of one of the dead walking among the living." Pinsker considered this an inevitable diaspora condition. "Judeophobia is a psychic aberration," he argued, and as such, "it is hereditary; as a disease transmitted for two thousand years, it is incurable."

Despite Pinsker's eccentric medical terminology, other early thinkers shared his pessimistic analysis. In 1893, Theodor Herzl, the father of modern political Zionism, wrote:

> The Jewish question exists wherever Jews live in perceptible numbers. Where it does not exist, it is carried by Jews in the course of their migrations. We naturally move to those places where we are not persecuted, and there our presence produces persecution. This is the case in every country, and will remain so . . . until the Jewish question finds a solution on a political basis.

This assumption was based on the conviction that the acts of violence against Jews, from the Crusades through the Inquisition, from the pogroms in Eastern Europe to the Blood Libel of Damascus, were connected; and this conviction was a part of the Jewish consciousness long before Israel came into being. "We are one people," Herzl wrote. "Our enemies have made us one. . . . Distress binds us together."

Herzl's belief, and that of other Zionist ideologues, was that the diaspora was primarily responsible for this exceptional condition, and that an independent state would put an end to it by turning the Jews into a normal people. At the end of World War II, this seemed to be the only hope. The Holocaust was the awful confirmation of Zionist doctrine, and what remained was a job of human and national reconstruction. National independence promised a new era, the end to two millennia of suffering and persecution. Despite the freshness of the scars, Prime Minister Ben Gurion and his fellow Labor Zionist leaders desperately wanted to turn the page, to let go of the past and move on to a new chapter.

This logic was at the heart of Ben Gurion's decision to accept financial reparations from Germany. Israel needed the money for practical reasons, of course, but there was more to the decision than simple economics. The Holocaust was a fact that couldn't be changed, but life had to go on and Ben

Gurion saw the danger in dwelling on such an awful catastrophe. He was prepared to believe that the Germans, and the rest of the world, could be truly remorseful for what they had done, and that accepting this remorse would benefit Israel, not only materially but spiritually.

Menachem Begin, on the other hand, considered the decision to accept reparations from Germany an act of moral lunacy. In a Knesset debate over the issue he said: "There are things in life that are worse than death. This is one of them. . . . There will be no negotiations with Germany." The debate over reparations was not Begin's finest hour; he led an emotional march on the Knesset to stop the government from accepting them. The Herut leader was prepared to threaten the very foundation of democracy over this issue—an act of irresponsibility that many Israelis never forgot or forgave.

Begin's opposition to relations with Germany was based on his conviction that human nature had not changed since the war, that Germany was not genuinely sorry for what it had done, and that in any case, no amount of remorse could erase its guilt. The task for Israel, as he conceived it, was not to get over the Holocaust but to absorb and learn its lessons.

At the time, it appeared that the Herut leader was hopelessly mired in the past, a captive of yesterday's demons. In those early years of statehood there were grounds for believing that Herzl's analysis had been correct and that Israel was well on its way to becoming an accepted member of the family of nations. True, the Arabs were still hostile, but even the occasional armed clashes with them, unwelcome as they were, served as a kind of confirmation that Israel had become a real nation and, like nations everywhere, could defend itself. Besides, it was widely assumed that Arab hostility would be temporary and that the conflict would be resolved within a relatively short time.

Beyond the Arab threat, there were powerful reasons for optimism. The mere existence of a Jewish state after two thousand years fueled the notion that things had fundamentally changed and that anything was now possible. Israel came into being with the agreement and support of both superpowers, and in its first years it had the friendship of Europe (excepting Great Britain). Immigrants were pouring in, just as

Zionist doctrine had predicted, and the country was progressing at an astonishing pace. Jewish history seemed a black canvas on which brilliant new colors were now being painted.

The euphoria of independence wore off gradually. In 1953 the USSR announced the discovery of a plot of Jewish doctors against Soviet leaders, and Russian propaganda described the alleged conspirators as "Zionist agents." Left-wing kibbutzim sadly took down the pictures of Stalin that had hung in their dining halls, and Israelis had their first intimation that anti-Semitism was not dead, that neither the Holocaust nor independence had put an end to Jew-baiting as a political weapon.

At about the same time, Gamal Abdel Nasser came to power in Egypt and made it apparent that Arab hostility to Israel would be more than a passing phase. From the mid-fifties, Israel has lived with the feeling of being surrounded by implacable and irrational enemies. Such a situation would give pause to any nation; but for Israel, with its special history and experience, the discovery cast a pall over the easy optimism of the country's first few years.

Not long after I came to Jerusalem I attended a concert featuring a group of young singers fresh out of one of the army's entertainment troupes. They whirled through a repertoire of typical Israeli sixties' tunes: sweet-natured love songs, patriotic numbers, humorous vignettes of teen-age life. Most of the audience was made up of young soldiers, and the atmosphere was relentlessly wholesome and upbeat—a far cry from the drug-ridden rock concerts that were popular at the time in the States. I looked at the energetic young sabra entertainers and thought of a phrase I had recently heard: *yaldai ha'shemesh*, "children of the sun," which had been used to describe kids like these—children raised not in the dark alleys of the ghetto but on the warm Mediterranean soil of the motherland. These kids had never been to the Huron Theater, I thought to myself, they had never known the fears I was hoping to escape.

As the show drew to a close, the group swung into an up-tempo number. *"Ha'olam ku'lo neg'denu,"* they sang. "The whole world is against us." The audience knew the song and joined in on the chorus. They clapped in the off-the-beat, splay-fingered Israeli style and sang: "The whole world is against us; never mind, we'll get by; we don't give a damn about them anyway." This was 1969; Israel was twenty-one years old. But the gilt-framed pictures and the curriculum of persecution and the years of isolation and warfare had taken their toll. Even the young people communicated in the common vocabulary of Jewish outrage and fear.

And then came the Yom Kippur War, a shock that blasted the national equilibrium and sent Israel into something very close to despair. The Arabs had a new weapon—oil—and it seemed to be frighteningly effective. Suddenly Israel was a pariah state. Forty or so Black African countries, many of them recipients of Israeli foreign aid, broke diplomatic relations within a matter of weeks. The Soviet Union supplied the Arab armies with weapons and led the political charge in the United Nations. Third World nations denounced Israel in every international forum. And, most ominously, Western Europe caved in to Arab pressure and refused to allow American planes carrying essential military equipment to refuel in their territory. In 1973, the last illusions about European remorse over the Holocaust disappeared. Only the Netherlands maintained a posture of public support for Israel; and Israelis were so pathetically grateful that the radio broadcast Dutch lessons to enable people personally to thank Dutch volunteers who had come to the country to help. Of course Israel wasn't quite alone; it still had the support of the United States. But how long, people asked themselves, would even the Americans hold out against the threat of Arab economic reprisal?

The Yom Kippur War relinked Israel with Jewish history, put the country squarely back into the chain of isolation and peril. This was an enormously frustrating and frightening development. In the diaspora, when the Jews had stayed to themselves they had been seen as a mysterious and threatening foreign presence, Christ killers, well poisoners, international plotters, fair game for pogroms and expulsions; and when they had tried to blend in, to become "real Germans," they had been marched to the gas chambers wearing their World War I decorations. The diaspora seemed to offer no third course; after Auschwitz, Jewish nationalism appeared to Israelis to be the last hope.

The early Zionist pioneers worked hard to make Israel "normal." They transformed themselves into farmers and soldiers; taught their children about the universal brotherhood of nations and kept their voices down when they talked about the old country; extended a helping hand to developing nations and played at international power politics. But now it appeared that the Zionist prescription for regular-guy status had failed. In the end, Israel was still a collection of Jews, unable to escape the historic fate of Jews.

With one great difference. There was now a Jewish state with an army. For the first time since the days of the Bible, the Jews were not unarmed. After the disillusionment of the 1973 war, military power became the irreducible bottom line for Israel. This was not the cult of military heroism that had followed the Six Day War. Yom Kippur produced no stirring anthems, no victory albums or glorious parades. It gave birth, instead, to an insatiable security hunger. The army was expanded, and people who had previously not been drafted— welfare cases, medical deferments, immigrants—were assigned to national service or reserve duty. Military spending, already high, grew far beyond the country's economic capacity, and Israel went heavily into debt to buy an ever greater number of weapons. No amount of security seemed secure enough now, no margin of safety too wide.

Shortly after the end of the Yom Kippur War, a series of PLO terror attacks rocked the country. Women flocked to pistol ranges to learn how to handle small arms. The steel security-door business flourished. Most Israeli men were already spending between thirty and sixty days a year in active reserve duty; now a new civil guard unit was formed, its volunteer members women and former soldiers beyond the fifty-five-year-old reserve limit.

The aftermath of the war left the country with a bitterness of spirit that has never quite departed. A few months after Yom Kippur, I went to visit a friend whose father was a concentration camp survivor. He was an old man with a blue tattoo, and like many survivors he almost never mentioned his experiences in World War II. We sat in the family's small living room and discussed "the situation," the national code word for whatever seems most wrong at the moment. My friend and I chugged Goldstar beer and argued—the accepted form of conversation in these sessions—while the old man sipped tea and listened. As I recall it, I was taking an optimistic approach: that Israel's problems were temporary, that diplomatic flexibility and sensible public pronouncements would eventually restore the country's faltering international position—something like that. Suddenly my friend's father broke into the conversation. "They didn't have enough fun with me in the camp, they've got to come after me here, too," he said in a sudden, horrible rage. "It's all the same. They won't let us alone anyplace."

It is impossible to underestimate the centrality of the Holocaust in the Israeli psyche, and it surfaces in the most unexpected places. Not long ago some friends and I were watching the news on television. There was an item about the closing of the Ata textile factory, and a reporter interviewed some workers who were about to lose their jobs. "I'll fight the management, the union, even the government if I have to," one indignant worker said. "I was in the Holocaust—you know what the Holocaust was. What do I have to lose now?"

"Imagine that," I said to the people I was watching with. "Just think of how obsessed he must be."

"That's nothing," replied one of the women. "One time I was going with this guy and he took me home to meet his mother. She took one look at me and said, 'It's not enough what Hitler did to me, you have to come here without a bra!'"

This sense of fear and rage is omnipresent. Every anti-Israeli or anti-Jewish statement or action feeds it, and people take a perverse pleasure in collecting examples. Not a day goes by without press reports of persecution of Jews in the Soviet Union, in Syria, Iran, Argentina, Romania. Nazi hunters appear on television to denounce Latin American dictators for harboring mass murderers, or the indifference of the West German government to their capture. There are reports of desecration of Jewish cemeteries in France, bombings of synagogues in Brooklyn, cooperation between the PLO and the Ku Klux Klan in Arizona. The anti-Jewish ravings of Idi Amin, Louis Farrakhan, the Saudi royal family, *Pravda,* the Ayatollah Khomeini, the German Greens, the radical right, the new left, the Arab center—all are noted and reported.

The sense of persecution remains the national glue, in much the same way that Herzl saw it almost a hundred years ago. When the Ethiopian immigrants began arriving in large numbers, many Israelis had a hard time identifying these Black Africans as fellow Jews. Then a senior government official was quoted as saying that "the traumas that the Ethiopian Jews have undergone are similar in many ways to the trauma of the Holocaust." Israeli physicians who treated Ethiopian children noted that they were suffering from the same kind of malnutrition that the concentration camp survivors had experienced. The public nodded understandingly. Holocaust, concentration camps, persecution . . . these exotic Africans must be Jews after all. They had passed the most fundamental initiation, and the stories of their persecution soon became a part of the national mosaic of pain.

Given Jewish history—ancient and modern—Israel would almost certainly have been a security-obsessed place even without real enemies. But from the moment of its creation, it has had to cope with a prolonged and unrelieved state of war. Not surprisingly, a great many Israelis have come to see the conflict in an emotional way, as a continuation of the Jewish condition. And, since anti-Semitism is a mysterious and irrational disease, the tendency is to view the conflict in irrational, almost fatalistic terms, to adopt a damned-if-we-do-and-damned-if-we-don't approach to the rest of the world. All that is left is the capacity to defend oneself from the hostile forces at work against the Jews; and this very quickly can lead to a kind of unreasoning militancy.

This irrationality offends and exasperates those Israelis who, through temperament or training, view the Arab-Israel conflict in mundane, political terms. Seen through their eyes, the Israeli predicament is simply a dispute between two competing nationalisms, or a struggle over territory. The world's attitude toward Israel is a function of international politics, understandable in terms of bloc interests, economic considerations, East-West tensions and so forth. They see the Israeli preoccupation with the past as a counterproductive obsession, one that leads to obstinacy, creates hostility and becomes ultimately self-fulfilling.

There is something extremely reassuring about this approach. It demythologizes the conflict, removes it from the realm of the supernatural, the inevitable. There is paradoxical comfort in believing that Israel is largely to blame for its problems, for if Israel has created hostility—through aggression, insensitivity or greed—then Israel has the capacity to repair the damage. Seen this way, Israel is not under some bizarre historical curse, doomed to struggle against irrational and immutable forces; it is simply another nation in a political dispute with its neighbors.

In political terms, the "emotionalist" attitude has come to be identified with the right, the "rationalist" approach with the left. Indeed, the left-right split—once an ideological dispute between socialists and nonsocialists—has become in recent years largely a matter of Jewish metaphysics. Most Israelis are educated in secular schools and taught to think in rational, logical ways about the world; and the notion that they belong to a cursed nation runs against their intellectual grain. There is also psychological aversion to accepting such a depressing idea. But then comes a moment, like my moment with my daughter, Michal, when we are forced to answer The Question; and, face to face with the idea that the world has a special attitude toward Jews, most Israelis find it almost impossible to deny that it has always been so, and remains so now.

There is an ambivalence that affects all but the most resolutely single-minded Israelis. Even an emotionalist like Menachem Begin was able to deal with Egypt in a practical, statesmanlike way; his decision to surrender territory for a peace treaty implied a conviction that Israeli policy could operate under normal international expectations. On the other hand, even a rationalist like Ben Gurion was not immune to mysticism. It was he, after all, who first said that to be a realist in Israel, you have to believe in miracles. It was a fine phrase, quoted at a thousand fund-raising meetings in America, but it had a dark side not usually noticed by the toastmasters. No one knew better than Ben Gurion that in Jewish history, not all of the "miracles" have been happy ones.

The struggle between rationalist optimism and emotionalist pessimism is one of the most constant elements in Israeli life. For the first twenty-five years it appeared that, for all the clouds, the sun would burst through. Then, on Yom Kippur, 1973, it started to rain. And when it did, the country, caught in the downpour, quite naturally turned to the man with the biggest umbrella.

The post–Yom Kippur War atmosphere was made for Menachem Begin, a man who had never detached himself from the dark past, never believed that the creation of New Jewish Men and Women would alter the essential national chemistry or the world's reaction to it. In a period of confusion, he offered certainty. At a time of international pressure, he bristled with defiance. Arab hostility was Israel's own fault? You might just as well argue that the Jews had brought on the Spanish Inquisition, the mass murders of the Crusaders, the Damascus Blood Libel. Jew-hatred, Begin maintained, was a crime without a motive, and no solution—changing the Jewish character, or social structure, or political position—could prevent it. In office, Menachem Begin often acted as if the whole world was wrong, and only Israel right, not because he doubted the wisdom of the international community, but because he questioned its decency.

Begin tapped into the country's security hunger, gave people a feeling of protection. This especially galled his opponents in the Labor party, who were, after all, warriors. While Begin had spent his life making flowery speeches, they had fought. Prime Minister Itzhak Rabin was a hero of the Six Day War, and one of the few military figures to emerge unscathed from the Yom Kippur debacle. Foreign Minister Yigal Allon, the boy commander of the War of Independence, was widely considered a brilliant military mind. Defense Minister Shimon Peres had been a close associate of Ben Gurion and was identified with the former Prime Minister's hawkish security policies. The Labor leaders simply couldn't understand how they, who had spent their whole careers fighting Arabs, were suddenly perceived as too soft. What they didn't realize was that after Yom Kippur the country wasn't primarily worried about the Arabs; it was afraid of ghosts. People were spooked by the demons of the past, and they turned to Begin, who had seen the apparitions all along. He wouldn't have understood the term, but to many Israelis, Menachem Begin was a ghostbuster.

In true ghostbuster style, Begin set out to spook the spirits. The only free-world leader ever to serve a term in Siberia, he lost no opportunity to bait the Soviets, reminding the world that Jew-hatred was a long and honored Russian tradition. When a bomb went off in a Jewish restaurant in Paris, Begin pointedly warned the French government that if it couldn't guarantee the safety of French Jews, he would have to look into it personally. The Prime Minister's domestic critics reminded him that his own government had been unable to catch some of the terrorists at large in Israel, but this demand for consistency made no impression on him whatsoever. Even the Americans came in for an occasional slap; during the war in Lebanon, when Ronald Reagan put a picture of a wounded Palestinian child on his desk, Begin retaliated by placing a photograph of a Jewish boy from the Warsaw ghetto on his.

Begin was at his most uncompromising when it came to dealing with the Germans. He hated them and he didn't care who knew it, refused to speak the language or meet with German journalists. Begin considered the new Germany a myth, and its pretensions to enlightened liberalism a grotesque fiction; and in Helmut Schmidt, with his tendency to moralize to Israel, he had a perfect foil.

In the spring of 1981, shortly before the Israeli elections, Schmidt visited the Persian Gulf and let it be known that his government was considering selling tanks and other weapons to Saudi Arabia. He also used the occasion to utter some pieties about Germany's moral obligation to the Palestinian people. This was all Begin needed to hear. He went off like a rocket, denouncing the idea that Hitler's successors would even dream of arming a nation at war with Israel or supporting an organization—the PLO—whose constitution called for the destruction of the Jewish state. His language was harsh, but when an adviser cautioned him about it, he replied that Germans are cowards who murder children and women, and that he wasn't worried about Schmidt's reaction.

Schmidt, who disliked Begin intensely, counterpunched

with some Marquis of Queensbury diplomatic jabs, a modern European gentleman confronted with a Jewish ruffian. Begin ducked the jabs and went for the jugular. "My family was murdered by the German Army," he told journalists, "and Herr Schmidt was a Nazi officer on the Eastern front. How do I know that he wasn't one of the murderers?" So much for the New Germany. Israelis, even many who normally cringed at Begin's rhetorical excesses, applauded enthusiastically.

Another event in the spring of 1981 pointed even more graphically to Begin's fixation with the Holocaust and his sense of Israel as a victim nation. In June, only weeks before the election, he ordered the destruction of the Iraqi nuclear reactor. When word reached Jerusalem that the attack had been carried out successfully, Begin explained his reasons to the country. For several years, he said, he had been haunted by what the *"meshuggeneh"* Saddam Hussein of Iraq might do with an atomic weapon. During that time he had looked at his own grandchildren and recalled the 1.5 million Jewish children who had been murdered, children who had turned to their parents, in vain, for protection. The bomb, Begin noted, even released a poison gas similar to the one the Nazis had used in the camps. Begin told of agonizing over the future of Israel's children and then making his decision. He was, after all, the Old Man, and he wouldn't permit another Holocaust. Never again.

The reaction of the opposition Labor party to the Iraqi bombing was a study in political ineptitude and showed how out of touch the party leadership was with the national mood. Labor hinted that the Prime Minister's true motive had been political—a charge that most Israelis, given Begin's long record of patriotism, found unbelievable. Worse, Shimon Peres criticized the operation, letting it be known that he had been in contact with the new French President, François Mitterrand, and had received assurances that France, the principal supplier of Iraq's nuclear technology, would act to prevent its use in making weapons. People didn't doubt that Peres had been given such assurances, but they questioned their value and Peres's common sense in seeking them in the first place. This skepticism was one of the primary factors in Begin's come-from-behind victory.

If Begin was not exactly unaware of the political value of his ghostbusting, neither was it a cynical manipulation, as many of his critics, especially outsiders, assumed. For one thing, in a country with so many traumatized Jews, he never could have got away with faking it. And for another, the tendency to identify the Arabs, and especially the PLO, with the Nazis was something that a great many Israelis—not all of them Beginites—could understand. Following the Yom Kippur War, army psychologists were astonished by how many soldiers involved in the first desperate days of fighting had imagined that the Syrian and Egyptian armies were Nazis, bent on carrying out mass murder. Many of the soldiers who saw the Arabs as reincarnations of the Germans were born after the end of World War II and a surprisingly high percentage came from families with no personal connection whatever to the Holocaust.

In May, 1974 a group of PLO terrorists crossed into northern Israel from Lebanon and seized a schoolhouse full of children in the border town of Ma'alot. As the country watched, the terrorists proceeded to murder the hostages. It is impossible to know what the PLO leaders who ordered the operation had in mind, if they realized the symbolism of what they were doing, but the massacre had an electrifying impact. Once again armed men had come for Jewish children; the nightmare had returned. The moment the first dead child came flying out of the second-story window of the schoolhouse, the chances of Israel's negotiating with Yasir Arafat ended for good.

Once Arafat became identified in the public mind with the Nazis, further comparisons were easy to make. After all, his predecessor and mentor, Haj Amin el Husseini, the Mufti of Jerusalem, had been an outspoken admirer of Hitler's Jewish policy and had spent World War II in Berlin trying to help the Nazi war effort. The Mufti and his fellow militants had played a key role in forcing the British to close the gates of Palestine to Jewish immigration during the war—giving them at least an indirect responsibility for the slaughter.

Many people became sensitive to every nuance of PLO-Nazi similarity. The Palestine National Covenant, with its uncompromising demand for the destruction of Israel, reminded them of Hitler's blueprint, *Mein Kampf*. The fact that German neo-Nazis were trained in PLO camps in Lebanon was duly noted. The 1976 airline hijacking of a French plane bound for Israel was carried out by a mixed team of Palestinian and German terrorists; and after the passengers were rescued at the Entebbe airport, a number of them told of their terror when the hijackers had separated the Israelis from the others. "They made a 'selection,'" a camp survivor told the press, "just like in the war."

And then, one night in 1979, a PLO hit team landed on the beach in Nahariyya, a resort town in northern Israel. They murdered Danny Haran and his five-year-old daughter while Haran's wife, Semadar, cowered in a utility room nearby.

Semadar Haran was a young kibbutz-raised Israeli, one of the children of the sunshine, a woman with roots in the soil of the Galilee. When she heard the voices of the PLO hit team and their automatic-weapons fire, she took her two-year-old daughter in her arms and hid. When rescue workers found her, the infant was dead, smothered by the hysterical young woman. She didn't understand what had happened—she could only mumble incoherently that the Nazis had finally come, and could someone please save her baby?

The PLO had sought to commit terror and they succeeded; Semadar Haran had been terrorized. A single knock on her door had transformed her from a vivacious young mother into a hunted victim of the Nazis. People heard the story and wept in sorrow and recognition. A lot of Israelis had been having the same nightmare lately.

Outsiders often imagine that Israel's bitter history and embattled present must make it a grim and forbidding place. But reality is more complex. Fear and insecurity exist on a plane of their own, separate from the daily lives of ordinary people, who make their own accommodation with their demons—people like the lady on the bus in Haifa.

I saw her only once, on a hot summer afternoon fifteen years ago. I was sitting across the aisle, one row back, when I first noticed her, and the thing that caught my attention was her painted toenails. They were manicured and lacquered a bright, shiny red, peeking out of stylish summer pumps, and they seemed wildly out of place among the gritty, sandal-clad feet of the other passengers. If the lady was aware of the incongruity, though, she didn't show it. She daintily rested her feet toes up, on the backs of her high heels to protect the paint job from the cigarette butts and sunflower-seed husks that littered the floor. She was close to fifty, but there was something fresh and girlish about her that made me think of Irwin Shaw's short story about the pretty women in their summer dresses. I began to wonder who she was, where she was going.

She could have been the wife of a banker hurrying home from an afternoon assignation, busing it because she had been afraid to leave her car parked outside her lover's apartment. Or an attractive widow on her way to her sister's place in the fashionable neighborhood at the top of the hill, dressed up to make a good impression on some eligible dinner partner. As I speculated I looked at her closely for the first time. Short brown hair carefully coiffed, soft-looking shoulders under the straps of an expensive summer frock, tan arms . . . Suddenly my gaze froze and I felt a jolt, a small shock of electricity. On her arm, blurred but unmistakable, was a blue tattoo. A concentration camp number. This elegant, pampered lady had been in Auschwitz, in Dachau, in Bergen-Belsen. She must have been a beautiful young girl, and I didn't want to think of what she had been forced to do to stay alive, to survive the war, to reach this Haifa city bus where she sat fresh in her summer outfit, a smile of secret contentment on her face.

The lady had no idea that I was staring at her, and when she got off the bus she didn't even glance my way. I watched her walk up the street, high heels clicking in a self-assured stride, and I wondered about her vitality, her vanity—how the red paint on her toes and the blue tattoo torn into her arm could possibly live together on the same body.

When Michali asked me why everyone wants to kill the Jews, I thought of the lady on the bus. What did she tell her children? Did she deny that it was so, say that Auschwitz was an aberration? Did she have a judicious, rational explanation that separated Haman from Hitler, parsed Pharaoh from the PLO? I longed to tell Michali that they had nothing to do with

108

one another, and certainly nothing to do with her. But I couldn't, because I'm not sure, and neither are most Israelis.

This uncertainty is what makes the country such a contradictory place, at once generous and mean, open and suspicious, happy and miserable. But Michali was only six, still too young, I thought, to understand that she lives in a country of blue tattoos and red toenails. And so I did what all fathers do when they don't know the answer: I told her she'd understand it all when she grew up, and I rubbed her back until she fell asleep.

PART II

HARD HATS AND HOLY MEN

6

"Not Nice Children"

In the spring of 1978, at the age of thirty-one, I became a Sephardic Jew.* The scene of this improbable transformation was the Jerusalem branch of the Israeli Rabbinate, located in a seedy building on Havetzelet Street in the city's downtown section. The Rabbinate is an office I rarely visit—the last time I had been there was in 1975, to get divorced. Now, three years later, I was back with my fiancée, Miri, to register for marriage. We sat down on a hard bench along with other couples on the way into or out of matrimony, and waited to be called.

When our turn came we were ushered into a small room and seated in a couple of wooden chairs across the desk from a black-hatted, black-bearded young rabbi-clerk. He produced a form and began filling in the blanks, starting with me. First name? "Ze'ev." Previous first name? "William." Last name? "Chafets." Previous last name? "None." One by one I answered the questions on the checklist. When he came to the space marked *Edah*, "ethnic affiliation," I saw him write "Sephardi."

"Excuse me, but you've got a mistake there," I told him politely.

"No mistake. You are a Sephardi."

* Sephardic Jews are literally Spanish Jews. In Israel the term is popularly used to connote Jews from African and Asian (i.e. Islamic) countries.

"Hardly," I laughed. "My entire family on both sides is from Eastern Europe. Russia and Poland. My grandparents spoke Yiddish at home. And I was born in the States. In fact, I never even heard of Sephardic Jews until I came to Israel."

"In that case, I have a pleasant surprise for you," the rabbi told me in a deepening Iraqi accent. "Your name is Chafets, your original name. And people with that name are automatically considered Sephardim. You see, back in the fifteenth century when most of the Spanish Jews fled the Inquisition and went east to Arab countries, a few headed for Eastern Europe instead. That's what your ancestors did. We can tell by the name."

The entire thing struck me as comical, but the rabbi was obviously offended by my laughter. "Discovering your roots is a serious matter," he said gravely. "We Sephardim are the original Jews, the heirs to the tradition of the great rabbis and wise men. Yehuda Halevi was a Sephardi, so was the Rambam. And Sadiah Gaon.

"You're going to need a Sephardic rabbi yourself now," he added, changing gears.

I must have looked at him quizzically.

"A rabbi. You're going to need one for your wedding. A Sephardic rabbi. As a matter of fact, I do weddings myself, as a special favor to certain young couples. Can I be of service?"

"I think we'll stick with the neighborhood rabbi, if it's all the same to you."

"As you wish." He turned to Miri. "Where are your parents from?"

"Germany," she replied. "And I'm afraid you can't make them into Sephardim. Our family name is Zamulevitch."

"In that case you will be registered as a mixed marriage—Ashkenazi bride, Sephardi groom. Excellent. They have the most beautiful children, you know."

"We'll name one after you, Rabbi," I promised.

"Excellent, excellent. Well, good luck to you. And remember, *habibi,* you're one of us now."

The whole thing was a joke, of course. Michali wondered if she could eat peas and corn on Passover, according to Sephardi practice. My prospective mother-in-law, whose two sons were already married to real Sephardic girls, sighed that she would never have an Ashkenazi grandchild. Friends who heard the story wondered if I had paid off the rabbi. "Being a Sephardi these days is in," a Baghdad-born neighbor told me. I laughed it all off, but it stayed in the back of my mind. Until now the ethnic divisions of Israeli society had had nothing to do with me. As an American Jew I never considered myself Ashkenazi or Sephardi—it was a distinction that hadn't really existed in Pontiac, Michigan. Now, suddenly, I was being offered membership in a club because of some unknown ancestor—taken in like a legacy pledge in a fraternity. Gradually, when new acquaintances asked me where my family was from—an inevitable question in Israel—I began to tell them the story of my mysterious Eastern origins. As a joke, of course, but still . . .

If you were going to become a Sephardi, 1978 was the year to do it. For three decades the Sephardim constituted "the Second Israel": a large, mostly silent mass of Middle Eastern Jews in a secular, Western-oriented society presided over by Eastern European founding fathers. During these years, as their number grew, they became a kind of marginal majority—so marginal, in fact, that Real Israelis barely thought of them as Israelis at all. But in 1978, after Sephardi votes had helped put Menachem Begin into office, there was a new militancy in the air. The defeat of the old leaders—who brought the Sephardim to Israel in the first place—let an ethnic genie out of the bottle, an angry and resentful genie bent on getting what it wanted most: respect.

When I had first arrived in Israel, I had been struck by the wild diversity of Jews I found. There were dark-skinned Indians, the women dressed in saris with red dots painted on their foreheads; powerfully built Kurdish stevedores who would carry a washing machine up four flights of stairs for a dollar a flight; a brown, hawk-nosed Yemenite with side curls and gentle eyes who rode the number 18 bus reading a newspaper upside down (a friend explained that in Yemen, children learned to read sitting in a circle around a single book). Israel was a country of great adventures, and one of the greatest, I thought, was the reunion of these long-separated tribes of Jews. To me, the entire process seemed romantic.

115

My fellow students at the university were mostly Ashkenazis, and they found my wonder at these exotic Jews
amusing. They had long since gotten used to the variety, and
they expounded on the mentalities and traits of each group
with an anthropologist's expertise. It was the Era of High
Certitude, and the evaluations rarely varied. As Yisrael had
taught me, each community was assigned certain characteristics: the Iraqis were intelligent and organized but cold; the
Kurds strong and stupid; the Moroccans, the largest single
group, were hot-tempered and primitive; the Yemenites,
everyone's pet, good-natured, bright and hardworking; and
so on.

There was near unanimity, too, about the prospects for
these Oriental Jews. They had made great strides since coming to the country, moving up from unskilled labor to trades
and even middle-level civil service positions. More and more
were going to high school, learning a skill, fitting into Israeli
society. A growing number were attending university, and
there were now quite a few Sephardi professionals. They were
still largely blue-collar people, of course, and would be for
some time, but this was to be expected. Most felt that the
Sephardi problem would be solved within a generation or two
when the Oriental Jews, through intermarriage and assimilation, became Real Israelis. It was generally assumed that the
Sephardim accepted this analysis, just as the students did
themselves, as obvious.

As time went on, I became accustomed to the hetero-
geneity of Jewish life in Israel. I served with Sephardi kids in
the army, gave orders to some and took orders from others.
In the middle-class building where we lived, about half our
neighbors were from Oriental backgrounds: Naim, a carpenter from Iraq whose daughter was my daughter's best
friend; Shaul, another Iraqi who worked as a clerk in the municipal court and moonlighted as a graphologist and fortune-
teller, and who was married to a woman from Argentina;
Melamud, a Moroccan refrigerator repairman who lived next
door; and half a dozen others. Neighbors get to know each
other in Israel, but we rarely discussed our different backgrounds. We all knew the stereotypes—I was aware that there
was one for me, an American, as well—and further discussion

seemed unnecessary. The ethnic assumptions were so universal and so invariable that it seldom occurred to me to question them.

These stereotypes, I later learned, had begun long before I arrived. In 1948, with immigrant camps stuffed to overflowing, a young reporter for the morning daily *Ha'aretz,* Aryeh Gelbloom, disguised himself as a newcomer and wrote a series of investigative pieces on the immigrants, which were largely sympathetic to the new arrivals. He described the difficult conditions of the absorption camps, the overcrowding, poverty and disease that plagued their residents. But in the last article in the series the young Israeli reporter turned his attention to the largest group of Sephardim in the camp, the immigrants from Morocco:

This is the immigration of a race that we haven't known before in Israel. We are dealing with a people of record primitiveness. Their level of education borders on total ignorance and worse, they totally lack the capacity to absorb anything spiritual. Generally speaking they are only slightly better than the Arabs, Blacks and Berbers among whom they used to live. In any case, they are of a lower order than the Palestinian Arabs we are accustomed to. Unlike the [Jewish] Yemenites, they also lack Jewish roots . . . they are totally given over to the wildest and most primitive instincts.

Gelbloom described the behavior of the Moroccans he had met:

In the corners of the camp where [they] live you find filth, gambling, drunkenness, and prostitution. Many of them suffer from serious eye, skin and venereal diseases. And all this without even mentioning theft and robbery. Nothing is safe from this anti-social element, no lock is strong enough. . . .

. . . it is not surprising that the crime rate in the country is rising. In some parts of Jerusalem it is not safe for young girls, and even young men, to go outside alone after dark. . . .

But more than anything else there is one basic fact—their total inability to adapt to life in Israel and, above all, their chronic laziness and hatred of work.

Gelbloom considered the Moroccans a particularly bad kind of material, but not too different from other potential newcomers from the rest of the Arab world. "Think about what will happen to this country if this becomes its population," he cautioned his readers:

One day they will be joined by the Jews from the [other] Arab countries. What will this country, and the standard of its population, be then?

The special tragedy of this immigration, as opposed to the poor human material from Europe [i.e., the survivors of the Holocaust], is that there is no hope for their children either. Raising their level from the depths . . . is a matter of generations.

Gelbloom's analysis of the "human material" of the Moroccans and other groups of Sephardi Jews was unusually extreme and blunt, but it was by no means unique. Two years later Amos Elon, who has since written movingly about the plight of the Palestinian Arabs, visited a group of Iraqi Jews in a camp and did for them what Gelbloom had done for the Moroccans, describing for the readers of *Ha'aretz* the unpleasant smell of these inferior Jews, whose odor, according to Elon, was a function of their primitiveness. (*Ha'aretz*, it is worth noting, favored "selective immigration," i.e., keeping the Sephardim out of Israel as long as possible.)

The sneering assessments of the young Ashkenazi reporters were exceptionally explicit; few Israelis felt—or at least said out loud, as Gelbloom had—that the Oriental Jews were inherently inferior. Most believed that their problem was grounded in their long sojourn in the backward Islamic world. Indeed, the great Hebrew poet Chaim Nachman Bialik was supposed to have jested that he hated the Arabs because they reminded him of Sephardi Jews.

Of course, the Sephardi immigrants were not the only ones to be stereotyped, assessed as human material and then fed into the system. During the first three years of independence, Israel roughly doubled its size through immigration, with half of the newcomers coming from Europe. Like the Sephardim, they were mostly penniless and disoriented. Few of them could claim a real Zionist education. Many were concentration camp survivors who still bore fresh emotional scars.

At first these European Jews were no better off than the Sephardim. They passed through the same tent cities, like the one Gelbloom had visited; were assigned the same make-work jobs and shoddy housing. But the Europeans had several advantages that enabled them to move ahead of their fellow immigrants. For one thing, they were from the same Yiddish-speaking world as the pioneer elite, and were thus considered culturally superior. Many, especially those from Central Europe, had professions that were useful in state-building. And, in the early fifties, when the first financial-reparations agreement with Germany was concluded, many began receiving regular pensions in foreign currency. The amounts were not huge, but in Israeli terms they were significant, and they enabled the recipients to improve their standard of living. If the Sephardi and Ashkenazi immigrants of the late forties had started even, by the mid-fifties there was already a considerable gap, and it was widening.

Throughout this period and later, when Mapai dominated the political scene, few if any of the new Sephardi immigrants were socialists. Their natural sympathies were with the religious parties, which represented their own traditionalist outlook. Nevertheless, a great many voted for Mapai, partly out of respect for the great David Ben Gurion, but at least partly from fear. Without *protekzia* from the Mapai ward heelers it was almost impossible to find a job, to change apartments, to enroll a child in high school. This was the system, at once generous and tightfisted, paternal and insensitive. Most of the newcomers were simply too weak, too awed by their new surroundings, too cowed by the glorious achievements of the pioneers and their sabra sons to protest. But by the mid-fifties, the first hints of dissatisfaction were beginning to surface.

The most dramatic and best-remembered came at Wadi Salib, a slum neighborhood in the city of Haifa. A barroom brawl turned into a riot, the police were summoned and one

Moroccan immigrant was shot and wounded. The next day the residents of Wadi Salib ran wild. They trashed public buildings, hurled rocks and bottles at the police and generally vented a frustration that had been building up for a decade. At the end of the day, thirteen policemen had been injured and thirty-two civilians were in jail.

In 1964, five years after Wadi Salib and a decade and a half after Aryeh Gelbloom's article on the Moroccan Jews, twelve-year-old Avi Zaguri arrived from Casablanca along with his mother and brothers and sisters. The Zaguris had been Zionists in Morocco, and they came with high expectations. Mrs. Zaguri asked the authorities to assign her to Jerusalem, where her sister lived. Instead the family was sent south to the Negev desert, to the recently founded town of Dimona. "They told us that it was only half an hour from Jerusalem," Avi recalls with a wry smile.

Today, Avi Zaguri is a huge, moon-faced man with a sunny disposition and a keen eye for the absurd. He and his brother Meir own and operate La Belle, a downtown Jerusalem tavern and restaurant that is the hangout for the press corps in the Israeli capital. It is the kind of place where you can get a phone call or avoid one, sit for hours over a beer, cash a check or, if you don't happen to have a check on you, cadge a loan from Avi. Like all good bars, La Belle has an attitude— friendly, upbeat, like the Zaguri brothers themselves.

Avi and Meir arrived in Israel young enough to be more Israeli than Moroccan. Meir was educated at a Herut-run boarding school, and he is a strong supporter of the Likud. Avi, on the other hand, is a Labor party man, which makes him something of a rarity among Israel's Moroccan community. But he doesn't hold the sins of the past against the establishment. He understands the well-meaning and largely unintentional nature of the pioneers' mistakes and, with congenital good humor, forgives them—until he remembers the day his mother, in total desperation, unable to feed her family or persuade the authorities to allow her to live near her sister, bundled up the Zaguri children and demonstratively abandoned them in the Dimona labor exchange. "You take care of them," she tearfully told the clerk, and although the children had been told in advance that it was merely a pressure tactic, Avi remembers it as a terrifying moment.

"They had no reason to treat our mother that way," he says, with a grim look in his usually warm brown eyes. "They dealt with us as if we were nothing, as if we didn't even exist. Just a few head of Moroccan immigrants. We were raised to love this country. We came because we wanted to, not because we had to. And then, when we saw what they thought of us here, how little they understood or wanted to understand, it almost broke our hearts."

Mrs. Zaguri eventually was reassigned to Jerusalem. She often comes into La Belle to say hello to her sons and to her daughter Aliza, who works evenings as a waitress. Meir is married to a girl whose family comes from Russia; his children, he says, are neither Moroccan nor Russian, just Israeli. Aliza goes out with a man named Fefferberg, whose family owns a Fiddler-on-the-Roof-style delicatessen not far from La Belle. They have adjusted to Israel, and the early years of struggle are just a bad memory.

The Zaguris' is not an isolated success story. Sephardim who were willing to adapt, who had patience and faith in the country, have been able to make their way in Israeli society. But the wounds of that period—when children were taught to disobey their parents, and parents were humiliated in front of their children; when traditional values were mocked and cherished customs became the subject of crude ethnic humor; when membership in the right party was the condition for getting along and getting ahead—those wounds have yet to heal.

In the early 1970s a group of young, mostly Moroccan, Sephardi activists sprang up in Jerusalem's Mussrarah neighborhood. They were street kids, tough kids, and many of them had spent more time in reform school than in any normal classroom, but they had a kind of genius for manipulating the media. With unerring public relations sense they called themselves the Black Panthers, a name that sent chills down the back of the pioneer establishment. The Panthers, after all, were an American group known for violent militancy, complete alienation from the mainstream and even, God forbid, anti-Semitism. And now there were Panthers in Israel.

Of course there had been ethnic protest groups in Israel before, but the Panthers were something new. For one thing, they were the first to challenge basic Zionist assumptions. The struggle for Soviet Jewry was then under way, and tens of thousands of Russian immigrants were arriving. In accordance with the country's improved economic conditions, and partially on the basis of lessons learned from the experience of earlier immigrants, the government offered these newcomers generous help and considerable personal choice in determining the conditions of their absorption. This rubbed the Panthers the wrong way. Why should Israel give choice housing, jobs and tax breaks to Russian strangers when they and their families were still stuck in big-city slums or in desolate outlying development towns? The country's first obligation, they argued, was to its own citizens, not a pack of foreigners. "Israel for the Israelis" was their motto.

In April 1971, Golda Meir met with the Panthers. It was a bizarre conference, for it would have been hard to find two more different outlooks than those of Golda and the Jerusalem street people. Like Chaim Laskov in his confrontation with Yehoshua Peretz at the port of Ashdod, the Prime Minister lectured the Panthers on the principles of Israel Major: pioneering, idealism, self-sacrifice, international Jewish solidarity. She was, in the words of her spokesman, "motherly but firm."

The Panthers, who had come to the meeting dressed in jeans and T-shirts, listened to the lecture with smirks on their faces. They bummed Chesterfield cigarettes from the Prime Minister and sat blowing smoke rings as she went on about the obligations of citizenship in the first Jewish state in two thousand years. Then they went back to the streets and staged a number of flamboyant and highly publicized demonstrations in downtown Jerusalem. Cops and Panthers, often kids from the same neighborhoods, clashed in the street in front of the Zion Cinema, bashing and cursing each other in televised fury.

A month or so after her meeting with the Panthers, Mrs. Meir was invited to address a meeting of the Moroccan Immigrant Society, an association of tame Sephardim who normally cooperated with the establishment. The old pioneer from Milwaukee was in a combative mood, and she gave her audience a piece of her mind. "These Panthers are not nice boys," she told them. "Perhaps they were nice boys once, and I hope they will be nice boys again, but they certainly aren't nice now."

Golda thought she was stating the obvious. So did Jerusalem Mayor Teddy Kollek, when he imperiously ordered a group of Panther demonstrators to get off the grass in front of his office. These old-line leaders didn't have a guilty conscience regarding the treatment of Sephardim. They knew that their motives had been good, that they had tried—and were still trying—to do the right thing. They saw the Panthers as a fringe group (which they were) and it apparently never occurred to them that the young protesters might be expressing a frustration and anger shared by "good boys and girls" in the Oriental community.

Perhaps the most disturbing and effective weapon in the Panthers' arsenal was their use of the term *Black,* with its implication of racial discrimination. Mrs. Meir and others were deeply hurt by this accusation. They pointed out that most of the Sephardi Jews, especially from North Africa and the Levant, were not necessarily darker-skinned than other Jews. Moreover, it had been a part of Zionist doctrine from the beginning to encourage "mixed" marriages between Ashkenazim and Sephardim as a way of promoting integration and fusing the disparate parts of the country into one people.

Actually, the status of Sephardim is much more like that of white southerners in the United States than of American Blacks. Like southerners, there are various kinds of Sephardim—a Yemenite can be as different from an Iraqi as a Tennessee sharecropper is from a Dallas businessman—but they share a common geography, history and religious tradition as well as an identifiable regional accent. And, like American southerners, the Sephardim have about them an aura of faded glory, a nostalgic pride in a great antebellum civilization. Their ancestors were advisers to caliphs; they were warriors and physicians who created a warm, gracious Mediterranean culture at a time when the Ashkenazim were huddled, freezing, in crude huts in the wilds of Russia and Poland. For centuries it was the Sephardim who were the Jewish aristocrats, and as recently as the end of the nineteenth century, when the first pioneers arrived from Eastern Europe, they were looked upon by the Sephardic grandees of Jerusalem as vulgar rustics. Many of these Sephardim made every effort to prevent social contacts between their children and the young radicals; and the first pioneer–Sephardi marriage in Palestine was so traumatic that the genteel spinsters of Jerusalem's drawing rooms remember it with distaste to this day.

Of course, most of Israel's Sephardic Jews are not personally descended from medieval poets and scholars, any more than most people below the Mason-Dixon line can trace their lineage to the planter aristocracy. The vast majority came from various Arab countries where their families lived for generations as merchants, artisans or farmers; and when they arrived in Israel they brought their traditional values—respect for religion, respect for family honor, respect for the authority of the community elders and the family patriarchs. They were social conservatives, largely untouched by the radical ideas of modernism, and they resented the intrusions of the state into their private affairs. But they found themselves in a modern, secular society without significant capital, political power or community organization, and they were more or less at the mercy of the establishment. Even today, a great many Sephardim remember their early days in Israel more or less the way that southerners a hundred years ago regarded Reconstruction.

Under the circumstances, the newly arrived Sephardim took whatever work they could get, whatever was assigned to them. At first, they were given jobs digging ditches, planting trees and picking fruit—often made-up jobs to give the immigrants something to do. Later, when the economy grew stronger, they became factory workers, small farmers, hard hats, mechanics, truck drivers. They filled the lower echelons of the police department and served as master sergeants in the army. Many of the women stayed home with their large families, but those who worked were waitresses and cleaning women, saleswomen and beauticians. The Oriental Jews became the Joe Six-packs of Israel. They had their own twangy,

Arabic-influenced accents, which became the butt of an un-
ending string of ethnic jokes; their own neighborhoods; their
own style of dress, of behavior; their own attitudes. They
were seen as crude, faintly ridiculous people prone to Satur-
day-night feuding, heavy drinking, large clans, sentimental
piety, raucous music, gaudy clothing—in short, a collection of
Jewish rednecks.

The Six Day War brought two important changes. First, the
occupation of the West Bank and Gaza provided a large pool
of unskilled labor, and many of the Sephardi workingmen became small contractors, foremen and supervisors. This meant
more money, more status and a chance to look down as well
as up. And second, after the war the first group of sabra
Sephardim came of age. These were the children of the generation of the desert, born and educated in Israel. Not all of
them made the great leap into Israeliness; a large number
were school drop-outs, scarcely better adjusted to Israeli life
than their parents. But a great many others were both ready
and able to enter the national mainstream, to adopt the trap-
pings and the attitudes of the Real Israel.

The process has proved surprisingly easy. As when a south-
erner moves to the North, there are no insuperable barriers of
race to overcome; the transition is accessible to everyone who
is flexible enough to take on the styles and habits of the establishment. Clean up your accent, take a new Hebrew name,
move out of the old neighborhood, buy some "Israeli" (i.e.,
American)-style clothes and for all practical purposes you
have made it. This doesn't mean that you pass for Ashkenazi—there's no need for that. You can remain proud of
your heritage, even toss in a few Arabic words or make a dish
of down-home food for friends, in the same way that a trans-
planted Georgian might regale his northern cronies with stories about Pappy's bootleg likker or serve chitlins at a
suburban party.

To a very large degree, *Sephardi* has become a cultural
rather than an ethnic term. Not long ago I pointed out to my
Jerusalem-born wife, whose own parents came from Germany, that three of her best friends are women from Oriental
families. "Who do you mean?" she asked. "Jenine, Leora and
Nava," I said, naming three high school classmates with

whom she is still close. "They're not Orientals," she said. "Their parents are."

Yet, despite the accessibility of mainstream Israeli identity, the majority of Oriental Jews have remained more or less within the confines of their communities, aware of the differences that separate them from their fellow Israelis. Unlike their parents' generation, however, they are disinclined to accept the notion that they are inferior. The collapse of the pioneer hegemony brought about by the 1973 war was a major factor in this new self-awareness and confidence, and the years since the war have brought not only assimilation for those who choose it, but a new ethnic pride for those who do not.

With this pride has come a new assertiveness and a sense of belonging. In the past decade the Oriental community has moved to something very close to full membership in Israeli society. It has accomplished this not by strikes or protests but through the classic tool of outsiders in a democracy: politics.

7

The Rise of the Rednecks

A few days before the 1984 Knesset election, a group of students in my wife Miri's computer programming course held an impromptu political bull session during a coffee break. They were all college graduates, many had advanced degrees, and as they talked it emerged that almost all of them were planning to vote for the Labor party. Until they came to Rachel. "I'm voting for Begin," she said, "and I don't care who knows it."

A couple of the students started to laugh. "You sound like all those characters in the Mechane Yehuda Market," one said. "They think that Begin's still running."

Rachel smiled but her eyes didn't. At twenty-five she was one of the youngest students in the course and probably the best, a real whiz on computers. She has a B.A. in economics from the Technion in Haifa, speaks Israeli Hebrew, dresses in the jeans-and-sweater style of the Jerusalem Yuppies. "Those characters selling fruit in Mechane Yehuda are my uncles and cousins," she said. "And no matter what you think, I'm voting for the Likud—for Begin."

"But why?" one of them persisted. "What about the war in Lebanon? And don't tell me you're for the Likud's economic policy because I've heard you talk about it. So what's the deal?"

"The deal is that my family is from Tunisia," she said, as if that were sufficient explanation, but her fellow students objected. "That's a complete non sequitur" one of them told her. "You're not a Tunisian; you're an Israeli. You grew up here. Who was in power when you went to high school, to college? What did the Likud do for you?"

"They let me and my family hold our heads up in this country," she said. "Begin did that for us. For me, the Likud, even without Begin, is Begin. I'll never forget what he meant to me and my family."

Only a few weeks before, I had heard that same point made in a somewhat different way by another young Israeli woman. It was in New York, in the ballroom of the Waldorf-Astoria Hotel, in May. Ari Rath, the editor of *The Jerusalem Post,* and I had been invited to address the annual convention of the American Jewish Committee on the upcoming elections in Israel. Ari spoke first, and predicted that the major issues would be the war in Lebanon and the economy. I agreed, but added a third factor: the Likud's strength among Sephardi voters, an emotional allegiance that transcends specific issues.

There were a number of young Israeli journalists in the audience that day, guests of the American Jewish Committee, and they were sitting in front, not far from the dais. When I finished my remarks, one of them, a pretty blond correspondent for one of the establishment morning papers, asked for the floor. Her face was flushed and her hands were shaking, and at first I thought it was from nervousness at addressing such a large gathering in English. But it soon became apparent that she was livid, not shy. She said (roughly) this: "I am a sabra, and the daughter of sabra parents. My grandparents came to the land of Israel as pioneers, to build a just, beautiful place. My family fought for the country, sacrificed for it. And now the people who vote for the Likud, the kind of people who want Begin, have ruined my country. These are brutal, vulgar people, people who have introduced violence and intolerance. I hate their values, their attitudes. They have destroyed our dream. They've stolen my homeland. I feel like a stranger in my own country."

There was a shocked silence in the audience. I had heard this kind of diatribe a dozen times in Israel, but it was a new experience for the American Jews, and it rattled them. More than a few of them, I guessed, were remembering similar sen-

128

timents expressed about themselves only a generation ago by America's bluebloods. Some of her fellow Israeli journalists shifted uncomfortably in their seats. This kind of talk was old stuff to them, too, but it didn't sound so good in broad daylight, here in a New York City ballroom.

The tone of the reporter's remarks was unusually harsh, but among Israelis of her class, the sentiments are hardly unique. Like northern intellectuals sneering at the south twenty years ago, a good many writers, journalists and social critics have become vocally contemptuous of Oriental Jews and their culture and aspirations. To a large extent this is a reflection of the classic view of Sephardi inferiority; to a lesser degree, hostility toward an increasingly powerful group that not only wants, but is able to get, a larger share of the national action.

This overt hostility toward the Eastern Jews is relatively new, an index of Sephardi gains during the past decade. In the fifties and sixties, when Orientals were merely raw material, there was no need to confront their culture or contend with their ambitions. Amos Elon could write his book about Israeli society and almost completely ignore their existence; or, on a political level, the Labor party could assign a single Cabinet portfolio to a Sephardi representative, despite the fact that Oriental voters made up almost half the electorate. In those days, the Sephardim simply didn't matter.

The 1973 war cracked the veneer of pioneer infallibility and superiority, let loose forces of dissatisfaction and anger that had been bottled up for a generation. Israel's Eastern Jews looked around and realized that their Ashkenazi fellow citizens were no wiser, no braver, no better than they were. And they saw something else: that they now constituted an enormous political force. These two perceptions came together in the mid-seventies, and radically changed the face of Israeli society and politics.

As elites suddenly confronted with insurrection from the ranks have always done, the Ashkenazi establishment began looking for an outside agitator who was responsible for stirring up the previously contented masses. And it wasn't hard to find one, not with Menachem Begin on the scene. Begin, the Black Pope of Zionism, was now blamed for having unleashed this revolt of the great unformed raw material from

129

the East against their betters. Bialik had said that he disliked Arabs because they reminded him of Sephardim; after 1977, it often seemed that the Real Israelis disliked Sephardim because they reminded them of Begin.

The fear of an alliance between Menachem Begin and the Oriental Jews didn't start in 1977. As far back as 1949, in his article on the Moroccans, Aryeh Gelbloom of *Ha'aretz* had voiced precisely that concern. "It is perhaps no wonder," he wrote, "that Mr. Begin and his Herut Party are demanding to bring them [the Sephardim] in the hundreds of thousands now. They know that these ignorant and primitive masses are the best material for them, and that only an immigration such as this can bring them to power."

Begin, for his part, was sensitive to the charge that he was primarily supported by the Oriental Jews. In his book *The Revolt,* written in the early fifties, he noted that some of his political opponents, "wishing to belittle us . . . whispered, or said aloud, that the whole of the Irgun consisted only of Yemenites." He went on to boast that "our comrades from the Eastern communities felt happy and at home in the Irgun. Nobody ever displayed any stupid airs of superiority toward them; and they were thus helped to free themselves of any unjustified sense of inferiority they may have harbored." Begin listed the large number of Sephardi commanders in the organization, estimating that Oriental Jews made up between a quarter and a third of the Irgun's membership.

Of course there were Sephardim in the Labor-led Haganah, too, and even some in the elite, kibbutz-dominated units of the Palmach; and later, after statehood, there was token representation in Mapai for "community leaders" of the immigrant groups. But they were appointed leaders, handpicked by the establishment, and their primary role was to act as a sop to fellow Sephardim and to serve as symbolic figures, Credits to Their People.

A great deal has been written about the seeming paradox of Menachem Begin's appeal to the Sephardi masses of Israel—how he, the very model of the Polish-Jewish middle class, won the affection and zealous support of these Easterners. The usual explanations—Begin's hard-line policies toward the Arabs, his flair for stirring oratory, the fact that he was a father figure for people looking for a patriarchial leader after Ben Gurion—are only a part of the story; none can account for the ties of emotion that bound large sections of the Oriental community to the Likud leader.

Above all, Begin's popularity was based on the ironic fact that he, almost alone among Israel's leaders, liked and loved Jews; and that from the very beginning the Sephardi masses realized that Begin didn't want anything from them—except their votes. In his view, Jews—Sephardi *or* Ashkenazi— didn't need any radical alterations beyond the natural changes that independence conferred. He certainly never accepted the notion of the New Jewish Man and Woman whom the socialists dreamed of creating in their Zionist laboratory. His mentor, Ze'ev Jabotinsky, had preached a kind of "Jewish Is Beautiful" philosophy. There was nothing wrong with the Jews that sovereignty wouldn't cure; and the first task of achieving it was to develop self-respect—not for what you might become, but for what you already are. Jabotinsky advocated (and Begin believed in) Jewish chivalry, the cultivation of the inherent Hebrew nobility of spirit that the diaspora had repressed but not destroyed.

Menachem Begin was perhaps the greatest public speaker of his generation, and he could use glorious Biblical rhetoric as well as or better than any Israeli politician, but in his long career he rarely, if ever, referred to himself as an Israeli. He was always "a Jew" or, later, "an old Jew"—and this, more than anything else, endeared him to the Sephardi masses. He didn't see them as incomplete, inadequate or primitive. He didn't want to alienate their children, mock their traditions, scoff at their religious beliefs. He didn't attempt to change their style of dress, their diet, their music. He couldn't have cared less if they kept their original diaspora names (as he kept his). Begin was a man who divided the world into three basic parts: Them, the goyim; Us, the Jews; and Me. From the start of his political career he had been able to communicate his indifference to distinctions within the "Us"; to Begin, Sephardim were just fellow Jews—and, it would be fair to say, fellow voters.

Like any sensible politician, Begin sought to consolidate and expand his electoral base. As Prime Minister he sup-

131

ported populist economic policies that enabled low-income workers to improve their standard of living dramatically, made urban renewal a national goal and placed a strong emphasis on social welfare programs such as the institution of free high school education. The Oriental Jews, still the vast majority of the country's poor and lower middle class, were the primary beneficiaries of this economic approach.

Occasionally, Begin's efforts to reach out to the Sephardim were embarrassingly corny. On one occasion, in a radio address after recovering from an illness, he lauded his physicians, reserving especially fulsome praise for "a young Moroccan doctor, only about thirty or so," who turned out to be, in Begin's considered opinion, "a genius." This kind of transparent ethnic pandering would, in any other Ashkenazi politician, have been construed as ludicrous (indeed, in the 1984 election, when Shimon Peres appeared on television with his half-Moroccan grandchild on his knee, there were howls of cynical laughter from one end of the country to the other), but Begin got away with it because people sensed he was, under the political corn pone, sincere.

Sometimes Begin's own efforts *were* laughable. Shortly after he came to office, President Ephraim Katzir's term came to an end. In Israel the President is a ceremonial figure, elected by the Knesset for a five-year term—a system designed to allow the governing coalition, which always has a parliamentary majority, to choose him. In the past, Labor has always been in power and its candidates—Chaim Weizmann, Itzhak Ben-Zvi, Zalman Shazar and Katzir—had all been Ashkenazim. Begin felt that the time had come to select a Sephardi for the highest office in the land, and he announced that he would do so.

The Prime Minister's decision was popular, but his choice of candidates wasn't. He apparently didn't know a single Sephardi of sufficient stature for the job, and he began asking around. Somehow he came up with the name of Professor Itzhak Chavet, a completely obscure Egyptian-born scientist at the Weizmann Institute whom Begin had never even met. Chavet was in Paris when the decision was made, and Begin asked his chief of staff, Yeheiel Kadishai, to get in touch with him and ask him if he'd accept the position. Kadishai reached

Chavet on the phone and told him he was being offered the presidency. "Of what?" asked the astonished professor. "The Weizmann Institute?"

Chavet's candidacy was so bizarre that hardly anyone supported it, including a number of Likud members of Knesset. Labor nominated Yitzhak Navon, also a Sephardi but, unlike his opponent, an extremely well-qualified candidate, and he was elected. Begin was not only embarrassed politically; it also looked suspiciously as though he had simply selected the first Sephardi he had stumbled on, as if they were interchangeable.

Begin's lack of sensitivity in the Chavet affair was a rarity, though; his instincts were usually much better when it came to scouting Sephardi political talent. This ability was especially evident in his decision to promote a promising young labor leader and community activist—David Levy from Beit Shean.

David Levy arrived in Haifa in 1957, along with his parents, brothers and sisters, from Rabat, Morocco. He was twenty years old—an awkward age, too young to be consigned to the scrap heap but too old to be turned into a Real Israeli. He and his family asked to be sent to Beersheba, in the Negev, where they had relatives. Instead they were assigned to the little development town of Beit Shean at the northern end of the Jordan valley, on the other side of the country.

Levy's father was a comparatively young man when he arrived in Israel. In Morocco he had been a carpenter, but his tools got lost in transit and he had no money to buy new ones. No one was interested in a has-been carpenter from Morocco, and anyway, there was no way a carpenter could make a living in Beit Shean. Instead, he was given a series of jobs picking fruit in nearby kibbutzim, or working on road gangs. A quarter century later, David Levy recalled the impact of the family's changed circumstances. "When I saw my father's terrible tragedy," he told a biographer, "saw how his honor was crushed in the dust, saw how in a few weeks he declined from a strong father respected by his family and community into a welfare case dependent on charity, I decided that I had no choice but to fight for my family."

During their first weeks in the country the family lived by

selling off Mrs. Levy's jewelry. David was unable to find work on his own, and he finally turned to the local government labor exchange. There he was subjected to a series of questions: "Why don't you have a job? What's the matter with you? What makes you think you meet the criteria?"

It was the normal hazing, designed to make the supplicant acknowledge the power of the establishment and to be properly appreciative of its eventual beneficence, but Levy snapped. He went berserk, turned over tables, smashed chairs against the wall, cursed and threatened in French and Arabic; finally he was subdued and taken to the police station. He was found guilty of creating a disturbance and sentenced to twelve days in the local lockup.

When Levy was released from jail he had two ambitions: to get a decent job and to get involved in politics. The first was comparatively easy. He became a building worker, a hard hat whose services were in demand at construction sites throughout the country. After work he taught himself to read and write Hebrew and was soon active in union politics. Following a brief, unsatisfactory experience with the local Mapai branch in Beit Shean, Levy crossed the lines and joined Herut.

There was nothing unique in this defection. For years bright young men from the Oriental communities had been approaching Mapai headquarters in towns and neighborhoods throughout the country. They were looking to get into politics, but Labor—the party of perennial control—didn't think it needed ambitious newcomers. Its ranks were already clogged with middle-aged activists waiting their turn, and new people meant new problems. There was no ethnic prejudice in this—young Ashkenazim weren't welcomed either, at least not if they wanted to do more than stuff envelopes or pass out campaign buttons. But young Sephardim, unfettered by ancient hatred of Begin or loyalty to Labor Zionism, had no problem in going next door to the local Herut clubhouse, where they were welcomed with open arms.

David Levy soon attracted the attention of the professional pols at The Fortress in Tel Aviv. He was still unseasoned and lacked political sophistication, but his cupid-lipped baby face and wavy pompadour—styled for him by his barber brother—didn't hide his toughness and ambition. Levy was a comer, a man who could organize fellow workers, talk to them in their own language, inspire them. On his next visit to the North, Begin made a point of seeking him out.

Menachem Begin instinctively grasped the importance of Levy. Labor's Sephardi politicians were little more than front men for the establishment, or, like Yitzhak Navon, they were too aristocratic to appeal to the blue-collar masses. Levy, on the other hand, was the real thing. He was a worker who knew how to use a set of tools and how far a paycheck would stretch. He was a real family man, on the way to twelve children, a husband who had taken out a part of his first month's wages to buy his wife, Rachel, a pair of red shoes. Although he wasn't orthodox, he had respect for religion, often putting on a skullcap when he sat down to eat with his family in their cramped apartment. Best of all, he lived in Beit Shean, one of the development towns that dotted the country and had become the centers of the blue-collar Sephardi electorate. Levy was only in his early thirties, but Begin saw to it that he was elected to the Knesset. And when the Likud came to power, Begin reached out for the forty-year-old Levy and appointed him minister of immigrant absorption, in the process bypassing more senior party officials, including a not-too-happy Yitzhak Shamir.

The reaction to Levy's appointment was brutal. Within weeks the country was flooded with David Levy jokes, based on the supposed ignorance of the young Cabinet minister. The jokes became a national craze, and on one memorable occasion a reporter for Israel television even asked Levy himself if he had a favorite. Naturally this was all done in good fun—for years ethnic put-downs rendered in thick Sephardi dialect had been a staple of Israeli humor, no offense intended—and people expected Levy to take it like a sport.

But David Levy wasn't amused; he was humiliated. He understood the political motivation for the put-downs, but they still hurt, especially when his name became a laughingstock among his children's friends. He rode out the wave of jokes with a stoic dignity, and as he did he also began to amass political support within the thousand-member Central Committee of Herut. By the time the David Levy jokes ran out of steam, Levy himself had built, but not yet unveiled, a formidable political machine. Just as important, he had been transformed from an anonymous politician into the symbol of the rising power of the Sephardi younger generation and the fear and resistance it inspired within the establishment.

In the 1981 election the joke was on the Labor party. The campaign was an acrimonious affair, in which the Likud made up an early deficit in the polls with a combination of election economics, foreign policy extravaganzas and stem-winding oratory by Begin in his last hurrah. The country was sharply divided between the Real Israelis, determined to recapture control from the interlopers, and Begin's coalition of outsiders, of which the Sephardi blue collars were a central element. Tempers ran high, sensitivities flared, misunderstandings abounded. Motta Gur, a Labor leader and reserve general who, as chief of staff, had once told an interviewer that it would be a long time before the children of Oriental families could match the technical level of the Ashkenazim, appeared at a campaign rally in a Jerusalem park, where he was rudely heckled by a group of young Sephardi Likudniks. "We screwed the Arabs," he shouted at them in red-faced fury, "and we'll screw you the same way."

Not long after, prime-ministerial candidate Shimon Peres told an unruly crowd of Begin supporters that they reminded him of the followers of the Ayatollah Khomeini. These analogies struck many Orientals as insulting references to their Middle Eastern origins. Peres and Gur denied that this was so.

Two nights before the election, Labor held a monster rally in the square in front of the Tel Aviv city hall. With the entire party leadership sitting on the platform, comedian-emcee Dudu Topaz, a stereotypical sabra son, welcomed the crowd. "It's a pleasure to see Real Israelis here tonight," he said, "instead of all the cooks and gatekeepers and *chach-chachs* over at Likud headquarters."

When Begin's advisers first heard the radio reports of the rally they couldn't believe it. Did you hear what Dudu Topaz called our voters last night? they asked the Prime Minister. Who is Dudu Topaz? Begin wondered, and what is a *chach-chach*? One of the advisers, aware of Begin's tenuous grip on

Hebrew slang, explained that *chach-chach* is a slur on North Africans somewhere between "redneck" and "trash."

That night, the night before the election, in the same public square, Begin addressed a crowd estimated at 100,000. In the midst of his speech the Old Man paused dramatically. "Do you know what they called you here last night?" he thundered, fishing in his jacket pocket and pulling out a rumpled piece of paper. Begin squinted at the page with incomprehension. "They called you *chech-chechim*," he hollered, mispronouncing the epithet. "Is that what you are?"

"No!" screamed the crowd.

The next day the Likud won an upset victory and Menachem Begin was returned to office.

When he set about forming his second government, after the election, Begin gave David Levy the impression that he was going to reward him for his part in the victory by appointing him Deputy Prime Minister along with his job as housing minister. At the last moment, however, complications set in and Begin changed his mind. He called in his protégé to explain the situation. He wasn't asking—in Herut, Begin's word was law—but was simply telling the young politician that the appointment wasn't in the cards. "Fine," Levy said, or words to that effect. "In that case, I'll pass on the Housing Ministry, too." The threat soon became public, and for a few tense hours the country watched the impasse between the two men. Finally it was Begin who gave in; and the former national joke became the highest-ranking Sephardi Cabinet minister in history.

In the aftermath of the highly charged 1981 election, there was a wave of alarmism about the relations between the Oriental and Ashkenazi communities. When a Tunisian-born Labor party member of Knesset observed that "gefilte fish makes me puke," pundits saw the remark as a sign of imminent social collapse. When some street vandals daubed anti-Ashkenazi graffiti on the walls in a Tel Aviv neighborhood, the incident was portrayed as a harbinger of ethnic violence. Op-ed writers in Israel's almost totally Ashkenazi press made dire predictions about the levantinization of Israeli culture, the ascendancy of the Oriental community with its presumed intolerance, crudity and anti-intellectualism. Some of these articles, written by respected liberal commentators, bordered on ethnic incitement; others were merely foolish. In one, a well-known columnist predicted that the 1981 election would mark the end of Ashkenazi political control in Israel, and that from now on, candidates for Prime Minister would be drawn from the Oriental community.

During this period, President Yitzhak Navon was the great Sephardi hope of the Labor party. Navon's term was due to expire shortly before the 1984 national election, and a number of Labor activists began a campaign to draft him as party leader. Navon, a man of great culture and intelligence, was uncomfortable in the role his fellow Laborites tried to cast him in. He had been a member of the establishment since the days when he served as David Ben Gurion's assistant. His wife, Ofira, was a classic sabra from a European family. Navon was a Sephardi, all right, and proud of his roots; but he was hardly a representative of the blue-collar masses.

He also lacked sufficient ambition for the job. After leaving the presidency, he deliberated for what seemed an endless time and finally called a press conference to announce that he would join the Labor list for the 1984 election, but not as its candidate for Prime Minister. On the way out of the conference, he gave a short interview to Israeli television. What was he going to do now? the reporter asked. "Right now?" Navon said, in his charming, aristocratic Sephardi accent. "I'm going to get my family and take them out for a good *hummus*." At which point, observed an Israeli satirist, he went home, collected his wife and children and took them all to a Chinese restaurant.

Navon wound up as the number two man on Labor's list, but it didn't have much effect. Labor, which desperately needed to overcome its image as an elitist, machine-controlled party, reinforced that image instead. One day in the spring of 1984, Shimon Peres, Yitzhak Navon, Itzhak Rabin and Chaim Bar Lev checked into a hotel near party headquarters, where they proceeded to fix the party's slate. Not surprisingly, the first four candidates on the slate were Shimon Peres, Yitzhak Navon, Itzhak Rabin and Chaim Bar Lev. The rest of the list was top-heavy with party hacks, only one of whom was under forty (the Likud, by contrast, selected eleven candidates in their thirties). The message to the country—and especially to the Sephardi masses—was clear. Navon had been selected by the bosses; he had no real power.*

As the 1984 campaign began, Labor based its strategy on the assumption that it had the establishment vote in its pocket and should therefore aim its efforts at the Orientals. Its secret weapon was to be Ha'Gashash Ha'Cheever, a beloved comedy team. The trio, two of whose members are Orientals, specializes in ethnic humor, much of it at the expense of the supposed stupidity and ignorance of the Sephardim. The group was selected to anchor the Labor party's television broadcasts, a decision that ought to have a special place in the annals of political insensitivity; it was like getting Amos and Andy to recruit the Black vote for the Republicans. (The Likud didn't exactly run a highbrow campaign, either; its anchorman was comedian Sefi Rivlin, best known as the host of a children's TV program. So it was Amos and Andy versus Captain Kangaroo.)

As I had predicted at the Waldorf, the Sephardi vote in 1984 went to the Likud; the Oriental Jews voted their interests and their emotional allegiance, just as the Ashkenazis did. But the passion that characterized the Begin era was strangely missing. Partly that had to do with the absence of Begin himself, and the potent emotionalism he brought to politics. But largely it was due to the recognition that, now that the dust had settled, the Sephardi drive for equality and respect had largely succeeded.

Ben Gurion had longed for a Yemenite chief of staff in some distant utopia, but in 1983, when Moshe Levy, the son of an Iraqi vendor, was appointed to the army's top spot, it occasioned very little comment. Not long after, Yisrael Kessar, born in Yemen, was selected by the Labor party to serve as head of the powerful Histadrut Labor Federation. The gov-

---

*They weren't wrong, either. Navon was supposed to become foreign minister; Rabin, defense minister. But following the election, when a government of national unity was established with the Likud, Labor had to give one of those jobs to their opponents. Rabin, theoretically number three, got Defense, while Navon was shunted to the Ministry of Education.

ernment of national unity that emerged from the 1984 election had so many Sephardi ministers and deputy ministers that nobody bothered counting. Most encouraging of all, when a Kurdish Jew was passed over for the job of chief of the national police in favor of a man named Kraus, no one seriously raised the possibility that the appointment had anything to do with ethnic prejudice.

Naturally, those prejudices have not completely disappeared. A considerable gap still remains between Oriental and European Jews in Israel. On the whole, the Sephardi community continues to be poorer, less well educated and upwardly mobile than the Ashkenazim. During the past ten years Israel has made astonishing progress in transforming itself from an elitist state into an egalitarian one, but like all such transformations, it has been a painful process and it has left residual resentments.

Not too long after the 1984 election, I dropped into La Belle for a drink. It was still early and I was the only customer, so I sat at the bar and made small talk with Aliza, Avi Zaguri's sister, and Michal, a social worker who moonlights as a waitress. The two women were sharing a chef's salad.

"How's the book coming?" Aliza asked.

"Not bad," I told her. "I'm thinking about writing about Moroccans. Are you an oppressed Moroccan?"

"Not me," she said with a smile. "The only one who oppresses me around here is Avi."

Michal was intrigued with the subject, however. She looks like the quintessential Israeli insider and she has a didactic way of talking that would let you guess she's a social worker even if you didn't know. "Why don't you ask me?" she said, smiling. "It's the Ashkenazim who are discriminated against these days."

"Oh, is that right?" said Aliza in a bantering tone. She has soft brown eyes and a wide, white smile; like the rest of the Zaguris she is blessed with a sunny disposition. She took a bite of the chef's salad, and thought it over. "I suppose we put ourselves in the slums when we came here," she said.

"Well, no, of course not," Michal said seriously. "And we all know now that a lot of mistakes were made. But the coun-

try was poor then, don't forget. There wasn't any choice."
She smiled reasonably.

"Well, somebody had a choice when they wouldn't let my
mother live in Jerusalem," Aliza said, and I could hear the
first faint edge in her voice. You can have this discussion with
the best-adjusted, mildest-tempered Sephardim in the world,
and you always get to that note of anger.

"Okay," replied Michal, "but she got a free apartment.
The country just couldn't pass out apartments in Jerusalem
and Tel Aviv, you know."

"Well, where did your family live?" Aliza asked.

"Mine? In Jerusalem. But that's different. I mean, we
bought our apartment." She smiled again, but the smile was a
bit tentative, and there was a hint of exasperation in it. "Be
fair, Aliza. People did their best. We shared. Your family got
an apartment, a job. You own this bar now. I work for you. Is
that discrimination?" She picked up the fork and took a
mouthful of the chef's salad.

"All we wanted was to be treated like everyone else. We
were respectable people in Morocco. In Israel, we weren't
treated with respect."

Suddenly the two women were in a full-scale argument. I
sat back listening, thinking of whether I could use it to show
how fragile the relations between even good-hearted, well-in-
tentioned Israelis can be. And suddenly I noticed something
else: As they argued, Aliza and Michal continued sharing the
chef's salad. From time to time one would stop talking long
enough to spear a tomato or a piece of salami and take a bite,
and then pass the fork to the other. When Avi came over a
couple of minutes later to tell them to go back to work, both
the salad and the discussion were finished.

"What were you all so excited about?" Avi asked me later.
I told him briefly about the argument and the shared supper.
"That's pretty amazing, don't you think?" I asked.

"What's so amazing about it?" Avi replied, gathering up
the dish and the fork. "We've got the best chef's salad in
town."

8

Ying Yang and the Rabbi's Daughter

Unlike La Belle, the Orient Café doesn't exist anymore, except in the memories of its former patrons—who include some of Israel's most prominent citizens, and some of its most notorious. But it was a real place back in the sixties, a kosher greasy spoon on a scruffy downtown Jerusalem street whose five-course-for-a-dollar dinners ("cheaper than food," we called them) attracted the impoverished university students who made up half its clientele. The other half—prostitutes and their pimps—were drawn by the fact that the Orient was Jerusalem's only all-night diner, and by the tolerant attitude of its owner, who made no apparent distinction between budding physicists and fading hookers. Off duty, the ladies would sit at rickety tables sipping arrack or tea and gossiping in loud voices while the pimps, oily-looking characters in matching Banlon shirt-and-sock outfits, gambled away their earnings in felt-ripping games of billiards in the Orient's back room.

A firm, if invisible, line divided the two groups. Most of the kids from the university were clean-living products of Mapai Calvinism, and they looked down on the pimps and whores with an absentminded distaste, as if they were performers in some especially bizarre freak show. Occasionally someone would notice a particularly garish outfit or overhear a Hebrew Damon Runyonism from one of the pimps, and then a laugh would go up from the student tables, but for the most part the young Israelis simply ignored their fellow patrons. If the girls minded, it never showed—they hardly even glanced at the students, and when they did it was normally in frank, uncomplimentary appraisal.

I was a student myself when I first started going to the Orient, but I was fascinated by the crowd on the other side of the room. I had seen plenty of Jewish undergraduates in my life, but Hebrew hookers were a novelty. I gradually established friendly eye contact with one or two of the younger girls, and after a week or two I was on arrack-drinking terms with several. At first they had hoped that I, a rich Amerikai, might be customer material; but even when they realized that I was simply an interested admirer, several of the girls were flattered enough to talk to me about themselves when business wasn't too heavy.

My favorite was Tikvah, a thin, pasty-faced girl in her late teens with dyed blond hair and large, feverish black eyes. Israeli prostitutes usually fall into one of two categories—gumchewers or nail biters—and she was, despite her frail appearance, a chewer, full of wise-guy wisdom which she laid on especially thick for me. Tikvah was capable of great flights of self-absorption, and in a bad mood she would simply ignore me, but when the spirit was on her she could keep me going for hours with stories about life on the streets of the holy city. Usually she displayed no curiosity about me whatsoever, but one night, during a lull in the conversation, she asked me what kind of a student I was.

"I'm, ah, studying Jewish philosophy at the university," I said. In this setting it seemed a rather sissified answer, and I suddenly wished I were majoring in engineering, agriculture, something virile and concrete.

Tikvah, to my amazement, was delighted, however, and suddenly respectful. "Jewish philosophy is my favorite subject," she told me, almost shyly. "It's in my blood. My family comes from Turkey, you know." I must have looked puzzled about the connection. "Turkey was the home of the Rambam. In fact, our whole family is descended from him. So, Jewish philosophy is in our blood."

The Rambam—perhaps the greatest medieval rabbi and Jewish thinker—was not, to the best of my knowledge, from Turkey. I had just made my mind up to keep silent on this

genealogical discrepancy when another one of the girls broke
into the conversation.

"The Rambam was from Morocco, you ignorant slut," she
instructed with loud good humor in a heavy North African
accent. "Turkey never produced a rabbi. Just a bunch of ignorant hookers."

"Kiss my ass," Tikvah replied, an edge in her voice. "You
don't even fast on Yom Kippur. What would you know about
the Rambam?"

"Oh, excuse me, madame. I forgot I was talking to the
daughter of the Chief Rabbi. What do you tell His Honor
when you get home at night, that you've been to the *mikveh*?

Several of the girls overheard and broke out laughing, and
there was a stirring on the other side of the room. Tikvah shot
the Moroccan girl a palm-up Middle Eastern version of the
finger. "Settle this," she demanded. "You're a student—you
tell her."

"Uh, well, he wasn't from Turkey, I don't think," I said,
watching Tikvah's face cloud with anger. "But he could have
been born in Turkey, or he could have come from a Turkish
family. Or maybe your family was originally—"

My lame effort at diplomacy was cut off by the challenger,
who banged her hand on the table and whooped in triumph.
"I told you he was from Morocco. All the great rabbis are
Moroccans: the Baba Sali, the Rambam . . ." She had run
out of rabbis, but the whole room was watching her now, and
she was not about to give up center stage. "Turkish men
aren't rabbis. They're a collection of child molesters and
homos," she brayed, and one of the students—probably from
Turkey himself—jumped up and made a little half-bow.

Tikvah glared at me, incensed by my betrayal. "Well, you
happen to be wrong, student: The Rambam *was* from Turkey.
And anyway, you don't even wear a hat—what kind of an
expert on Judaism are you supposed to be?" She pushed her
chair back angrily, and it fell over as she stomped out on her
high heels, much to the amusement of the young Israeli students. When she got to the door she turned and addressed
them for the first time. "What are you laughing at?" she demanded imperiously, her brassy poise back in place. "You're
all a bunch of godless infidels." She gave the room the finger

once again, and then clomped out into the night to earn her living.

In Israel, and especially Jerusalem, you can't get too far away from religion. The world's most hallowed sites are, for Israelis, just places. The Via Dolorosa, for example, is a street most Jerusalemites think of in terms of Abu Shukery's *hummus* restaurant, although on Easter a large crowd usually turns out to watch the black-clad Greek pilgrims ascend the rough stones on their knees, balsa-wood crosses on their backs and regulation crowns of thorns—which sell for $7 each or three for $20 at the Seventh Station Boutique—on their heads. Mount Zion is a good place to park for the rock concerts held in the natural amphitheater located in the valley of Gehenna. The Israeli softball league was founded on a kibbutz in the Ayalon Valley, where, in less prosaic times, Joshua made the sun stand still. Even King David's Tomb becomes a familiar landmark, as in "To get to the Chinese restaurant, drive down to David's Tomb and hang a right."

Religion is the great dividing principle of Israeli society. Each community—Jewish, Christian, Moslem, Druze—has its own courts for matters of personal status, such as marriage, divorce and burial. Children attend public schools that combine secular subjects with religious studies. There is a separate orthodox public school system for Jews, and private, state-funded Talmud academies for the hyper-orthodox; but even in the nonreligious, secular public schools, Bible, Talmud, rabbinic literature and Jewish history—and of course Hebrew—are required subjects.

Once, when my daughter, Michal, was in the fourth grade, I took her to lunch with an American rabbi friend. Used to dealing with American kids her age, he asked her if she had ever heard of Abraham and Sarah from the Bible. She looked at him as though he were crazy, but when she realized that it was a test, she entered into the spirit of the thing. "Okay, rabbi, who were Hofni and Pinchas? Who was Hur? What happened at Timnat Serach?" Now in the ninth grade, and not in the least orthodox, she has, without trying or even noticing, acquired an easy familiarity with Jewish texts, history and customs that the students of the most prestigious

146

American Jewish day schools can never approach. Unlike Tikvah, she knows where the Rambam was born, but I doubt if she cares enough to get into an argument over it.

Israelis have a shared Jewish vocabulary that flows naturally out of the educational system, common experience and the very nature of the country. One Chanukah, for example, *Moked,* the Israeli *Meet the Press,* hosted four politicians for a discussion on the lessons of the Maccabees for Israeli foreign policy. All four displayed an easy grasp of the intricacies of the period, and the audience was equally comfortable with events that took place, after all, more than two thousand years ago. Between songs at a rock concert I attended recently, the star of the show cracked up his teen-age fans with a joke about studying Rashi—the medieval rabbinic sage—in school. Soldiers eat off of blue plastic plates for meat and yellow for dairy, under mess-hall signs that say: KEEP KOSHER—THIS IS AN ORDER. At the movies, when a rabbi says the kaddish for Rocky's departed Jewish manager, the audience murmurs, "Amen."

Recently, one of the country's leading DJs offered a special service. In the days before Yom Kippur, Jews traditionally ask forgiveness from their fellow man for any transgressions they may have committed during the year. The DJ invited his audience to send in postcard forgiveness requests, which he read over the air between tunes by Culture Club, Talking Heads and Tina Turner. The average Israeli teen-ager saw nothing incongruous about it at all.

Religion is omnipresent in Israel but it is far from universally practiced, something that was evident when, in late 1977, less than a month after President Anwar Sadat's visit to Jerusalem, an Israeli delegation was invited to attend preliminary peace talks in Cairo. It was a moment of high excitement—the first visit in history by Israeli officials to Egypt—and the delegation, headed by Eliahu Ben-Elissar, was determined to use it to forge links with the Egyptian government and public. I was a member of the delegation, which left for Cairo accompanied by thirty Israeli journalists and several hundred foreign correspondents.

Our Egyptian hosts were as anxious for success as we were,

and they went to great lengths to be hospitable. They put us up in the Mena House Hotel, a luxurious establishment built during the colonial period next to the pyramids in Giza, and they laid on a series of tours for the official party and the accompanying journalists.

One of the first places we went was Alexandria. After a meeting with the regional governor, a distinguished ex-artillery officer who had commanded a sector of the canal front during the Yom Kippur War, we were taken on a tour of the municipal museum, the Jewish old-folks home and several other sites of civic pride. At lunchtime our hosts brought us to a seafood restaurant near the beach, where a crowd of Egyptian passersby cheered as our group—two tour buses full of Israeli officials, security men and journalists—trooped inside.

The restaurant was a large, airy place with long tables festively adorned with flowers. The head of our delegation, Ben-Elissar, and the Egyptian governor toasted each other with mango juice, in deference to the Muslim prohibition against alcohol, and then red-jacketed waiters began to serve the first course. They led with their strength: huge shrimps fresh from the Mediterranean, fried in a light batter. The shrimp were obviously the specialty of the house, and our hosts—unaware that shrimp are not kosher—glowed with pleasure at the treat they had prepared for us.

Israeli officials abroad are not allowed to eat nonkosher food at official functions, and the presence of dozens of journalists made this a very public occasion. Normally we would have asked for something else, but that seemed impossibly impolitic under the circumstances. We were goodwill ambassadors, and the idea of offending Egyptian hospitality at this delicate juncture in the relations between the two erstwhile enemies was too grim to contemplate. I shot a look at Ben-Elissar, and I could tell he was visualizing headlines in the Egyptian press about the rudeness of Israelis who rejected Egypt's most prized delicacy. This was obviously a moment for diplomacy and flexibility. Ben-Elissar hesitated a long moment and then, smiling at the governor on his left, took a bite of the prohibited shellfish. I breathed a sigh of hungry relief, and we all dug in. The shrimp was delicious and I wolfed it down, bathed in the special glow that comes from personal sacrifice in the cause of international understanding.

The glow lasted until the next day, when word of our luncheon menu got back to Jerusalem. The reporters, many of whom had asked for second helpings, wrote about the non-kosher debauch in the fleshpots of Egypt, and the religious politicians let out a mighty scream of protest. They were joined by hundreds of rabbis from Brooklyn and Queens who had read accounts of the meal in *The New York Times* and sent heated telegrams to Prime Minister Begin. There were tense telephone calls from Israel, and for an awful moment it appeared that Chief Rabbi Shlomo Goren might personally fly to Cairo to supervise all further eating.

Back in Cairo we quietly informed the Egyptian protocol people that from now on there could be no more shrimp, and that we would appreciate strictly kosher food. They were understanding—Islam has its share of dietary restrictions—but somewhat at a loss; kosher food is not exactly a widespread commodity in Egypt. Finally someone came up with the idea of getting prepackaged kosher meals from one of the international airlines that service Cairo.

The next day at lunch we found a table next to the door of the opulent hotel dining room where we normally ate our meals. The table was stacked with seventy-five cartons of kosher beef stroganoff plus trimmings. With a certain reluctance each of us took a package, struck with a sense of loss caused by the delicate aromas that wafted out of the kitchen. Regret turned to consternation when we unwrapped the foil. Whatever the lunches tasted like at twenty thousand feet, at ground level they were very close to inedible.

From then on until the end of the conference, each day we entered the dining room, passed the pile of kosher dinners on the table near the door, and ordered our meals from the hotel menu. Ben-Elissar, Meir Rosenne and one or two of the other more conspicuous members of the delegation confined themselves to the acceptably kosher smoked salmon. The rest of us, uninhibited by piety, protocol or political ambitions, feasted on the hotel's regular Indian and Continental fare. During the next couple of weeks I saw only one Israeli—the correspondent from an ultra-orthodox newspaper—take a tray from the stack near the entrance.

On Friday night the delegation had a ceremonial sabbath dinner in the hotel's Nawas Room, to which we invited not only the accompanying journalists but also a number of Egyptian functionaries with whom we had been working. Most of us weren't normally sabbath observers, but this was a special occasion and we laid it on thick. Meir Rosenne, who had attended a religious school in his youth, chanted the prayers over the wine—kosher from Carmel, specially flown in for the occasion—and then led the entire group in singing sabbath melodies.

In the midst of all this unaccustomed ceremony, one of the Egyptian protocol officers seated across the table smiled at me warmly. "You know," he said, "at first I didn't understand very much about your religion, but I think I'm beginning to now. It is very beautiful, really."

"Yes, well, it's quite intricate," I told him. "Probably some of the customs seem strange to outsiders."

"Not at all," replied the Egyptian diplomat, a fine spirit of ecumenicism in his voice. "I'd like to ask you a question about the kosher laws, though."

"Go right ahead," I told him, hoping it wouldn't be anything I didn't know or couldn't fake.

"Well, as I understand it, your religion requires that the food be present during the meal, but only one person actually has to eat it. Is that correct?"

At the time, the question struck me as hilarious, but on second thought I wonder if the Egyptian diplomat wasn't onto something: Religion, Israeli-style, is something that the few do for (some would say *to*) the many. Orthodoxy is less a set of spiritual beliefs than a life-style, and it divides the country into those who are and those who aren't. This distinction is less sharp among Sephardim, who, untouched by the European notions of Reformation and secularism, tend to have a soft, southern acceptance of human frailty in the discharge of religious duties. Ashkenazim, on the other hand, approach the subject with a stern northern consistency, drawing the line between *religious* and *secular* in the dirt with a sharp sword. Today, Israel is what it has been since its inception: a secular

150

state with significant religious influence; the orthodox parties would like to turn it into a religious state based on rabbinic law.

The clash is as old as Zionism, which many rabbis originally deplored as an attempt to usurp the role of the Messiah in restoring the Jewish people to the land of Israel. The first pioneers were, by and large, self-proclaimed atheists, opponents of the religious traditionalism that they believed had kept European Jewry politically passive for generations. They foresaw a progressive secular society guided by socialist principles, in which the role of the rabbis would be, at most, a peripheral one. And yet the pioneers were ambivalent about detaching themselves and their movement from Jewish religious tradition. They challenged the theology and clericalism of the rabbis, which they saw as antiquated and paralyzing, but they wanted to reinterpret, not totally discard, the spiritual element of Judaism. They were, in a sense, Reform Jews.

If most of the rabbis saw the pioneers as atheistic louts, one, Rabbi Avraham Zvi Kook, recognized their potential in achieving a national basis for Jewish religious life. Kook became the chief rabbi of Palestine, and he forged ties with the young radicals, ties he explained to his own disciples by means of a parable. During the time of the Temple, he said, only the high priest had been allowed to enter the Holy of Holies, and even he had to purify himself before going into the chamber. But, according to the rabbi, every few years the sanctuary fell into disrepair, and then workmen had to be brought in. They tracked mud and dirt into the holy premises, hammered at its hallowed walls and then left—at which time it became once more a sacred and unapproachable place. Kook told his rabbinic critics that the pioneers were workmen, readying the holy land for its true role as a sanctified Jewish country. Not all the orthodox bought this explanation, but gradually religious Zionism became reasonably widespread. In the first parliamentary election, in 1949, religious parties received approximately 12 percent of the vote—a proportion that has remained more or less constant ever since.

David Ben Gurion could have set up a ruling coalition without them, but he was anxious to co-opt these orthodox parties. For one thing, they made accommodating political partners, concerned primarily with religious legislation, and content to provide parliamentary support for the Prime Minister's foreign and security policies. Then, too, Ben Gurion realized that a great many Jews around the world were orthodox, and the presence of rabbis and skullcapped politicians in his government would lend it a greater legitimacy in the diaspora. But most importantly, Ben Gurion saw that there was too much residual religious sentiment among Israelis themselves to ostracize the orthodox parties or turn them into parliamentary pariahs in the same way he had Begin's Herut. Religion was too strong; it had too much of an emotional hold over Israeli and foreign Jews alike to be fought. Coexistence was necessary, and coexistence meant compromise, a national *modus vivendi* that would allow orthodox Jews to become involved in Israeli life.

And so Ben Gurion, the socialist, established a partnership with the religious Zionists that lasted almost thirty years, a partnership that yielded the basics of the country's current orthodox influence. A long list of blue laws was enacted, banning public transportation, government and business activity and entertainment on the sabbath and Jewish holidays. A separate public school system for religious children was established. Special exemptions from military service were set up for yeshiva students and orthodox girls and the army undertook to observe the dietary laws strictly. Matters of personal status were placed in the hands of special religious courts supervised by a rabbinate headed by Sephardic and Ashkenazi chief rabbis. This arrangement became known as the "status quo," and it has existed more or less untouched until today.

The status quo is enforced by the country's orthodox political parties, which have proliferated in recent years and now offer a faction for every taste. There is the National Religious Party (NRP) for the knit-yarmulke "modern orthodox" disciples of Rabbi Kook; Agudah Israel, governed by the modestly named "Council of Torah Sages," which appeals to the black-hatted and bearded ultra-orthodox Ashkenazim; Shas, an Agudah breakaway led by the equally humble "Council of Torah Wise Men," whose support comes from ultra-orthodox Sephardim; as well as several smaller splinter groups. Taken altogether they represent a small minority (in the 1984 election, they received barely 10 percent of the total vote) but numbers don't accurately reflect their political power. No major party in Israeli history has ever received an absolute majority in a national election, and governments are always coalitions. The religious parties are past masters at making this system work for them.

Israel is not the only country where organized religion is primarily about power, but there are few democracies in the world where spiritual leaders are so blatantly involved in the action. Some of Israel's most venerable rabbis are power brokers who cut deals with the secular pols over money, legislation and patronage with all the restraint and dignity of Tammany ward heelers. The sight of these divines haggling over cash for their charitable institutions or maneuvering through the political thicket in order to gain some new piece of legislation has given many Israelis a jaundiced view of their religion and its guardians.

This attitude is reinforced by the fact that Israeli religious figures rarely address spiritual issues, at least not in a way recognizable to anyone outside their own orbit. Military chaplains are not counselors or advisers; they are there to police the arrangements for sabbath observance, kosher food and other rituals. Religious courts have a Judge Roy Bean ambience in which the letter of the law often takes precedence over common sense and common decency. Even major rabbis rarely speak out on spiritual matters; most of their public utterances deal with questions of Talmudic scholarship, which the average Israeli finds irrelevant. There are, of course, orthodox Jews, rabbis and laypeople, who are truly devout, but they are seldom seen by the secular majority, who are kept at arm's length by the self-segregation of the religious.

Far more apparent are the public high jinks of rabbinical leaders, who often seem at war with one another, their fellow citizens and the twentieth century. Almost every Israeli has a favorite "crazy rabbi" story. Mine, told to me by a very senior Israeli political figure, concerns the Jews of Ethiopia.

For years the rabbinate of Israel refused to recognize the Ethiopians as real Jews, a fact that made their immigration almost impossible. But in the mid-seventies, Sephardic Chief Rabbi Ovadia Yosef declared them to be authentic. This decision coincided with the election of Menachem Begin, who was determined to bring the Ethiopians to Israel, and by the late seventies the first groups began to arrive.

Despite Rabbi Yosef's ruling, however, there were still some doubts about the Jewishness of these exotic Africans. Clearly they were descended from ancient Hebrews, but a good part of their religion had been lost during the centuries of isolation. Some of the more extreme rabbis demanded that they undergo a conversion ceremony; but others ruled that a symbolic circumcision, in which a drop of blood is extracted from the penis, would be sufficient.

"Nobody knew if these Ethiopians were Sephardim or Ashkenazim," my friend the politician told me. "But Rabbi Yosef simply assumed that they were his, especially since he was the one who had dealt with their problem. And so he scheduled the circumcision ceremony at one of the towns in the Galilee where a group of Ethiopians had been brought."

Somehow, however, the Ashkenazi rabbis got wind of this ceremony, and a day before it was scheduled to take place, they launched a preemptive strike. "They brought all the men together, pricked each one to draw a drop of blood, shook their hands and welcomed them to the Jewish people. The Ethiopians didn't really understand what it was all about, but they accepted it good-naturedly. After all, it was a small enough price to pay.

"But then, the next day, the Sephardi rabbis showed up. Once again they gathered all the men together, and once again they took out the equipment for drawing blood. Of course the rabbis didn't know that the Ashkenazi rabbis had been there first, but when they found out, they decided to go ahead with their ceremony anyhow.

"The Ethiopians went along with it, too, but by this time they were getting a rather strange notion about Judaism. Every day another prominent rabbi wanting to take blood from their penis—that can be disconcerting, you know?" My friend laughed, remembering the scene. "Imagine those poor Africans. And we thought *they* were primitive."

Yet, despite the antic and sometimes grotesque behavior of

the orthodox establishment, its rigidity and insensitivity to the needs and moods of the people, there is still an atavistic respect for rabbis and religion. This respect is a central factor in the power of certain religious figures who, unknown to the general public, wield an invisible influence that astute politicians do well to take into account. Once in a while one of these power brokers surfaces, however, and people become aware of a new force on the political scene. That is what happened in the little Negev town of Netivot in early 1985, when the country first learned that an ex-con named Baruch Abu Hatzira was now a miracle worker and political manipulator to be reckoned with.

Like many of the powerful rabbis of Israel, Ashkenazi and Sephardi alike, Baruch Abu Hatzira owes his influence to his father, a saintly figure named Yisrael Abu Hatzira, known as the Baba Sali. The old man was the greatest Moroccan rabbi to immigrate to Israel, and he spent his years in the holy land in meditation and prayer. Thousands of Jews, not all of them North Africans by any means, venerated the Baba Sali, crowding his home in Netivot in order to ask for a miracle cure, a desperately wanted pregnancy, a word of advice or a blessing for good luck. The ancient rabbi never turned anyone away, and thousands of Israelis swear to this day that he was responsible for great and good changes in their lives. When the Baba Sali died, well into his nineties, he was one of the country's most beloved and admired figures.

The Baba Sali's death left a void, and his son Baruch stepped in to fill it. As the only surviving son of the holy man, he was the logical successor, despite his somewhat checkered past. As a young man he had gone into politics, where the family name had helped him become the leader of the National Religious Party in Ashkelon. But like many another son of a great man, Baruch failed to live up to the family tradition; in office he became, not to put too fine a point on it, a crook, whose activities landed him in jail for fraud, bribe taking, counterfeiting court documents, attempting to influence witnesses and various other crimes and misdemeanors. Baruch passed his years in prison teaching Talmud to his fellow inmates and writing impassioned love letters to his young mistress in Tel Aviv, who later rewarded his fine sentimentality by publishing them in a local tabloid.

Baruch Abu Hatzira was given an early parole in order to be with his dying father, and when the old man passed away, the son stepped from his prison stripes into the Baba Sali's white robes, crowning himself "Baba Baruch," the new holy man of Netivot. The story was spread that just before the old man died he had predicted that Baruch would have four times his power, a prophecy that Baruch humbly accepts.

The first thing the young Baba did was to build a quarter-of-a-million-dollar mausoleum for his father—the largest and most expensive grave site in the country. This monument was financed, as are most of Baruch Abu Hatzira's projects, by the contributions of grateful admirers. Every day, hundreds of supplicants line up at his door with empty canisters and plastic bottles. These are passed along to the wonder worker, who fills them with tap water, mumbles a ritual incantation and, in return for a contribution, hands over the sanctified and empowered liquid. Baruch reportedly takes in several thousand dollars a week—one of the most lucrative uses of holy water since the early sixties, when Prophet Jones conducted mass baptisms with a fire hose at the Detroit Fair Grounds at five dollars a head.

In early 1985 the Baba Baruch staged a monster memorial service for his father. More than 150,000 people traveled to the Negev to attend the ceremony, and tap water flowed as famous rabbis and politicians joined the ex-con on the platform to pay tribute to the Baba Sali.

Following the ceremony the Baba Baruch consented to appear on television, although he sat mute, too ethereal for mere conversation, while his cousin Aharon spoke for him to the TV correspondents. Aharon Abu Hatzira is himself a well-known politician, a former minister of religious affairs who had his own brush with the law and was forced to resign his Cabinet post. The two cousins were not always on the best of terms—during his incarceration Baruch felt that Aharon, then a government minister, might have done more to ease his life in prison, such as coming to visit him—but now they were an entity. Aharon Abu Hatzira, whose buckteeth and knowing eyes make him look like a cynical vampire in a yarmulke, smiled at the camera and told the interviewer that the Baba Baruch's past was of no importance, that his followers believed he had been purified by the tests and trials of his youth. The holy man himself looked silently on, his face showing the benign satisfaction of a man who can get 150,000 voters out for any reason at all.

Not every rabbi has this kind of following, but the important ones—Sephardic and Ashkenazi—all satisfy the first commandment of politics: They can deliver the vote. Once, before Israeli elections became real horse races, this power was valuable but not crucial; but in the more competitive era that followed the Yom Kippur War, with the major parties at rough parity, the orthodox parties' support can mean the difference between government and opposition.

Certainly they were the difference for the Likud in 1977. The decision of the National Religious Party to break up its longtime partnership with Labor, and the preference of the ultra-orthodox Agudah rabbis for Begin, gave him the narrow margin of victory necessary for setting up a coalition. Each of the parties represents a different trend within the orthodox community, and Begin appealed to each for different reasons.

On election night, 1977, Menachem Begin appeared at Likud headquarters to address his supporters. With the nation watching on television, he donned a black skullcap and began his remarks by quoting from the psalms. This simple act electrified the orthodox black hats (many of whom heard about it the next day, since there is a rabbinical proscription against watching the "devil box"). Finally, here was a political leader who looked and talked like a real Jew. In the world of the ultra-orthodox, where fashion is all-important and Chassidim can come to blows over the proper length of a caftan or the right texture of a kugel, Menachem Begin displayed an unerring sense of style. He courted the Israeli Torah Sages and prominent rabbis in the United States; in his meetings with them, the sixtyish Prime Minister would put on a black fedora and an angelic expression and somehow manage to transform himself into a bar mitzvah boy. He was a conservative on social issues and spoke often of Jewish values and tradition. And he was generous. During his administration, money was lavished on orthodox schools, charities and other institutions, shoveled into orthodox hands with only the mildest effort at public accounting. Naturally, the Labor party screamed bloody murder about this form of political bribery, but no one took its indignation too seriously. At one point Reb Avraham Shapira, the Agudah leader who looks like Burl Ives playing a corrupt cardinal, rose in the Knesset and reminded Shimon Peres that the Likud was only following Labor's precedent. "And Shimon," he admonished, "you know perfectly well that we aren't getting anything you didn't offer."

Begin's courtship of the ultra-orthodox community paid him a real political dividend: He became the first secular politician in history to attain genuine popularity with Agudah's followers. This gave Begin a stick, as well as a carrot, in his dealings with the rabbis: Both he and they knew that Agudah's constituency wouldn't allow the party to desert the Likud-led government. The fact that the Begin years were lean ones in terms of the Agudah agenda—during his two terms in office hardly any significant religious legislation was passed, certainly nothing approaching the gains they had made under Ben Gurion—was a tribute to the leverage this popularity gave him.

The ultra-orthodox voters forgave Begin his inability to get them major legislation, just as they forgave him his own impieties. Overseas, Menachem Begin had the reputation of a religious fanatic—the foreign editor of *The Washington Post* once compared his religious zeal with the Ayatollah Khomeini's—but in fact, Begin wasn't even orthodox. He went bareheaded (perhaps the single most significant mark of non-orthodoxy in Israel), rarely attended synagogue and maintained only some of the sabbath restrictions—for example, he didn't drive but he wrote and turned on lights, a distinction that doubtless escaped *The Washington Post* but was not lost on the black hats of the ultra-orthodox world. They were prepared to accept these deviations and to embrace him for much the same reason that the Sephardim did—because he was a fellow outsider and because he treated them and their values with affection and respect. Previous Prime Ministers had given up far more in terms of actual concessions, but what Begin gave he gave willingly, with a sad shrug for his inability to do better. Even more, he never gave them the feeling that they were worthless or that their way of life was a doomed anachronism. And as a result, the Agudah politicians and rabbis, most of whom were far to the left of Begin on security issues, found themselves the victims of a political kidnapping.

Begin's attitude toward the modern orthodox, especially the activists in the Gush Emunim settlement movement, was more ambivalent. Unlike the Agudah black hats, they looked like Israelis, wore jeans and sneakers and cute little skullcaps that the girls knitted for their boyfriends. They were patriotic, served in the army, worked in normal jobs, went to the movies and sometimes even lived in "mixed" neighborhoods. By all outward indications they were Real Israelis who happened to believe in God and observe religious commandments.

But the sabra knit-yarmulkes were (and are) deceptively different from the other Real Israelis. They attended separate schools and separate youth movements where, without anyone noticing for a long while, they were instilled with a new kind of religious nationalism. The reason it went unnoticed is that during the Mapai dynasty, the opinions of the religious community on national-security issues were considered unimportant. It was only with the Yom Kippur War that the modern orthodox, like the Sephardim or the Agudah people, began to assert themselves.

The primary focus for this assertiveness became the struggle over the future of Judaea and Samaria, the West Bank. For the generation of modern orthodox children educated before the Six Day War, there was never any question that Judaea and Samaria—which contain some of Judaism's most sacred sites—are an integral and indispensable part of the national patrimony. For that generation, any compromise over the future of this hallowed ground would be not only a strategic mistake but a violation of religious law. The emergence of the Gush Emunim movement shortly after the Yom Kippur War constituted a double opportunity for the young orthodox sabras: to defend the God-given patrimony and, for the first time, to become centrally involved in the country's political life. Pioneering had always been the key to "Israeliness," and Gush Emunim seized the technique and vocabulary of the early Labor Zionist settlers in its efforts to "create facts" in the disputed territory.

Menachem Begin was one of the first politicians to grasp the potential importance of this development. (Shimon Peres, who as defense minister in the Rabin government acted as a patron for the movement, was another.) Between 1974 and 1977, Gush Emunim served Begin as shock troops in the battle for Judaea and Samaria; it provided the Herut leader with a sabra settlement movement he had never had before.

In office, Begin continued to use the young religious settlers and derived an ironic pleasure from having taken the pioneering high ground from the Labor movement. But he was a legalist as well as a nationalist, and he resented the superlegal pretensions of the Gush's leaders, as well as their pose of moral superiority. More than once, close aides heard him grumble about "these young messianists who think they can teach me about the Land of Israel."

Despite the NRP's new prominence in political life, the Begin years were not happy ones for the National Religious Party and its leadership. In 1977 the party elected twelve members to the Knesset, more or less their traditional showing. In 1981, after four years of Begin, its strength was halved, to six. And in 1984, after three more years of Likud rule, it got only four seats. Many of the defectors went over to the Likud, on the grounds that they might as well vote for a major party instead of a splinter group; while others, impatient with what they saw as the moderation of both Begin and the NRP, moved farther to the right and joined the secular, anti-Camp David, annexationist Tehiyah party.

As for Gush Emunim, the attention it has attracted both in Israel and abroad proved vastly disproportionate to its real size or strength. More than a decade after its founding the movement is divided and, to a large extent, discredited by its extremist behavior, particularly the involvement of some of its most prominent activists in terrorist operations against West Bank Arabs. Gush Emunim has failed dismally in its efforts to become a mass movement; despite the open door of the Begin years, it never attracted large numbers of young orthodox Jews to its settlements in the West Bank. In fact, most of the West Bank's Jewish residents are ordinary nonideological Israelis drawn there by the low prices of government-subsidized housing. The country remains divided over the wisdom of surrendering any portion of the area; but many, perhaps most, of those who favor keeping it are secularists like Tehiyah leaders (and former Laborites) Yuval Ne'eman and Rafael Eytan, who see it primarily in security terms, or young Israelis who can barely remember a time when the territory was not a part of Israel.

Yet, despite the political failures of the orthodox parties and the loss of momentum that Gush Emunim suffered as a result of its involvement in terrorism, the religious community of Israel remains a potent force in national coalition politics. The sight of Menachem Begin donning a black yarmulke and reciting psalms on election eve, 1977, was a novelty; eight years later, on the eve of coalition negotiations, Shimon Peres put on a similar skullcap and went, accompanied by photographers, to pray at the Western Wall. His prayers were rewarded with a government of national unity and with a partial re-creation of the traditional alliance between Labor and the National Religious Party. A few months later, Peres, the disciple of David Ben Gurion, turned up for what he announced would be a monthly Talmud lesson from Rabbi Ovadia Yosef, who is, coincidentally, the spiritual adviser of one of the new orthodox parties. Israel may not be a God-fearing nation, but its politicians have a healthy respect for His voters.

The power and presence of the orthodox (and particularly the ultra-orthodox) is especially obvious in Jerusalem, where they are a potent factor in municipal politics, pursuing policies that would have made them a welcome addition to the city council of Calvin's Geneva. They managed to keep public swimming pools out of Jerusalem until 1958, and more recently they have been an effective lobby against the building of a new soccer stadium. They are a force for intolerance, and when politics fails, they often resort to other means to impose their wishes.

There is, for example, the matter of sabbath observance. Young yeshiva students customarily stone cars that come anywhere near their neighborhoods on the sabbath; and they have also been known to use strong-arm tactics on merchants

and theater owners who open their premises before the third
star becomes visible on Saturday night. Shopkeepers who ignore written warnings are visited by two or three burly, black-
coated enforcers who drop in to discuss the high price of fire
insurance. Many of these bearded toughs come originally
from Brooklyn or Queens, a fact that often lends a Cagney-
esque flavor to the sacred shakedown.

Nor is the violence limited to nonbelievers. Dyspeptic rabbis with fifty-year-old grudges excommunicate each other by
plastering notices on the walls of their ghetto. Sometimes rival
Chassidic groups clash in the alleys of Mea Shearim, Yiddish-
speaking Sharks and Jets who cut off each other's beards and
daub swastikas on the doors of each other's synagogues. The
Jerusalem police department has a special unit that monitors
ultra-orthodox violence, but they rarely catch anyone. "They
all look alike to us," a hapless police officer once told me.

The political maneuverings and sporadic violence of the ul-
tra-orthodox have not made them overly popular among
Jerusalem's nonreligious citizens. Once, in a fit of frustration,
Jerusalem's outspoken and brilliant mayor Teddy Kollek, in-
formed that there was a fire in Mea Shearim, said that he
wished the whole damn neighborhood would burn down.
Kollek apologized for the remark, but a great many
Jerusalemites applauded the sentiment.

And yet there is something about Jerusalem that gives the
ultra-orthodox minority a home-court advantage. Jerusalem is
an austere mountain fortress on the edge of a desert, the kind
of place that would give you pause even if it weren't the official Holy City, and if you live there, you live by the city's
rules. From time to time there are feeble attempts to upgrade
the capital's somber night life, but they are invariably futile—
a nightclub in Jerusalem seems as incongruous as a kosher
deli in Butte, Montana. If by some feat of magic, all 400,000
Jerusalemites were suddenly replaced by the population of
Las Vegas, within a matter of weeks the blackjack dealers
would be busy making green felt prayer rugs and the cocktail
waitresses would be sewing long sleeves on their bunny outfits.

Outside of Jerusalem the influence of religion is far weaker.
But throughout the country there is a struggle—ultimately the

struggle between the majority, who want the country to be a secular Jewish democracy with traditional overtones, and the minority, who hope to turn it, by incremental steps, into a state ruled by religious law. This contest is carried out in the public arena, in the Knesset and city councils, and behind closed doors where politicians cut their deals. It is acted out on the West Bank, where settlers who know the Eternal Truth struggle with governments whose authority rests in law and popular support. But the battle extends beyond politics and affects the lives of ordinary Israelis who are searching for ways to accommodate these conflicting views and to live together in some semblance of harmony.

At 64 Rothschild Boulevard in Tel Aviv stands a two-story building, set on the wide tree-lined avenue whose gracious houses, now in their sixth decade, have lapsed into a state of genteel decrepitude. At the entrance to number 64 are two signs that announce the building's tenants. One says: YE-SHIVAT BE'ER MAYIM HAIM—the Well of Living Waters Rabbinical Academy—which is located on the second floor. The other is for the yeshiva's downstairs neighbor, and says: YING YANG CHINESE RESTAURANT. The Well of Living Waters is run by Rabbi and Mrs. Loufovitz and their married daughter, who immigrated to Israel from Hungary after World War II; Ying Yang's proprietor is Yisrael Aharoni, the son of Bucharian immigrants who grew up in Haifa's Wadi Salib slum area, the site of the 1959 ethnic riots. Both the Loufovitzes and Aharoni have come a long way to meet at number 64 Rothschild Boulevard.

From his earliest boyhood, Aharoni (no one calls him by his first name) was fascinated by the Far East, especially Far Eastern cooking. After finishing his military service, he spent a few months in Taiwan, sampling local dishes and dreaming of the day that he would be able to bring Chinese cuisine to Israel. Strangely, it was Menachem Begin who made his dream come true.

When Begin came to office in 1977, almost his first act was to order the admission to Israel of several hundred Vietnamese boat people, most of whom turned out to be ethnic Chinese. Begin looked at the boat people and saw the homeless and unwanted Jews of the 1930s; Aharoni watched them arrive and thought of *dim sum* and moo shu pork. Within days he made contact with the first group of newcomers. Could any of them cook? Did anyone want to work? Before long, Ying Yang was a reality, and Aharoni found himself as a kind of foster father to a large clan of Israeli Chinese.

Yisrael Aharoni looks somewhat Oriental himself, round-shouldered and plump as a won ton, with a Fu Manchu beard and moustache combination and a long pigtail that reaches all the way down his back. This, along with the superior quality of his restaurant, has made him a familiar and popular figure, and his picture has even been used by one of the country's largest banks as an advertising gimmick. Under his tutelage, his Chinese staff and their families have made a rapid adjustment to the country. Most of them now speak excellent Hebrew, many have taken out Israeli citizenship and begun to raise families—giving their sabra children Israeli names—and several have opened restaurants of their own. They have little concern about the religious issues that plague Israel—most of them are Buddhists—but they *are* interested in politics, and despite the dovish Aharoni's best efforts, they are strong Beginites, a small and largely unknown component of the Likud's ethnic coalition.

During the last few years, Ying Yang has become both a busy restaurant and a meeting place for the country's Chinese community—developments that have perplexed and dismayed the students and rabbis of the Well of Living Waters. Their dismay saddens Aharoni, who is the kind of person who thinks everyone should love one another as much as he loves them. But despite his best efforts, he has failed to ingratiate himself with his upstairs neighbors, who persist in seeing him as what they call a "beatnik" and his establishment as a godless emporium of forbidden foods and sabbath-violating revelers.

When the War in Lebanon broke out, Aharoni was called up with the rest of his reserve unit. Despite his rather eccentric appearance he is a good enough combat soldier that his commanding officers have resisted the temptation to turn him into the company cook, and he took part in some of the heaviest fighting of the campaign. When his unit was sent home, Aharoni changed out of his uniform into a red silk jacket emblazoned with dragons, let down his pigtail and went to check on his restaurant. At the entrance to 64 Rothschild Boulevard he met the rabbi's daughter from upstairs.

"I haven't seen you around for a long time," she said, a note of hope in her voice. "You're thinking of selling?"

"No, I was in the reserves. In Lebanon."

"In Lebanon?" she said with disbelief. "What were you doing there?"

"I was fighting," said Aharoni.

The rabbi's daughter looked at him with genuine amazement. "I don't understand. If you were in the war, then why weren't you killed?"

"I guess she couldn't believe that God would let her down like that," Aharoni laughs.

In Tel Aviv, where the orthodox are in retreat from the forces of sweet-and-sour hedonism, it is easy to laugh at this sort of thing. In Jerusalem, where it is the secular Jews who feel pressure from the political power and assertiveness of the clerics, the situation is different. But in both places, and throughout Israel, the relations between the secular and orthodox communities are usually best described in terms of competition and struggle. The Israeli middle class, the ultimate battleground for these forces, remains caught in the center, neither militantly secular nor noticeably observant.

In fact, forty years after independence, neither side has won a decisive victory in their struggle over the character of the Jewish state. Rabbi Kook's secular workmen have yet to turn the country into a Holy of Holies, and the Torah Sages of Mea Shearim have failed to transform Israel into Minsk-on-the-Mediterranean; but neither has the Zionist revolution rendered religion an artifact of the diaspora. Like Ying Yang and the Well of Living Waters, these rival impulses share the same premises in an uneasy equilibrium. Meanwhile, the vast majority of Israelis go about their business, willing to applaud the Talmudic scholars for their dedication and the Chinese chefs for their Peking duck.

PART III

HUSTLERS

9

A Service for His Country

Israeli history has been made in some improbable places. The first Zionist Congress was held in Basel, Switzerland. The Balfour Declaration, which promised a homeland to the Jewish people in Palestine, was promulgated in London. The decision to establish that state was taken by the United Nations at Lake Success, New York. But none of these distant scenes was as unlikely as the back room of P.J. Clarke's saloon on Third Avenue in Manhattan, where a few years ago an unsung pioneer named Shaul Evron got the inspiration for his own contribution to his country.

Shaul Evron is not a native New Yorker. On the contrary, he is a child of Tel Aviv, born in the mid-forties and raised in a small apartment above his father's pharmacy on Allenby Street. The Tel Aviv of his boyhood was an austere place, a kind of Jewish Salt Lake City that held the pioneer values in high regard and encouraged its citizens—especially its children—to abide by them. Shaul Evron was such a child, but from the very beginning he rebelled against the earnest conformism of his generation. Even as a young boy he was a dreamer, and his dreams were mostly about food. (Lately, according to him, women have begun playing a larger role.) Shaul is a patriot and, in his own way, a pioneer; but he is also a constructive critic, and he doesn't understand why the Jews, having waited two thousand years for sovereignty, now find it necessary to overcook their meat.

. In his mid-teens and restless, Shaul Evron shipped out as an apprentice seaman, and while he didn't learn much about sailing, he became an expert on the bars and restaurants of the port cities of four continents. He would return from his voyages and, like a sabra Sinbad, regale his friends with tales of exotic banquets and beverages. The average Israeli in those days of Zionist minimalism was taught to regard eating as a necessary but unpleasant duty, and Shaul's culinary enthusiasm was considered more than a bit eccentric. Like anyone ahead of his time, he knew ridicule at the hands of his peers; but unlike many other visionaries, he has lived to be vindicated and to have the satisfaction of seeing them come begging for the recipe for steak *au poivre* and the ingredients of the perfect martini.

In the small-town atmosphere of Tel Aviv, Evron became something of a legend—a sabra son in good standing who was more interested in having a good time than in shouldering the burdens of state-building. Of course certain duties were inescapable. In the army, for example, his background and education made him officer material, and he became a lieutenant in the armored corps. He displayed scant aptitude for tanks, however, and was soon appointed commander of the armored corps's male glee club, perhaps on the theory that his hedonism included a love of music. In fact, as Evron recalls it, a music lover was the last person who should have been assigned the job, since the "glee club" consisted of a randomly selected basic training platoon deputized *ad hoc* whenever a musical performance was required. Shaul took the job without complaint, but he usually managed to anesthetize himself against the trainees' singing with a vodka or two before each show.

After the army and a stint at the Hebrew University, Evron became an economics reporter for *Ma'ariv* newspaper, and during these years his reputation grew. Ombibulous in a country so abstemious that it has no drinking laws, fastidious about his food among people who considered steak and French fries the epitome of fine dining, he was, in those early days, prepared to go anyplace and pay any price in a constant search for what he called "satisfaction for my mouth." More than once he drove his battered gray Peugeot 204 convertible for hours through the Negev desert, past bleak outposts where a can of tuna fish is considered a gourmet item, to Eilat, on the basis of a rumor that oysters had been sighted in one of the restaurants near the port. On one memorable occasion, during a food and beverage safari in the United States, he took an early-morning flight to Chicago in order to taste kielbasa at O'Hare's snack bar, flew on to the Dallas airport to sample its raw bar ("The oysters weren't much," he later explained, "but I've always wanted to eat in a place with a sign that says 'please check your firearms'"), and then flew to San Francisco, loudly praising the time zone system that allowed him to fit in a late *dim sum* lunch in Chinatown.

It was during this trip to the States that Shaul Evron made a discovery that was to affect the life of his fellow countrymen. One night, in the back room of P.J. Clarke's saloon, he had his first taste of 101 proof Wild Turkey. His round, ruddy face lit up with pleasure as he washed down the Kentucky whiskey with a Miller High Life, and by the time the second double had arrived, Evron had decided with quiet resolve to bring the stuff to Israel.

Tel Aviv, in the years since Shaul's boyhood, has made a quantum leap forward, and it is now possible to find cheeseburgers and tacos, sushi and fried calamari where once only gefilte fish and gray, unclassifiable meat held sway. Likewise, the grip of Johnnie Walker Red has been broken by a variety of beverages that the city's increasingly sophisticated citizens now demand. Evron, who knows the bars and nightclubs of his native city the way his pious ancestors knew the Talmud, was aware, that night in Clarke's, that Israelis who wanted a drink of Kentucky bourbon were stuck with Four Roses, and although he had, until then, considered it a fair whiskey, he now decided that it was his responsibility to introduce his countrymen to something better.

This unselfish pioneering impulse came as a shock to those who had known Evron only as the commander of the armored corps male glee club, or as a patron of Tel Aviv's seedier night spots; but it was no surprise to anyone acquainted with Evron's family history. His father's father was Abramsky, an old Jew who owned a small mill and bakery on the Polish-German border. Back around the turn of the century, old

171

man Abramsky, a pious and prodigious patriarch with eight sons and a daughter, had a vision: The crazy young socialists in Palestine were right; a Jewish country would arise in the ancestral homeland. The old man realized that the new state would need trained personnel, Jews with Gentiles' skills. And so, as his sons grew to manhood, he took them aside one by one and assigned them professions. He dispatched them to distant cities to learn seamanship and agronomy, engineering and pharmacy, preparing them for citizenship in a country that did not yet exist.

Two of Abramsky's children rebelled and went to America. Three more stayed in Europe and were murdered by the Germans. But four sons made it to Palestine. Uncle Moshe became a sea captain on the Zim line, Uncle Yisrael an oil man, Uncle Yeshyahu a banana farmer. Old man Abramsky himself escaped Hitler and came to Palestine, where he died when Shaul was just a baby. But although he never knew his grandfather, Shaul claims that he has inherited the old man's patriotism, which for many years lay dormant until that day in Clarke's when he had a vision of sufficient power to bring it alive.

Not long after returning from the United States, Shaul opened a restaurant of his own, The Kiosk, in Neve Tzedek, one of Tel Aviv's oldest neighborhoods. Almost his first act was to contact the liquor distributor. "Get me a dozen bottles of Wild Turkey," he commanded. "Make it the 101 proof. And damn the cost." When they arrived, special delivery, he lined them up on the bar with the fondness of a general inspecting crack troops. "They look almost too good to drink," he told his friends as he poured us all complimentary samples of the stuff.

The Kiosk got rave reviews, but Shaul was unable to concentrate on money in the presence of so much food and drink; and ultimately he gave up the restaurant and went back to journalism, as a food critic. (Here, too, he has a problem. It is almost impossible for him to say a harsh word about anything edible, a weakness he balances by bad-mouthing owners and chefs.) But by the time he retired as a restaurateur, Wild Turkey had caught on. It is available today in two dozen Tel Aviv bars (as well as in Jerusalem's La Belle, the closest thing to a Tel Aviv bar east of Latroun), and Shaul can often be found in one of these places, blue eyes twinkling behind his steel-rimmed spectacles, a beatific smile on his cherubic face—a man content in the knowledge that he has done something for his country.

Shaul Evron is a man of parts—patriot, journalist, gourmand, officer and gentleman ("Put down 'family man,'" he told me, when he heard I was writing about him; "I've got a cousin in Beersheba"), but he is first and foremost a Tel Avivi. He leaves his native city on rare forays after some provincial delicacy—mixed Jerusalem grill of cow and lamb innards prepared on skewers and wrapped in Iraqi pita bread, for example, or southern fried chicken at Vered Hagalil, an American-owned dude ranch overlooking the sea of Galilee—but he almost always returns to the city by sundown. There isn't much to do outside of Tel Aviv after dark, certainly no other place that offers the dizzying variety of restaurants, bars, nightclubs, concerts and theaters that make the city a combination Broadway, Nashville, Sunset Strip and Miami Beach.

Unlike Jerusalem, Tel Aviv is a city built on sand, a shifting, experimental place whose balmy Mediterranean climate gives it a sensual, entirely human feel, wholly different from the austere mountain capital forty miles to the east. During the years of Evron's boyhood it was a somber city, not only in the grip of the socialist puritan ethos but still in mourning over the Holocaust. Most of Tel Aviv's residents come from European backgrounds, and it would be hard to find many who were not personally affected by the war. Even the modern, post-independence architecture of Tel Aviv is, at first glance, depressing: a collection of Lego-like housing blocks made of poured concrete, resolutely utilitarian and unadorned. The city's main avenues run parallel to the Mediterranean beach, as if to protect the citizenry from soft breezes and the sight of bare flesh.

In the past decade, however, Tel Aviv has blossomed into a place of almost manic energy, much of it channeled into the pursuit of the good life, Israeli-style. New entertainment districts sprout up almost as fast as the suburban housing tracts that surround the city and serve as its bedroom communities. A class of newly prosperous businessmen has emerged, and Tel Aviv has accommodated their recent prosperity with an array of entertainments—some gaudy and garish, others experimental and culturally ambitious—which have wrought what a friend of mine once described as "urbane renewal." The city remains ugly, sometimes hideously so, but with age it has taken on character, even a sort of charm. Jerusalem is the symbol of the heroic Israel, but Tel Aviv is capital of Israel Minor, a city no larger than the sum of its parts. A journalist friend once explained the difference this way: "If you live in Jerusalem and forget the city, then your right hand loses its cunning and your tongue cleaves to your palate. But if you live in Tel Aviv and happen to forget about it for a few days, nothing happens. Why should I take any chances?"

The rivalry between the two cities is legendary. Back in 1968, for example, the Coca-Cola company opened its bottling plant in Israel, and for the first time Coke, with its distinctive signature in Hebrew, became available. I was a student at the Hebrew University at the time, and I remember the first ad I saw for the soft drink in *The Jerusalem Post*. I didn't especially like the stuff, but having grown up in America I considered it a natural element, like water or oxygen, and somehow its availability made Israel seem more like a real country.

The ad had promised that Coke would be in the stores on April first, and early that morning I went to the supermarket on Agron Street to buy a tangible symbol of Israeli progress. Much to my disappointment, however, I was told that it hadn't yet arrived. "They're not selling it in Jerusalem yet," the checkout girl said. "For the time being, you can only get it in Tel Aviv." Then, noticing my look of disappointment and apparently taking it for wounded civic pride, she patted my arm. "It's not fair," she consoled me. "They get everything before we do. But never mind. When the Messiah arrives, He'll come to Jerusalem first."

If the Messiah does come, and he gets to Tel Aviv, He'll have his work cut out for Him. During the past decade, while foreign correspondents and other such experts have been report-

174

ing on the supposed increase in religious fundamentalism, Israel's largest city has undergone a process of blatant secularization. Until the 1973 war, Tel Aviv was almost as sabbath-observant as Jerusalem, but since then the city has opened up, with movies, theaters and night spots running full blast. Hundreds of restaurants operate in the city, and most of the good ones are nonkosher, so much so that their menus have abandoned the euphemistic "white meat" for the more straightforward "pork chops," or "spare ribs." On Yarkon Street near the luxury hotels on the beach, a flourishing strip of porno movies, streetwalkers, B-girl clubs, pool halls and fast-food joints offers temptations not sanctioned by the Torah.

Tel Aviv gets away with this kind of sacrilege because, unlike Jerusalem, it is a city with no inherent religious importance and no significant orthodox population. It was founded as the provincial capital of a socialist enterprise, and a majority of its residents are, as they always have been, nonobservant. It is rare to meet Chassidic Jews on the streets, but not uncommon to see elderly Jews in khaki shorts and old-fashioned European-looking caps chatting on park benches in Yiddish-inflected Hebrew, or riding past on rickety bicycles. Tel Aviv has a great many old people, and their presence lends atmosphere and authenticity to the city's pioneer past.

Many of these old-timers are far from pleased by the changes that have swept over their city in the past few years. Coca-Cola and Wild Turkey are only the tip of a giant Western iceberg that has washed up on Tel Aviv's shore, informing it, and the rest of the country, with a previously unknown materialism, modernity and sophistication. Things that were unheard-of until the Six Day War have become commonplace: Chinese carry-out, air conditioning, color TV, traffic jams (when I first came to Israel, cars were so rare that they had the respectful designation of "privates"), tennis stadiums, bagels and lox, gay bars, slick magazines, world-class basketball, milk in cartons, direct-dial overseas phone calls, surfers, nautilus clubs, Hebrew rock 'n' roll, diet soda, color coordination, laundromats, super-highways—changes that have made Israel less quaint for tourists but more interesting and comfortable for its citizens.

Before 1973, many of Israel's cultural imports came from Europe, especially France—there was a time when every shop became a boutique, every dance hall a discotheque—but the general disillusionment with Europe that followed the war opened the way to a process of Americanization that has increased over the years. Sometimes it takes the form of simple imitation—there is a chain of hamburger joints called McDavid's, which serves its own Big Mac (pronounced locally "Big Mek"), and not long ago someone opened a break-dance school in Tel Aviv. Sometimes it is a matter of borrowing finished products, such as American television shows—*Dallas* and *Benson,* MTV videos and NBA play-off games—that appear regularly on Israeli TV. But a good deal of America's influence is felt indirectly, as cultural and technological trends from the United States become absorbed into Israeli life and are given a particularly local twist.

Nowhere is this process more evident than in the growth of Hebrew rock 'n' roll. Until the mid-sixties, the pioneer cultural commissars kept the lid on rock music. Israel's pop scene was still in the accordion age, and it consisted mostly of morale-building ditties, moving ballads about the beauties of the Land of Israel, or psuedo-cabaret tunes. The radio, government-controlled until 1965, offered a rich fare of these songs, as well as classical music. Foreign pop tunes were for the most part confined to easy-listening pap, although an occasional Cliff Richard, Elvis or Platters song slipped through.

The pitiful state of rock 'n' roll was one of the first things I noticed when I arrived. A few weeks before coming to Israel, I attended a Wilson Pickett concert in Detroit with some friends. During Pickett's classic rendition of "In the Midnight Hour," one of my companions turned to me and with more than a little malice said, "Bet you don't hear too much of that over in the Holy Land."

I was feeling patriotic, and I just laughed. "We have our own music," I told him. "We don't need this diaspora jive."

He looked at me skeptically. "When you get to Jerusalem," he said with finality, "you may walk around singing *bim-bom-bim-bom-bom,* but I know that in your heart you'll still be going *boogedie-boogedie-boogedie-boogedie-shoo.*"

In the excitement of coming to Israel I forgot this grim prediction, but it came back to me when I turned on the radio for the first time and heard Patti Page's rendition of "Where Will the Baby's Dimple Be?" Even in the midst of my Zionist enthusiasm, I couldn't help thinking there was something seriously wrong with a country whose national radio would play such a song—or "Sixteen Tons" or Dean Martin's "That's Amore"—over and over.

Luckily for me I arrived right at the tail end of the accordion era. Shortly after the Six Day War a number of small rock clubs opened up on Hamasger Street, a gritty strip near Tel Aviv's Central Bus Station. The bands who appeared there were made up of local kids who had heard enough rock music to want to make it themselves. These bands—the Blue Stars and the Churchills—sang in comically bad English and played with all the sophistication of a high school combo whanging away at "Louie, Louie"; but they are remembered today with affection and nostalgia by a whole generation of Israeli musicians. Yehuda Eder, a kibbutz-bred lead guitarist who has played with some of Israel's best bands, recalls coming into town to listen for hours to the new sounds of Hamasger Street's pioneers. And it wasn't long before the music reached his kibbutz as well.

"The American volunteers who came after the Six Day War brought it," he remembers. "They came with electric guitars—who had ever seen an electric guitar? They had Jimmy Hendrix records; they smoked grass. For us, they were like invaders from another planet."

A few years later, after his military service, Yehuda Eder joined Tamuz, a Rolling Stones-like band that helped launch a new era in Israeli music. Despite the fact that both Eder and Shalom Hanoch, one of the group's lead singers, were kibbutz kids, Tamuz had a bad-boy image that appealed to the disillusioned young veterans of the Yom Kippur War. Part of this image can be attributed to the group's other lead singer, Ariel Zilber. Zilber lost a leg playing with a grenade as a youngster, and despite his rather genteel background (his mother was a well-known Yemenite singer, his father a classical musician with the Israeli Philharmonic), he managed to convey a menacing, peg-legged rebelliousness, like a Semitic Gene Vincent. His biggest song was *"Holech Batel"* ("Hanging Out"), a blues-influenced portrait of a street character in search of drugs, sex and stealable auto parts. It was an almost unheard-of theme for Israeli music, and just as important, it was sung in simple, straightforward Hebrew.

The father of the idiomatic style is another kibbutz-born musician, Danny Sanderson. When he came on the scene in 1973, the cultural establishment was so conservative that it actually banned one of his songs from the radio for bad grammar. Undeterred, Sanderson sang about everyday experiences, linking them with wry humor to the great themes and pretensions of society. His lyrics made him a one-man Leiber and Stoller, a good-natured Dylan who captured the unique flavor of ordinary life in the shadow of extraordinary events and effortlessly blended the past with the present. In one, for example, David beats Goliath and "the whole Pentateuch came out to cheer . . . if you want to be our king, at six give us a ring."

Sanderson opened the way for other artists to explore the contemporary connection with the Bible. One of the most memorable was Ariel Zilber's song about a loser sitting and wondering why "Samson of Eshteol, he was such a buck; and here I am in Ashkelon, working on a garbage truck." These songs were a departure from the heroic treatment of Biblical themes in the pioneers' music, and they expressed the fusion of Western and Jewish influences that are at the heart of contemporary Israeli pop culture.

Danny Sanderson's first group, Kaveret, was the Beatles to Zilber's Rolling Stones, a collection of seven shaggy-haired, lovable kids who sang upbeat, funny songs about things other kids could identify with. Their first album sold 100,000 copies, an almost unbelievable number in a country of less than 4 million, but Sanderson's American-born parents were not convinced. At the height of his first popularity, when he was already a national figure, Mrs. Sanderson invited her son to a Friday night dinner. "It's still not too late to become an architect," she told him over chicken soup.

This is Danny Sanderson's kind of humor. At five foot two, he is a Paul Simon look-alike, but his public persona is closer to Woody Allen, with a touch of Groucho. He is a wise guy who laughs at himself, a first cousin to the borscht-belt comics, a rare Israeli practitioner of *shtik,* conceivably the only serious rock musician in the world who mixes stand-up comedy with his music. He learned both—the humor and the music—in New York, where he lived for eight years while his father managed El Al's office there. Sanderson attended Manhattan's High School of the Performing Arts, formed his own band and absorbed the various currents in American music before returning to Israel at age eighteen to join the army.

After leaving military service, he formed Kaveret with a group of army buddies who had played together in one of the entertainment troupes, and went on to become the biggest thing in Israeli show business, not only the seminal lyricist of modern Hebrew rock but a musical innovator as well. He borrowed from the materials at hand—his American background, the chants of the synagogue, Arabic music—and welded them into a distinctive, and distinctively Israeli, style: Jimi Hendrix rhythm lines with a Chassidic or Near Eastern flavor, good-time music in a minor key. Like Tel Aviv itself, the music was bittersweet, experimental, energetic, eclectic. He wrote the first Hebrew surfing song, dedicated to the teenagers who pack the Herzliyah beach in summertime; bouzouki-flavored Mediterranean tunes about stuck-up girls; an old-fashioned Zionist pioneer number that suddenly ends in a sweeping big finish reminiscent of the Five Satins; a haunting Bedouin song about a shepherd who wants to invite his girl friend to the movies until he realizes that it's impossible because they both live in the Bible. "You can do anything in this country," Sanderson says, "as long as you keep the amplifier below five."

Sanderson's parents came to Israel in 1948 to help fight for independence and, later, to settle on a kibbutz on the northern border. Like old man Abramsky they were pioneers, and they never dreamed their son would become an Israeli rock 'n' roll star. But Sanderson, in his own way, is no less patriotic than his parents, and his pioneering spirit is infectious. Which is how I came to be the co-writer of the first Hebrew doo-wop song in two thousand years.

It all started when I was still the head of the Government Press Office. Once a week or so, a group of American foreign correspondents used to gather in someone's house, break out guitars and sing songs from the fifties and sixties. It was strictly for fun, but nothing stays private in Israel for long, and one day a member of the group, Marcus Eliason of the Associated Press, told us that Sanderson, whom he knew, had heard about the sessions and wanted to come. Several of us objected strenuously—we didn't want to be relegated to singing the *wah-wahs* in the background—but Marcus insisted that Sanderson wouldn't monopolize the evening, and he was right. He came with one of his sidemen and contented himself with accompanying us on an electric guitar, occasionally requesting a song from his New York boyhood. Not surprisingly, the addition of Sanderson and his sideman noticeably improved the quality of our performance and he soon became a regular. Over the course of time, we became good friends.

One day we were sitting on my porch in Jerusalem talking about nothing in particular, and listening to music. "Know what this country needs?" he said suddenly. "It needs a good doo-wop song, like we had when we were growing up. The kids here have never had one. How about writing one together?" A couple of hours later we had *"Bo'i Motek,"* a Hebrew version of the Dell Vikings' "Come Go With Me." That week he went to a recording studio where he cut the song, singing all the voices *a capella*. When the tune was released, Sanderson explained in a radio interview why he had done it: "In Israel, everybody brings something from home. Doo-wop is Zionism, too."

10

Swish! It's the Law of Return

If Tel Aviv measures itself against New York and L.A., the rest of Israel measures itself against Tel Aviv. The city is an island bordered by the Mediterranean on the west and surrounded on its other three sides by faceless bedroom towns and interchangeable suburban housing tracts, raw Levittowns for the newly prosperous where a three-bedroom bungalow with an "American kitchen" on a tenth of an acre goes for $150,000—in cash—and up. These suburbs are no more Tel Aviv than Paramus or Hoboken is New York. The real Tel Aviv, the Israeli Big Time, sits at the heart of this urban sprawl in an area small enough to cross by foot in any direction in half an hour.

Within this vortex are the centers of a dozen interlocking establishments. The Ministry of Defense, the Histadrut Labor Federation, the offices of the major political parties, the largest newspapers, the stock market, the smart galleries, theaters and concert halls, the expensive shops of Dizengoff Street— all are crowded, Manhattan-like, in neighborly proximity. Jerusalem may be Israel's eternal capital, but Tel Aviv is the seat of its national activity, the home of Big Politics, Big Army, Big Labor, Big Culture, Big Spending—and even Big Crime. Not long ago my brother-in-law Eli, who headed the Jerusalem police's narcotics squad, arrested a local drug dealer. He found only about half a gram of heroin, but the arrest was so unusual that it was reported on the radio. When

I congratulated him, however, he was mortified. "A lousy half gram," he fumed. "The Tel Aviv cops are probably laughing their asses off. We just don't get a chance up here—all the real hoods are in Tel Aviv."

One of the pillars of Tel Aviv's major league status is the Maccabi Tel Aviv basketball team, the perennial national champion and a power in European Cup competition. When Maccabi takes the floor against Spain or Italy, ten thousand screaming fans fill the stands at the Yad Eliahu sports arena, and the rest of the country comes to a halt to watch on television. When they beat the Russians, or win a European championship, as they have twice in recent years, the nation erupts into spontaneous and uncharacteristically uninhibited celebration, delighted by the evidence that Israel is once more, in the words of former team captain Tal Brody, "on the map." ·

The Maccabi mania began shortly after the Six Day War when Brody, a former all-Big Ten guard from the University of Illinois, arrived in Israel as an immigrant and signed up with the team. Brody introduced a new, sophisticated style of American fast-break basketball. Even more important, he provided the inspiration for some creative Zionism. European and Israeli rules limit the number of foreign players per team. But Brody, who is Jewish, was eligible for automatic citizenship under the Law of Return. The Maccabi organization saw to it that their star player became an Israeli, and then went out to beat the bushes for other American Jewish hoopsters. Other teams followed Maccabi's lead, and within a few years they recruited Barry Leibowitz out of the old ABA, Phoenix Suns' center Neil Walk at the end of his career, seven-foot Dave "Nice News" Newmark from Columbia, Lou Silver from Harvard, former NBA-er Joel Kramer, and a dozen other Jewish ballplayers from the States. One of Maccabi's rivals pulled off a coup when it found out that Willie Sims, a Black college star, was in fact born Jewish; and Sims soon found himself back in his ancestral homeland with a basketball in his hands.

Despite the American Jewish imports, however, Maccabi still had a height problem. Israelis tend to be short—good backcourt material, fine outside shooters, but not tall enough to compete with the giants from Russia, Yugoslavia, Spain and Italy that Maccabi regularly faces in the European Cup. The American Jewish big men mostly arrived at the end of their careers and couldn't provide much help. Maccabi's solution was to look for a good non-Jewish giant who could help under the boards. After several misadventures, one of their scouts finally came up with Aulcie Perry, a willowy Black center from New Jersey. Perry arrived in 1977 and led Maccabi to its first European championship, becoming an instant national hero in the process. But the following year, the team was unable to defend its title. Perry was an outstanding shooter and defensive player, but he proved too frail to fight for rebounds against the European big men. Maccabi's management realized that what it needed was a power forward, and it found one in Earl Williams, a Sonny Liston look-alike who had played briefly in the NBA. The problem was that the rules permitted only one foreigner, and the Israeli champs didn't want to give Perry up.

Maccabi's dilemma was solved with characteristic Israeli ingenuity. During the off-season the center went to the United States for a visit, where he was apparently overcome by a religious experience and converted to Judaism. He had left Tel Aviv as Aulcie Perry; he returned Eliasha Ben Abraham, and claimed Israeli citizenship under the Law of Return. Few religious events in recent history have been so fortuitous, or have paid such immediate dividends. The combination of Eliasha and Earl Williams proved unstoppable and Maccabi went on to win its second European championship.

Perry's conversion was contagious. Within a short time American basketball players in Israel experienced a mass religious awakening that raised the national median height by an inch or two. None have proven as valuable as Eliasha Ben Abraham, however, and with him, Maccabi maintained its supremacy for a decade. Perry retired in 1985, but the club still fills its arena night after night. The players get rich, the team gets richer, the fans get world-class basketball and everybody, with the possible exception of Maccabi's opponents, is happy. The early pioneers dreamed that the exiled Jewish people from the four corners of the earth would gather in Israel and pool their skills to rebuild the homeland. Maccabi Tel Aviv is a testament to the fact that the pioneering vision still lives, as well as to the fact that in Tel Aviv these days, pioneering often goes hand in hand with Big Business.

Of all the changes that have washed over Israeli society since the Six Day War, and especially since Yom Kippur 1973, the emergence of business as a respectable and even honored pursuit is surely one of the most important. During the period of the pioneers and the sabra sons, making money was regarded as a debased and selfish endeavor, at odds with the socialist ideology of Labor Zionism. Merchants and shopkeepers were considered necessary, but the people who dedicated their lives to the pursuit of money were looked upon as not really good enough for anything else.

As for the sabra sons, the best and the brightest went into activities related to state-building: the army, agriculture, engineering or government service. Throughout the fifties and early sixties, the emphasis was on conspicuous austerity, self-sacrifice and occupations that yielded concrete, tangible results. The only acceptable business activity was in the public sector, which, given Israel's highly centralized economy, was—and remains—the dominant economic sphere.

From the very beginning the pioneers conceived of the economy as a tool for creating the state and reforming the Jewish personality, an approach reflected in their priorities and the economic system they devised. The government dominated virtually every part of the national economy, and used its power to shape society and the country's borders. It controlled (and still controls) nearly all the land, all the capital and—along with the General Federation of Labor, also dominated by the Labor party—most of the jobs. From the outset and until now, the system has been geared to meeting national tasks—attracting and keeping immigrants, populating outlying areas and so forth—and not necessarily to making a profit.

A recent example of this attitude came during the war in Lebanon. Finance Minister Yoram Aridor met with Prime Minister Begin and warned him that the cost of the war, and of simultaneously continuing settlement activity in the West Bank, would be prohibitive. Begin, in the tradition of Prime Ministers since Ben Gurion, simply disregarded Aridor's advice. "The cavalry charges ahead," he told his finance minister, quoting Charles de Gaulle, "and the supply mules follow behind." Begin viewed the economy as wholly secondary to the nation's essential goals, and more than once he dismissed the rampant inflation of the early eighties by telling aides that in fifty years no one would remember the inflation rate but everyone would know if Judaea and Samaria had become a part of Israel.

Despite the power of the government in economic affairs, Israeli Prime Ministers have traditionally taken little notice of the economy, preferring to concentrate on foreign and security issues while leaving money matters in the hands of powerful finance ministers. Perhaps the most formidable was Pinchas Sapir, a master builder and bureaucrat who ran the economy during the Eshkol and Golda Meir administrations. During Sapir's heyday Shaul Evron was a reporter for *Ma'ariv,* a major Israeli daily, and he once described covering a meeting in which the bald, bearlike Sapir appeared before the Israeli Manufacturers Association: "Sapir had made them some promise or another on tariffs, and then he simply broke it. The manufacturers were furious, and they kept making speeches about how the government had lied, but Sapir just sat there with this disdainful look on his face, like he was watching a bad play or something.

"Finally they asked him for a reply, at which point he got up and started telling them anecdotes about his boyhood, making a joke of the whole thing. You could see the head of the association, who was sitting next to him, getting redder and redder. When he was through, the chairman stood up and started sputtering: 'You've gone too far this time! We won't stand for it! We're going to fight this until the bitter end!' He was ranting away and Sapir just sat there with this ironic smile on his face.

"Then Sapir got back up to reply. 'I know you realize that I can't make a decision on this by myself,' he told them, which was ridiculous—everybody in the room knew that Sapir made *all* the financial decisions—'but I'll take it up with the Prime Minister, tell her what you said. I only have one request though. Mrs. Meir is an elderly lady, and she hasn't been feeling well lately. When I report on the meeting, let me change

185

"fight to the bitter end" to "oppose"—I don't want to scare her to death.'"

In Sapir's day it was still possible to get away with this sort of thing. The government controlled everything: capital, labor and land and, most importantly, the moral high ground. Any confrontation between the national leadership and mere business was bound to end in a victory for the government. But the 1973 war opened the way for a reexamination of the old values, which in turn set loose forces of personal economic ambition and materialism. Suddenly it became respectable to want a better standard of living and say so, to earn more and have more. The Yom Kippur War was the pivot on which Israel turned from a highly controlled, pioneer economy and began developing into a more open, Western one; and this— along with the resolve of the outsiders to get a piece of the action, and the new security hunger—was responsible for bringing the Likud to power in 1977.

Within the Likud there was a tacit division of function. Begin was in charge of foreign affairs and security; Simcha Ehrlich and the Liberals took over the economy, which was supposed to be their area of expertise. The problem was that after a lifetime in the opposition, the Liberals in general—and Ehrlich, who became Begin's first minister of finance, in particular—had no real idea how to work the levers of power. Ehrlich came to office with little more than a vague set of middle-class values and a fragmentary understanding of Milton Friedman's economic theories. He was certain that these could be translated into a new economic order that would encourage private enterprise, dismantle the country's burdensome bureaucracy and open the way for a quantum rise in production. One of his first acts was to remove the strict foreign-currency regulations that made Israel a kind of economic ghetto, and open the economy to the forces of the international marketplace. The message was that middle-class values were not only acceptable but laudable, and that they could infuse new life into the economy, which had stagnated since the 1973 war.

The country took to this new approach with a vengeance. The stock market boomed, new enterprises opened their doors, Israel was flooded with foreign luxury items, and after fifty years of struggle and stern ideology, people took a breather. Israelis reacted the same way everyone does when the standard of living rises precipitously—with delight. People bought new cars, larger apartments, color television sets. They took trips abroad, crowded restaurants and nightclubs, acquired new tastes. Inflation skyrocketed, but individuals were protected by a system of indexing that linked salaries and savings to the cost of living. Economists warned that the nation was living beyond its means, that the huge foreign debt would eventually cause the bubble to burst, but people weren't listening. By Western standards the boom was modest enough—even at the height of the consumer binge the average Israeli was earning only $500 or $600 a month, paying enormous taxes on luxury items (duties on automobiles are often almost twice the cost of the car, for example) and acquiring things that people in the West take for granted. But for luxury-starved Israelis, it seemed a new day of unlimited potential, a chance finally to sample some of the good things in life.

The bubble burst, as the economists had predicted, in the fall of 1983, shortly after Menachem Begin retired from office. The stock market crashed, inflation seemed to be spinning entirely out of control and Finance Minister Yoram Aridor was forced to resign. Consumerism was not the main problem; Israel's defense spending, and the debts it had accumulated in order to pay for the 1973 war, were the primary drain on foreign currency reserves. Fully two thirds of the national budget went to military spending and debt service. But personal consumption was the most visible element of Israel's economic difficulty, and color television came to symbolize it.

The 1984 election was the first in Israeli history to turn primarily on economic issues. Labor attacked the Likud's mismanagement of the economy. The Likud responded with a "you never had it so good" campaign. Both were right and the country divided its votes almost equally between the two major parties, creating a situation in which a national unity coalition with a mandate to fix things up—but not too drastically—came into being. The Likud had clearly gone too far in its liberal economic policies, but there was no turning back.

The country, having tasted Western economic freedom, was in no mood for a return to the austerity of the fifties and early sixties. Nor was the Labor party prepared to advocate such a change. The generation of the pioneer leaders was gone, replaced by a set of technocrats and politicians whose economic philosophies differed little from the Likud's. In the new government, the Labor party's Cabinet ministers included a wealthy lawyer from Haifa, a millionaire industrialist, and Ezer Weizman, the quintessential Israeli aristocrat. Weizman, who left the Likud to run on his own slate, joined the Labor alignment after the 1984 election. When a reporter asked him how he could ally himself with a socialist party, Weizman scoffed, saying: "David Levy is more of a socialist than anybody in the Labor party."

A few days before the 1984 election, Israeli novelist Amos Oz wrote an article in the tabloid *Yediot Ahronot* about the issues at stake. Oz, who is often referred to as Israel's foremost novelist, is handsome, wellborn, sensitive and talented—in short, the kind of man others find insufferable. He lives on a kibbutz and is active in the Labor party, on whose Knesset slate he was given an honorary place in the '84 election. Like a number of other Israeli intellectuals, Oz lives in a state of perpetual dissatisfaction with his country and its people, and in the *Yediot Ahronot* article he gave this view full expression, berating the voters for their philistinism and selfishness. This is how he put it:

> Perhaps one of the greatest sins of the Likud government is that during these past seven years the government has not demanded anything except applause and wild cheering. . . . Aside from this applause, the citizens have not been requested to do anything beyond fulfilling their elementary civic duties. . . .
>
> For seven years the people of Israel have been taught to be a pack of hedonists with big stomachs and little heads. Anyone who doesn't have—let him yell with all his might, and he'll get. And anyone who doesn't have the strength to yell, or to take for himself, is pitiable, hapless, luckless. So, an entire nation of builders and cre-

ators has been transformed into a nation that mortgages and feasts on the future of its children.

Oz went on to suggest that Israelis adopt the slogan of John F. Kennedy, and begin to ask what they can do for their country, and not what the country can do for them.

The article had little effect on the outcome of the election, but it went a long way toward explaining what separates the Israeli intelligentsia from the rest of the country. The "elementary civic duties" that Oz belittled consist of thirty-five to sixty days a year of active military reserve duty—often in frontier conditions—for almost every man in the country under age fifty-five; income taxes that reach 66 percent at around $1,000 a month; an entire series of government levies from a 15 percent value-added tax on all purchases to a special payment for the ownership of a television set; and customs duties that double and often triple the cost of "luxury items" such as refrigerators, stoves and small appliances. These military and financial obligations are accepted as more or less natural by Israelis, as the institutionalized requirements of citizenship. Thus it is perhaps understandable that most readers found Oz's call to sacrifice somewhat gratuitous, and more than a little divorced from reality.

It would be easy to dismiss Oz's attitude as the patrician disapproval of a world-famous and economically secure author for his less worthy countrymen, but that would miss the point. Oz is an authentic representative of the pioneer puritanism of the founding fathers, a man whose dour perspective is actually an expression of dissatisfaction with human nature—Jewish human nature, unreconstructed by Zionist transformation. In this, Oz's view reflects that of the Israeli intelligentsia, a group alienated from the national mainstream and almost wholly without influence. Their trademark is intolerance of everything that deviates from their own view of the world, and contempt for the "little heads" of the average Israeli. People, for example, like Shimshi Cohen.

Shimshi isn't exactly a friend of mine, but I've known him for almost ten years, every since he started dating Leora, one of my wife's childhood girl friends. Shimshi and Leora met at the

Hebrew University, where she studied art history and he majored in international relations. His studies were just a cover story, though; Shimshi spent most of his time in the library cafeteria putting his beach-boy good looks and wolfish grin to use picking up girls. Although he is a sabra raised on the shores of the Sea of Galilee, in those days he seemed more like the president of some Zeta Beta Tau chapter on a Big Ten campus.

Shimshi and Leora got married in 1975. She cut short her career as a stewardess with El Al and he found a job with an insurance company in Jerusalem. Like other young Israelis they borrowed money from their parents and from the government to buy a small apartment and a small car. From the start they were interested primarily in little things: making some money, getting ahead, living the good life, Israeli-style.

During the next ten years I saw Shimshi and Leora from time to time. Usually they were preoccupied with some new material acquisition: a bigger apartment, a new car, a trip abroad. Shimshi always had some new way to make money, a stock tip or an idea for a killing in real estate. Occasionally, after a couple of whiskeys, he would tell funny stories about growing up in Tiberias. This knack for stories, along with his fresh good looks and hail-fellow attitude, made him a successful businessman. Leora, as much to keep busy as to add to the family income, became an insurance appraiser.

By the time they reached their mid-thirties, Leora and Shimshi Cohen were practically the quintessence of the small-headed Israeli. Square jobs, two cars, two kids, a three-bedroom apartment in a good neighborhood which, because it is on the top floor of a three-story building, can qualify for the prestigious designation of "penthouse." Dinner with the parents on Friday nights, Saturday afternoons at the soccer matches, vacations abroad every summer. They live in Jerusalem, but many of their values and dreams are not too different from those of suburban Jewish couples in Shaker Heights, Scarsdale or Bloomfield Hills.

Shortly after finishing college Shimshi worked in Arik Sharon's 1977 campaign, organizing his native Tiberias, but Sharon never paid the salary he had promised and Shimshi quit. Today he considers himself a Labor party supporter, but he isn't active in politics and rarely gives it a thought. Great issues of war and peace are debated in Friday-night get-to-gethers, and then put aside during the rest of the week. Great issues are for Amos Oz or Arik Sharon, for the messianists of Gush Emunim or the dreamers of Peace Now.

During his national military service Shimshi became an officer, and he left the regular army, shortly before the Yom Kippur War, with the rank of lieutenant. Like all Israelis he was assigned to a reserve unit, in which he has served ever since. For the last few years Shimshi, now a major, has been the company commander. It is a tight-knit unit, now reaching middle age, and its members have children and mortgages and spreading potbellies. About a third of them are in business, and when the unit is in the field they leave their late-model Fiats and Peugeots parked next to the company headquarters. Advancing age has changed the company's ambience and attitudes, but it hasn't affected its professional competence. In their mid-thirties and beyond, Shimshi says with pride, his men are still fine infantry soldiers.

Some of them are social friends as well as comrades-in-arms. They play tennis together, meet for coffee on the weekends, give one another discounts and send one another business. They have been together since they were in their twenties, seen one another under pressure, watched one another mature and start to age. They have celebrated weddings and the birth of children, consoled one another through divorces, observed the soap operas of one another's lives in six-month installments. Shimshi, who went to officers' school as a boy, is their commander, but in civilian life he isn't different from the others. He leads a company of little heads in an army of little heads.

When the war in Lebanon broke out, Shimshi's unit was not called up. That suited him and his men fine. He had fought in the Yom Kippur War, and had long since lost any youthful enthusiasm for military tests. During the first two and a half years of the war, Shimshi and his fellow reservists were mobilized a number of times, but always sent for duty someplace else.

Finally, in early 1985, Shimshi Cohen's company was assigned to Lebanon. As usual, Shimshi cleared his desk, leaving his secretary to take care of the routine insurance business. He went to the bank to make sure that Leora would have enough money and that the bills were paid. He canceled his regular Friday-afternoon court at the Tennis Center, and did his other pre-reserve chores. Early on a Sunday morning he put on his uniform, got in the car and drove the four hours from Jerusalem to the Lebanese border, where he joined his unit.

A few days later Leora was out when the telephone rang. Her father answered. "Tell Leora to come to the hospital in Nahariya as soon as possible. Shimshi fell off a half-track and has been badly scratched." That was the message.

"I knew very well that they wouldn't have called me over a scratch," says Leora. She is a very good-looking woman, thin and well-groomed, and vain about her appearance. She spends her mornings at the Hilton Health Club, where she works out on the Nautilus machines and dances her body through aerobatics. She was attracted to Shimshi because of his good looks, and she knows he was attracted to her for the same reason. Leora has big brown eyes that appear vulnerable until she smiles. Like her husband she has a killer smile, and when the two of them are amused at the same time, they can light up a room like a matching pair of Jack Nicholson table lamps.

Despite her premonition that Shimshi was seriously hurt, Leora didn't panic. She called a doctor friend and the two of them drove to Nahariya, on the Lebanese border. There they found Shimshi in the local hospital, with shell fragments embedded in his face and his left eardrum shattered. Leora was relieved that her husband's life wasn't in danger, but frightened to learn that he would probably never hear out of his left ear, and perhaps out of his right as well. She looked at Shimshi's handsome face, now pimpled with shrapnel, and she fought back tears. How much longer does this go on? she wondered. Thirty-six years old, an insurance executive with a little potbelly despite the tennis, father of two. Veteran of two wars already, and now this . . .

Leora didn't cry in front of Shimshi. She went back to Jerusalem and explained to her daughters that their father had been hurt in the army. She called his office and told his partner what had happened. And she began to get the house ready for what she feared would be a long convalescence.

The word from the hospital in Nahariya was better than expected. Shimshi had been on patrol in south Lebanon when an explosive charge, detonated from a distance, had blown up almost next to him. But he had been lucky: The damage, except for some of the embedded shrapnel, appeared to be temporary. After a week or so the doctors sent him home to his penthouse apartment and his Danish furniture and his good-looking wife.

A couple of days after Shimshi was discharged from the hospital, I saw him on television, on the nine o'clock evening news. One of the soldiers from his company, Tuval, a forty-two-year-old former goaltender for the Jerusalem Beter soccer team, had been killed in Lebanon, not more than a few hundred yards from the border. Tuval was Shimshi's Friday-afternoon tennis partner. He had three kids and a job in the computer department of the Jerusalem city government. He and Shimshi used to drink beer after their Friday tennis games and shoot the breeze—mostly talk about work and family problems and how to make a little extra money in the stock market. They almost never discussed politics or philosophy. Now, Shimshi Cohen was on the nine o'clock news because his friend and tennis partner had been killed in his third war, and Shimshi was supposed to give the eulogy. He managed to mumble something, the military cantor chanted the prayer *"El Ma'ale Rachamim"* and they buried Tuval. Shimshi and Leora went home and sat in the dark.

A few weeks later I called Shimshi to tell him I was planning to write about him, and to check some of the details of his injury. "How do you feel?" I asked.

"Played two hours of tennis today," he boasted in his Zeta Beta Tau voice.

When would he be able to see me? I wondered.

"Come on over tomorrow," he said. "I'll grill up a couple of steaks on the porch. And I've found a new Scotch whisky you'll like. It's twenty percent cheaper than Johnnie Walker Red and just as good, if not better."

"You sound pretty chipper for a casualty," I said, and he chuckled, a happy survivor.

"Look," he told me, "we both know it happens."

When we got together the next day, I was surprised to see that Shimshi looked as good as he had sounded on the phone. He admitted that he had had a few rough days, but said he was feeling fine now. "Are you going to stay with your outfit?" I wondered.

Shimshi grinned. "Leora wants me to get into a rear-line unit, and at first I was considering it. But hell, I'm not a rear-line officer. Yeah, I'll go back."

Sometime soon, Shimshi Cohen will get a brown envelope in the mail; in it will be his orders for the next term of reserve duty. He knows he may well find himself back in the line of fire. Leora has a sister and brother in Panama City, and Shimshi's sister lives in Geneva. They are all well-off, and would be happy to help Shimshi and Leora start over in a place where middle-aged businessmen don't risk their necks playing soldier and bury their tennis partners in military funerals. But Shimshi wouldn't think of moving. "Because you're a Zionist?" I ask him.

"Yeah, I guess I am, but that's not the main thing. The main thing is, I like my life here."

"Has it ever occurred to you that you're crazy, that all of us are crazy?" I asked him. "Half the time we're Yuppies; the other half we live like peasants in Southeast Asia, with a rifle in our hands and an endless war. At least the peasant is stuck out there. They won't let him out, and even if they did, where would he go? But you—you speak English, you have family abroad. You're an insurance man with two kids. The Shi'ites in Lebanon are supposed to be crazy, but maybe we're crazier. They take a few pills, get stoned and drive a car full of TNT into somebody. That's a one-shot deal. But we go back time after time, live our lives as if we're going to have to get into that suicide car any minute. Ten, twenty, thirty years of mobilization! How do you explain that?"

Shimshi Cohen's eponym is Shimson—Sampson—the Biblical hero. Shimshi is no hero, although he behaved heroically that day in Lebanon when his patrol was attacked, calmly directing the battle with blood pouring off his face until he was relieved, about fifteen minutes after he was wounded. "I've never thought of it like that," he laughed. "I guess when you

194

put it like that, it does seem a little crazy. But you know how it is—it's just a part of life. You don't add up the time or think about it that much." He paused and took a sip of the Scotch. "Hell, maybe we *are* crazier than Shi'ites—who knows? But you know what? This is the end of the line. You've got to stop running sometime."

Shimshi Cohen's father came to Palestine in the 1930s as a pioneer. He built roads and houses, did manual labor as a matter of ideological conviction. Shimshi is proud of the old man and feels a twinge of guilt for his own life-style. It would never occur to him that he, like Shaul Evron or Danny Sanderson, is a pioneer, a member of a generation that has become the first middle-class permanent revolutionary society in history. Israelis of his generation are people who have internalized their revolution and institutionalized the sacrifices it requires, turning impossible taxes and constant tension and sporadic military duty into a way of life that coexists somehow with tennis and color television, with Wild Turkey and doo-wop and the square values of the middle class. Children are raised to question, to argue, to think for themselves; and when these children reach eighteen, they volunteer for combat units in numbers that make it impossible to accept them all. Men spend a third of their lives in uniform, and retain a relentlessly civilian attitude. The country is engaged in a perpetual battle against the Arab world, but it resists every attempt to put its political life or national debate on a "war footing." Israelis are as militant as the most fevered Viet Cong cradling a Kalashnikov assault rifle in a rice paddy, and as mundane as the guests at a Philip Roth wedding.

Once upon a time the pioneers of Palestine wore khaki shorts and lived on crude settlements. They spoke the language of ideals and lived for redemption through toil. Their grandchildren wear khaki only for gardening or washing the car, and their notion of self-improvement runs to Italian lessons and Weight Watchers. More than anything, they are what the old man told me they were almost twenty years ago: ordinary people in extraordinary circumstances.

11

Fear of Frei-ing

When the War in Lebanon began, Danny Sanderson got a call to report to his reserve unit. "Bring your equipment," the commanding officer told him. "You're going up to the front." Sanderson started putting together his stuff—Fender electric guitar, Marshall pig-nosed portable amplifier, a Chuck Berry songbook and other gear essential to a rock star on his way to a neighborhood war—and drove to his base, near Tel Aviv. His sidemen were already waiting, and they were issued flak jackets, helmets and Uzi submachine guns, which they loaded in a jeep along with their instruments and speakers. Four hours later they were on the front lines, ready to entertain the troops.

"Some genius came up with a new rock 'n' roll strategy for the war in Lebanon," Sanderson recalls. "It used to be that they would bring the troops to some rear area where they could get a shower, a hot meal and a little rest and relaxation. But somebody decided that it was a waste of time, that the thing to do was to bring us right up to the front, and let us put on our show during lulls in the fighting."

When Sanderson's jeep reached the first audience—a weary-looking collection of artillerymen on the eastern front—the soldiers had no trouble recognizing him. Danny Sanderson has one of the best-known faces in Israel and the exhausted soldiers cheered when the little redhead and his sidemen showed up to entertain them.

197

"It was weird. I mean, these guys were sweaty and filthy from firing their guns all day long and here we are, guitar cases and all, saying, 'Hey, guys, wanna hear some music?' We plugged ourselves into the field generator and they all gathered around, so we started the show. Sounded pretty good, too, although the flak jackets kind of slowed up our moves.

"Then suddenly, in the middle of a song, someone hollered 'incoming' and the audience scrambled for their battle stations. Me and the other guys hit the dirt, one hand over our helmets, the other on our Fenders. We must have laid there for about five minutes, and I finally decided that this was ridiculous. I mean here we were, four Israeli soldiers, just lying there watching. I crawled over to one of the officers, a young kid with a scraggly beard, and yelled, 'Hey, is there anything we can do to help?' 'Yeah,' he said. 'When this stops, can you play some Rolling Stones songs?' I broke out laughing, and one of the other guys in the band looked at me and said, 'Do you think Mick Jagger has to put up with this kind of shit?'"

It isn't easy being a star in Israel. The country is tiny, everybody seems to know everybody else, and nothing gets you in trouble faster than putting on airs, known in local parlance as *shvitzing*. "There are certain things you just can't do here," Sanderson explains. "Like, for example, there's no way I could write a song about sitting on the dock of the bay, wasting time. If I did, everybody would say, 'Bullshit. I see that little guy running all over town, paying bills, doing the shopping—where does he get that kind of time?'"

Israel is a relentlessly informal and egalitarian place, where privates call generals by their first names, citizens phone Cabinet ministers at home to complain about government policy, and waiters drop silverware on the table with a surly clang. The lack of ceremony is symbolized by the national dress code; most Israelis—at least most Israeli men—wear what my mother used to refer to as "school clothes," and it is not exceptional to see people at a wedding in jeans and a T-shirt. In Israel the term *white-collar worker* has almost no literal meaning.

Nor are Israelis much inclined to see themselves as uninvited to any national event. During the state visit of President Jimmy Carter, Prime Minister Begin gave a dinner for him in the Knesset's Chagall Hall. The event was off limits to the press corps, but a table was set up in a roped-off area for a small press pool—two Israeli correspondents and two Americans—that was assigned to cover the banquet. As the head of the Government Press Office I was responsible for the media arrangements, and during dinner I looked over at the pool area to make sure that everything was all right. I saw the two American reporters eating alone, and I went over to find out what had happened. "Where are the Israelis?" I asked.

"Over there," one of the American journalists said, pointing to the round tables on the other side of the rope where the invited dignitaries were sitting. "One of them said that he wasn't going to sit around watching a bunch of politicians eat. 'They're no better than we are,' he said, and then he and his friend picked up their chairs, went over and made a couple of people move aside." The American smiled. "Good system you've got here," he said.

Old-timers often lament the decline of the intimacy that characterized the *yishuv* before the founding of the state; but despite the country's rapid growth from about 650,000 in 1948 to almost 4 million today, Israel remains an irreducibly small country, the kind of place where the average person can't stand on a downtown street corner in any of the big cities for more than a couple of hours without running into someone familiar. And, not surprisingly, there are both advantages and disadvantages to this kind of small-town intimacy.

On the one hand, Israel is a country in which you simply can't get lost. People know each other, and even if they don't, it usually takes them about five minutes to discover a whole array of mutual acquaintances from school, the youth movement or the army. And even if no common ground can be established, people still have no hesitation about approaching one another, getting involved, even asking for help. It's the kind of place where you can stop someone, explain that you've forgotten your wallet, and expect to get an instant loan; but it's likely that by the time you get home, your neighbors will know that you've borrowed money from someone who turns out to be their cousin.

And that is the negative side of the national intimacy—the fact that life in such a small country can be confining, especially for individualists. For one thing, people have long memories. On one occasion I was walking down a main street in Jerusalem with a friend who was born and raised in the capital, when a very well known criminal attorney passed and the two nodded to each other. "I didn't know you knew him," I said.

"Him? Sure, we grew up together."

"What's he like?" I wondered.

My friend looked over his shoulder contemptuously at the famous lawyer. "He's a pisher," he said. "Once we got into a rock fight with some kids from another neighborhood and he was so scared he wet his pants." My friend snorted, remembering the incident of thirty years ago. "Nothing but a pisher," he said.

Standards for women are even more demanding. Israeli men are encouraged to be macho, and a little wildness is considered the mark of a regular guy (*bachur tov* is the Hebrew expression, connoting something like a "good ole boy"). Women, on the other hand, are expected to behave themselves. "I'd love to have a 'bad girl' persona," Yehudit Ravitz, one of Israel's most popular female rock singers once told me, "but I can't. The public isn't ready for a woman who sings about casual sex, or getting drunk just for the fun of it. When I go to the supermarket, old ladies are constantly coming up to me and straightening my collar or smoothing down my hair. 'Look how you look,' they tell me. 'You should take better care of yourself. You're from the television.'"

There is a square, almost constipated air about many Israelis, especially those over thirty. "In this country there is a prejudice against having a good time," says Sanderson, who appears in concert more than a hundred times a year. "An Israeli entertainer has to contend with three inhibiters: the Holocaust, the security situation and good old-fashioned Jewish guilt."

When Israelis do go out, their recreation often has a forced, aggressively festive air about it. "Sometimes, when people get up to dance at my shows, I can almost hear their teeth gnash-

200

ing," says Yehudit Ravitz. "Kids are a little looser, but people in their late twenties and up just aren't able to let go."

Entertainers like Sanderson and Ravitz spend a good deal of time thinking about the Israeli public and how to reach it. Once, after a trip to the United States, Sanderson returned with an insight into one of the differences between Americans and Israelis. "In the States, everybody's got a *shtik*," he reported. "They just project personality—'have a nice day,' whatever the latest phrase is. Garage mechanics tell each other jokes from the borscht belt that they heard on the Johnny Carson show. Everybody's in show business." He didn't need to add that in Israel, nobody is. Excessive displays of personality, charm or even good manners are considered suspect, manifestations of superficiality or worse. If you are in a good mood, you show it; and if your feet hurt, you show that too. Little show-biz ruffles and flourishes, winks and whistles, bits—all are considered a form of affectation and lead to immediate and uncompromising ridicule.

With outsiders, Israelis tend to be both friendly and withdrawn. There is a small circle of highly sophisticated people, especially in Jerusalem and Tel Aviv, who are at home with foreigners and seek them out. Foreign correspondents, diplomats and other visitors tend to meet them, and through them derive a wildly mistaken notion about what Israelis are really like. Most outsiders leave thinking that they have met a good many Israelis and have a fairly clear notion of what they are about, but this is rarely the case, and for those who can't speak Hebrew, it never is.

The average Israeli may be superficially friendly toward foreigners, but he rarely allows them to see too much or get too close. The "us" and "them" syndrome is still very strong, and it is Hebrew, more than any other single factor, that determines who is which. Because it is spoken only in Israel, Hebrew is more than simply a language—it is an exclusive code. Most Israelis speak English and many know several languages. (I had a garage mechanic who once proudly told me that he spoke four languages: Hebrew, English, Yiddish and Gothic. He claimed he had learned his Gothic "during the war." He might have meant German, but I liked the notion of having a Gothic-speaking auto mechanic so much that I didn't press him.) But there is a pronounced difference between what people will say in a foreign tongue and what they say to each other, in Hebrew. This is one of the reasons why foreign correspondents are so frequently mistaken in their reporting about Israel, especially reporting that purports to deal with the Israeli "soul." (For some reason, this subject is especially popular with journalists who don't know Hebrew; and it usually comes out about as sensibly as a story on the American "soul" by a French correspondent who doesn't know English.) Hebrew is central to the Israeli mentality and experience—they cannot possibly be understood without it. People on the other side of the language gap—including immigrants who do not master Hebrew—are doomed to have an incomplete and often distorted view of the country and its people, no matter how hard they try or how many English-language conversations they carry on.

With each other, Israelis often have what is known in some neighborhoods in America as "an attitude." This is a defensive posture that stems primarily from the anxieties that Israelis delight in fostering in others. The most reasonable request can send a government clerk scrambling for reasons why it can't be done. A plumber will force you to beg before coming to deal with a leaky pipe, and then make you believe that it cannot possibly be fixed before he fixes it. Voluntary cooperation, the effort to be accommodating or reassuring, these are the most un-Israeli of characteristics. *Le'ho ci et ha'mitz*— literally, to squeeze the juice out of someone—is the phrase for this process, in which the simple is made difficult in order to let you know that you are dealing with someone who can't be taken for granted.

Not long ago, on a trip to New York, I lost my wallet, which contained a return ticket to Israel on El Al. I went to the airline office in Rockefeller Center to report the loss and request a new ticket. The lady behind the counter—an American—was friendly and helpful. She assured me that it was a routine matter, that a telex to my travel agent in Israel would clear everything up and a new ticket would be issued. I called the next day and she pleasantly informed me that there was a technical problem in Tel Aviv, nothing to worry about, and that everything would be ready in the morning. The next morning—my last in New York—I went to get the ticket and was informed, in a polite, distressed tone, that the confirmation had yet to come through and I would have to miss my flight.

Naturally I asked to see the manager, an Israeli. He was an officious little man who curtly informed me that it was absolutely impossible to issue me a ticket without approval from Israel. "I'm expected home tomorrow," I told him. "What am I supposed to do?"

He noted my concern with satisfaction and said, "That's your problem." ("That's your problem" is a Hebrew phrase so common that it has its own abbreviation.)

This was a classic Israeli confrontation, and two things were clear to both of us. First, he was not going to leave me stranded in New York. Eventually he would find a way to let me fly, even without a ticket. And second, he was going to wring the juice out of me all day long. The ball was now in my court, and I did what all Israelis do in such situations: I asked myself the key question "Who do I know?"

In this case, since I desperately wanted to avoid spending the entire day wrangling with the manager, I skipped the preliminaries and called the Israeli ambassador in Washington, Meir Rosenne, who is an old friend and fellow delegate to the Mena House conference in Cairo in 1977. Despite our friendship I felt foolish about calling with such a petty problem, but he told me not to worry in a tone that indicated this wasn't the first time he had dealt with such things. Everything would be settled immediately, he said, and when I returned to the El Al office a few minutes later, it was. The manager was obviously disappointed that I had deprived him of an afternoon's sport, and he regarded me sourly, like someone who has cut through the park in a cross-country race.

Later that day I told this story to an Israeli friend who lives in Manhattan. "What do people do who don't know the ambassador?" I asked, a bit self-importantly.

"Then they know the ambassador's secretary, and she gets them the ticket," my friend answered. "Everybody knows somebody. Only a freier would go to El Al without some *protekzia*."

*   *   *

To be a freier is the greatest of all Israeli sins. A freier is a sucker, a patsy, someone who can be taken advantage of. An honest tax declaration qualifies you as a freier. Paying retail is a cardinal act of freierdom. (One of the national pastimes is to ask someone how much something cost—anything from a house to a bag of oranges. No matter what the amount is, you let him know that he has paid too much and is a freier.) Ask a fellow worker to help with some assignment and he may say, "I'm not your freier."

In fact, the entire Israeli wage system is based on this principle: It doesn't matter what I make, as long as I make more than you do. The wages of doctors are linked to engineers, who are linked to professors and so on down the line, with each group maintaining a sharp eye on the gains of every other. To allow another group to forge ahead, to widen its advantage or narrow its gap, is a cause for action. Most strikes and labor disputes in Israel have less to do with objective wage demands than with the fear of being a freier.

The only exception to the paralyzing dread of freierdom comes during times of emergency or stress, to which Israelis respond with amazing acts of cooperation and good citizenship. I got a chance to witness this transformation firsthand during the visit of Anwar Sadat to Israel in November 1977.

Sadat's initiative caught the entire country by surprise. On Wednesday afternoon, less than ninety hours before the Egyptian President was scheduled to arrive, I was called to a meeting in the Prime Minister's Office and informed that I would be in charge of the press arrangements for the visit. I had been in my job as director of the Government Press Office for less than three months, but even if it had been three decades I wouldn't have been prepared for the task of providing logistical and technical facilities for the more than two thousand journalists, camera crews and photographers who descended on us. In the meeting I nodded in the appropriate places and tried to appear confident, but I went back to my office convinced that it would be impossible to make the necessary arrangements by Saturday night.

When I got back I found a mob scene outside my door.

Dozens of people, most of whom I had never met, were waiting to volunteer their services. A prominent businessman whom I knew only by reputation showed up and put himself, his car and driver at my disposal for the duration of the event. A professor of political science got out of a sick bed to help out in the press center. Eventually we had a secretary working full time just fielding phone calls from people who wanted to work, or bake a cake for the journalists, or offer home hospitality to an Egyptian, any Egyptian.

The director of the Jerusalem Theatre simply canceled four days' worth of shows when we called to ask if we could put a press center there. The Egged bus company took buses off their regular routes so that we would have transportation for the army of journalists. The Communications Ministry, which usually takes weeks, months or even years to install a telephone, put in three hundred, equipped for direct dial abroad, within forty-eight hours. For four days I made the most outrageous requests, and never was turned down. Suddenly everything was possible, everybody willing to help. It was as if I had a magic sword, and with it I cut through the layers of bad manners and orneriness, all the way through The Attitude to the core of the national spirit.

In the end, the arrangements went well and the journalists found everything in place when they arrived. It was an exhilarating experience, and when it was over I called a staff meeting to thank all the people who had worked so hard. "You couldn't have done any better if you had had four months instead of four days," I told them emotionally. *"Habibi,"* said the businessman, who had barely changed his shirt in the last ninety hours, "if there had been four months, we couldn't have done it at all."

Fear of freierdom is at least partly grounded in the extreme competitiveness that is the result of a large number of talented individualists crowded into a tiny country. Resources are scarce—there is only so much airtime, so many jobs, only so much money to be made—and people fight over their shares of the comparatively small national pie. This partially explains the seeming inability of many Israelis to say a good word about their fellow citizens. In general, praise is not an Israeli custom, and even when it is given it is often accompanied by a somewhat barbed note. Many new immigrants, especially idealists from the West, are taken aback by this and frustrated by the country's failure to appreciate their skills. This frustration could well be called the Abba Eban Syndrome, in which talented people are allowed to languish in jobs for which they are overqualified while others with less ability go on running things. But like Eban, these new immigrants are at least partly at fault for not understanding the system. In Israel, people aren't given positions of authority and responsibility; in almost every case, they have to seize them.

Fear of competition mixes with the general Israeli compulsion for security, to influence the country's social and economic life. The socialist fathers, in an effort to neutralize individualism as well as to promote social welfare, created a system of tenure that guarantees most salaried employees a job for life. Civil servants—the largest single category of workers in Israel—normally receive tenure after one year on the job, at which point they become virtually unfireable for anything less than grand larceny or high treason; and even in the private sector it is extremely difficult to let an employee go. On the other hand, Israeli salaries are small and usually unrelated to productivity, and advancement is mostly a matter of seniority. Even in their mid-twenties, many Israelis are already on the lookout for a tenured job, and it is not unusual for them to stay in the same workplace for their entire careers. The educational system tends, despite a recent liberalization, to be vocationally oriented, and the great ambition of every Jewish parent is for their children to have a *miktzoa b'yad*—a profession or trade they can count on.

Advancement in Israel, when it is not a matter of simple seniority, is most often a question of connections, or *protekzia*. In the early days of the state that meant the right party credentials—a slip of paper from the local Mapai functionary very often meant the difference between work and unemployment, the key to a larger flat or some other prestigious goodie. In recent years, as the grip of Mapai has weakened, the party aspect of *protekzia* has given way to a somewhat more complex pattern of exploiting family, communal and personal ties to beat the system. This pattern was once explained to me by a former Israeli general: "If you have important friends, you don't need *protekzia*."

Confronted with any kind of restriction or problem, it is second nature for Israelis to wonder who they know—or can get to know—that might be of help. "Who have you got in the police?" or "What kind of connections do you have with the post office people?" are normal questions. Often Israelis will go to great lengths to find such contacts in order to settle matters that could be more simply handled by a direct, impersonal approach to the authorities, but to go unarmed with *protekzia* to deal with authority puts you in danger of being a freier.

Given the intimate nature of Israeli society, finding the right contact is relatively easy. Members of Knesset are elected on an at-large basis and thus have no fixed constituency, but most people know at least one; and it is considered perfectly reasonable to ask them, or even Cabinet ministers, to intervene in the most petty matters. Of course government officials are under no compunction to listen to the blandishments of these VIPs and they often ignore them; but just as often, such intervention is effective. After all, the government clerk never knows when he himself might need a favor that requires a little *protekzia*.

There is another, more unselfish side to *protekzia*. In the summer of 1985, Israel traded more than a thousand security prisoners—many of whom were convicted killers—for three prisoners of war who had been held in Syria during much of the war in Lebanon. The government offered a number of reasons for the deal, which was widely perceived as unwise and even dangerous; but in private, Israeli leaders admitted that it had been made primarily because they could no longer stand the entreaties of the prisoners' tearful parents. These parents were ordinary Israelis, without any special personal contacts or party leverage, but they were able to achieve a form of *protekzia* simply through their persistence and by exploiting the extreme sensitivity of Israeli leaders to this sort of pressure.

The prisoner exchange was a prime example of the Israeli system, which is largely based on the extremely personal relationship that citizens have with the country and its governing institutions. It is not unusual for people to quarrel with the country in more or less the same tones of wounded expectation that one would use with a relative or lover. "If that's the way it's going to be around here, I'm leaving" is one of the most common expressions of frustration, even from people who would never dream of really going anyplace else.

The prisoner of war exchange also demonstrated the powerful role of guilt in the Israeli decision-making process. There is a widespread expectation that the government should behave like a parent and take responsibility for preventing individual tragedies. "What will I do for a job?" is not merely a rhetorical question; it is a direct demand that the government protect the individual's financial security and, no less important, his self-respect. This expectation, and the government's willingness to see itself as responsible, is one of the keys to Israel's inability to take the "hard economic decisions" that foreign and local experts often propose. Simply put, there are very few Israeli politicians who are able to look people in the eye and remain indifferent to their suffering. This is partially a matter of politics, of course; not many politicians enjoy being seen as hardhearted in the face of a mother's plea for help. But to a surprising extent, this sentimentality, and the *protekzia* it generates, are genuine. The tradition of Jewish self-help remains powerful in Israel and accounts, as much as Labor Zionist ideology or Revisionist populism, for the government's commitment to individual well-being.

Under the Israeli system this sentiment is there, ready to be tapped; but the initiative must come from the individual. The authorities expect that people will begin to holler when they get upset. Silence is taken as a sign of contentment, or at least acquiescence (to remain silent when you are in trouble is the sign of a freier).

There are some who view this as the government's way of making people grateful for services and help that they are entitled to, and this, indeed, is sometimes the case. But most often the process is far less Machiavellian. Grab the government's attention, show your pain or anger, and you are likely to get a personal and highly sympathetic hearing.

This is true even in the army, the country's most pervasive and best-organized institution. A great deal has been written over the years about the impact of universal military service on the Israeli character, but as much as the army has shaped the Israeli personality, it has been shaped by it. The army is the great national meeting place, the single experience that most Israelis share, and it serves as a kind of national organizing principle. To outsiders, Israel often seems hyperactive and somewhat chaotic, but it is, in fact, one of the best organized societies in the free world, thanks to the requirements of the military. Everyone is assigned to an army unit that knows your whereabouts and status at all times. Trips abroad, changes in address, health problems, psychological difficulties—all have to be reported to the army. People can't get lost in Israel or simply drift. They are accounted for, known about, engaged in a personal relationship with at least one major national institution.

The obligations of reserve duty are not universally unpopular. Many men, especially salaried employees whose full wages are reimbursed by the government, find their annual military service to be a welcome change from the humdrum routine of daily life—and many wives welcome the chance for a breather from their husbands. The army can also do wonders for the sagging male ego, allowing men engaged in boring pursuits to taste a bit of adventure or, at least, play soldier. The Israeli Army, like all armies, brings out the juvenile, locker-room side of people. A very dignified diplomat once amazed me by confiding that every time he puts on his uniform he gets as horny as when he was an eighteen-year-old recruit. The notion itself wasn't surprising—it's an experience common to most of us, much to the amusement of the real eighteen-year-old soldiers—but the barracks atmosphere that allows strangers to trade such confidences is often a liberating break from the constraints of life in a small country where everybody sees and no one forgets.

There are, of course, unpleasant aspects to the reserve experience that go beyond the simple possibility of finding yourself in a war. The Israeli Army is an extremely loose and easy place, and veteran units often come very close to being self-run, with the officers providing a bare minimum of discipline, and no spit and polish whatever. (Once, for example, during reserve duty on the northern border, I shared a hut with three other enlisted men and two officers, a lieutenant and a major. The first thing we did was to make up a roster of duties—floor scrubbing, cooking and so on—in which the officers were naturally included.) Still, despite the generally relaxed atmosphere, reserve service is an interruption, and the army a place where you temporarily lose control over your own life. Most Israeli men learn and retain a sufficient talent for vulgarity and conformity to get along in the collective environment of military service, but it is tough on the eccentric or sensitive. Extreme misfits can be excused from duty, but that kind of exemption carries an almost ineradicable stigma.

Not too long ago I was sent for a brief army training course in the Negev desert. On our first night I found that I couldn't sleep and went outside the tent for a cigarette. It was midnight or so, and I was surprised to find half a dozen others standing around in a small group, smoking and talking. One of them was a smallish man in his late thirties, a professor of philosophy from the Hebrew University, who was busy lecturing one of the guards on the impact of Heidegger on Jewish thought. The guard, a young soldier from the base doing his national service, obviously had no idea what he was talking about, but the professor, undeterred, went on in a low, intense voice. After a while he left the soldier and turned his attention to me. I was in no mood for German philosophy at that hour, and said so. "We can talk about anything you like," the professor offered, a hint of desperation in his voice. "It's going to be a long night."

"Why don't you go to sleep instead?" I asked him.

"I can't. I'm not able to sleep with other people in the room, especially strangers. I'm sure I'll be up all night."

"All night?" I wondered. "You mean you never sleep in the army?"

"No, just at first," he confided, a touch of embarrassment in his voice. "Not for two or three days, until I'm totally exhausted."

"Well, why don't you tell one of the officers?" I asked him. "Maybe they'll transfer you into a different kind of unit, or at least excuse you from the exercise."

The little professor looked at me in horror. "No, I couldn't do that. I want to do my part, just like anybody else. Don't worry, this happens every time. I'll get through it all right."

I watched him during the next couple of days, and he did get through the training, but I left wondering what he feels every time he sees that brown envelope with the reserve notice in the mailbox.

The army is the great meeting place of Israeli society, probably the only place the young soldier in the Negev will ever hear a lecture on Heidegger, or the professor come in contact with a nineteen-year-old whose idea of good reading is the sports page of *Yediot Ahronot*. But the integrative impact of military service—like that of schools who draw their students from dissimilar neighborhoods—is often exaggerated. Israelis share a small country, and in some ways they know one another very well, but they also manage to find ways to give one another space.

One of the ways is by forming and maintaining close friendships within a more or less closed circle, known as the *hevra*. These friendships are formed early; it is not unusual for adults to socialize primarily with people they have known from grade school, and these relationships have very little to do with social status, money or other such concerns. Israeli friendships are deep and important, and go well beyond what is considered usual in other modern industrialized societies. At the same time, the *hevra*, once established, tends to be inhospitable to outsiders, and even spouses of long duration are often treated as nonmembers. A friend of mine married a girl from a kibbutz whom he met after she returned from a year in London, but despite the fact that they have been together for more than five years, she is still referred to as "the English girl" by his friends, who have yet to accept her as a permanent member of the group.

When I arrived in Israel, I became acutely aware of family in a way that Americans—including American Jews—simply are not. The first question everyone asked was "Are you here with your family?" and when I answered in the negative I evoked genuine concern and pity, even from strangers. For me, the product of the Easy Rider ethos of the American sixties, being on my own seemed a necessary rite of passage; but for Israelis, including many Israelis my age, it was simply unnatural.

For Israelis, family is even more important than *hevra;* it is the essential kernel of society, both the source of and refuge from many of the pressures of daily life. It is the primary support system, the basic economic unit, the single most fundamental institution and, for years, the only one not under the control of the pioneer establishment and its Israeli-making machine. Indeed, the bitterness that many Sephardim feel toward the Labor Zionists stems mostly from what they see as the attempt, a generation ago, to integrate them into society by alienating them from their parents and their traditional family values.

In a sense, there is nothing surprising about the extremely close family ties that exist in Israel. The world, after all, has long been aware of the close-knit nature of Jewish kinship, not to mention the Jewish mother stereotype made famous by American Jewish writers and comedians. In Israel, Jewish motherhood (even for fathers) reaches new heights, largely, I think, because of guilt.

My son, Shmuelik, was born on the fourth day of the war in Lebanon. I was present at the delivery and had the thrill of watching the birth—and an almost immediate shock of fear about his future. Shmuelik wasn't more than ten minutes old when I started worrying about his going into the army. I didn't say anything about it but obviously my wife was thinking along the same lines, because later that day, still slightly doped up from the delivery, she fixed me with a determined stare. "Don't you encourage him to do anything dangerous," she told me, as if he were going to be drafted next week.

The problem is, of course, that we both knew we would wind up doing just that. Military service is the single most important measure of social status for young men. To volunteer for an elite combat unit is the equivalent of attending an Ivy League university, (regular combat units are the Big Ten, and a desk job or noncombat position is strictly junior college). This means that if you raise your son to be achievement-oriented, well-adjusted and patriotic, you wind up with a paratrooper or a pilot. The result of this dilemma is a great measure of guilt, which makes Israeli children among the most spoiled in the world.

Israelis are child-obsessed. You are, for example, expected

to know and remember the names and vital statistics of other people's children, even people with whom you have a relatively casual relationship. Ignoring children in social situations is considered rude and, in some circles, an *ipso facto* demonstration of inhumanity. Children call adults, including their teachers, by their first names and are encouraged to express themselves, at school and at home, with freedom and self-confidence.

Child rearing is considered the foremost responsibility of adulthood. Women who are not married at twenty-five begin to feel uncomfortable, and by thirty an unmarried woman is the object of pity. It is a little easier for bachelors, but not much. Men without families are thought of as strange and, after forty, somewhat pathetic. Israeli society simply assumes marriage and children as natural and necessary aspects of adult life, and this assumption extends across ethnic, religious and class lines.

I remember taking some American friends to see Menachem Begin when he was Prime Minister. A husband and wife in their mid-thirties, they were very excited about meeting a world leader, and they prepared a few questions on international policy that they thought would be appropriate. Begin greeted them warmly, offered them tea and then asked how many children they had. "We have one son," the husband said proudly.

Begin looked at them with genuine concern. "Only one son? That's not enough. You need more children." He went on in this vein, lecturing them about the importance of a large family, for several minutes, and at the end of the visit he returned to the subject. "Don't forget to make more babies," he admonished them as they shook hands at the door.

I later told this story to another friend who had been close to several Labor party leaders. "Only Begin could have come up with something like that," I laughed.

"Are you kidding?" he said. "Eshkol and Golda used to do exactly the same thing."

Child rearing takes precedence over almost everything else in Israel. Working mothers are entitled to leave work early in order to spend time with their children, and during school vacations it is not at all unusual for them to bring the kids to work with them. And the idea of leaving a sick child for any reason at all simply wouldn't occur to the average Israeli parent.

When Shmuelik was a baby he came down with a case of croup. We bundled him up and took him to Bikur Holim, a somewhat decrepit institution in downtown Jerusalem which was the duty hospital that evening, and the emergency room doctor immediately ordered him to be hospitalized. It was late at night when he was wheeled into the ward, a crowded room with beds against every wall. Once he was in place, the nurse brought in a mattress and put it under the bed. "You can sleep there," she said to Miri, and it was then I noticed that every bed in the room had a mother sleeping under it.

In the morning the mothers—about half of whom turned out to be Arabs—took turns watching one another's children while they went out to take a shower and change clothes. Jewish and Arab parents were suddenly united in a common concern which took precedence over any cultural, political or personal differences that might otherwise have colored their relationship, and for a week we all lived together in the children's ward in the kind of harmony that would have been unlikely in other circumstances.

Israeli children are encouraged to remain dependent on their parents long after the age when young people in other countries strike out on their own. It is considered a parental obligation to help young married couples buy an apartment, and parents have been known to bankrupt themselves in order to do it. It is also normal for parents to give their children financial assistance for years after marriage, even if the children themselves are doing well. It is not unusual for a forty-year-old professional man to expect his aged father to lend him the money for a larger flat, a new car or even a trip abroad. This is done with no seeming embarrassment—the middle-aged child will, after all, do as much for his own children someday.

The close relationship between children and parents is accentuated by the small size of the country. No one lives more than a few hours from home—close enough for weekend visits, holiday celebrations and frequent phone calls—and most Israelis live considerably closer. This proximity, combined with financial dependence well into adulthood, can be a source of comfort—and of tension. Children remain accountable to their parents or, if they are not, often feel a sense of guilt. In the pressurized atmosphere of Israel, family obligations frequently lead to friction.

It is extremely difficult to escape the pressures of life in Israel. A recent rock 'n' roll song told about a new invention that could turn the radio off for five minutes at the top of every hour so that you wouldn't have to hear the news, but even if such an invention were possible, it still couldn't shut out the tensions of a small, embattled, competitive and in many ways parochial society. Getting away from it all is practically impossible in Israel.

This feeling was once expressed by Yehuda Eder, one of the country's leading rock sidemen. "Sometimes I feel like I'm in a straitjacket here," he told me. "In Europe or the States, rock musicians can go wild. They break up their instruments, even take their clothes off if they feel like it. Then they hop in the limousine after the show and disappear. Nobody ever sees them again. Can you imagine me doing something like that here, with half the kibbutz in the audience and my parents sitting in the front row?"

In order to escape the pressures of daily life and find a real measure of privacy, Israelis turn to foreign travel. *Hutz le'aretz* (or *Hul,* as it is affectionately abbreviated) means abroad—anywhere abroad. In recent years as many as three quarters of a million Israelis—out of an adult Jewish population of fewer than 3 million—have traveled overseas annually. Some go for business or to visit family in distant parts of the world, but for most it is simply to escape the daily grind, to "breathe some air," in the local phrase. *Hul* is the magic place where you can forget the news, try out new styles, have fun in public without running the risk of making a fool of yourself, or having it get back to the neighbors. *Hul* is where you don't have to pay a 100 percent purchase tax on luxury goods, where there is no reserve duty, no need to open your purse for a security inspection before entering a theater, no obligation to show up at the folks' on Friday night for some of Mom's patented sabbath chicken.

Many Israeli parents try to send their children to *hul* for the first time before their military service, to give them a treat before their army duty. Many more young people travel abroad after completing their stints (three years for boys, two for girls), and a not inconsiderable number stay for studies or to make some easy money. If they remain permanently, they become what is known as *yordim*—literally, "those who have descended." No one knows precisely how many Israelis have emigrated but various estimates put the number at between 250,000 and 350,000 since the founding of the state. This is not an abnormally great number for a country whose population is largely made up of immigrants and their children—especially considering the Jewish tradition of mobility and rootlessness—but it disturbs other Israelis who see the *yordim* as slackers (and themselves as freiers for picking up the slack).

The general disapproval of *yordim* is expressed in a classic Israeli joke about a man who visits a brothel in an isolated town in the American Midwest and informs the madam that he is prepared to pay $100, but only for an Israeli woman. "That's an amazing coincidence," says the delighted proprietor, "because we happen to have one right here."

The man is taken to her chamber, where they silently make love. When they are finished, the customer thanks the prostitute in Hebrew. "Don't tell me you're an Israeli, too?" says the lady.

"Yes, I'm from Haifa."

"That's wonderful," says the prostitute. "I'm from Haifa, too. My brother still lives there. Maybe you know him— Chaim Cohen?"

"I do know him," says the man. "I know him very well. As a matter of fact, he gave me a hundred dollars to give to you."

In recent years, the attitude toward *yordim* has softened somewhat, as Israeli society has become more open, tolerant and individualistic in its outlook. It's no longer true, as it once was, that emigrants are considered traitors; nor do most Israelis believe that the Jews of the diaspora will be moving to Israel any time soon. The official doctrine of Zionism continues to view the presence of Jews abroad as an historic aberration and the diaspora itself as a temporary condition; but in fact, Israelis have become resigned to the idea that they will, for the foreseeable future, coexist with, and to a certain extent compete with, the Jewish communities of America, Europe and the rest of the free world.

When I came to Israel in the summer of 1967, there was a widespread expectation that the Jews of the United States were on their way to the homeland. The Six Day War created an atmosphere of victory and historic inevitability. For a generation, Israelis had been the object of charity from their American and European cousins—as a boy I donated a quarter every week at Sunday School in order to plant trees (in honor of my grandfather, Al Kaline, Soupy Sales and, later, Smokey Robinson and the Miracles); and I had been encouraged to finish my meals by the threat that the leftovers would be sent to starving orphans in Palestine. This attitude pervaded much of the diaspora-Israel relationship. Many Israelis in their thirties and forties remember visits by their American relatives as humiliating—uncles and aunts ensconced in luxury hotels disbursing foreign goodies like toilet paper and instant coffee and sighing in Yiddish about how hard life seemed to be in Israel. Pity was often mixed with admiration, of course; but on the whole it was a disconcerting experience to see one's parents gratefully accepting trinkets from the *mishpocheh* from abroad.

The balance shifted briefly after the Six Day War. Israel was a victorious nation with a sense of solidarity and confidence, while American and European society appeared on the verge of imminent collapse. Israeli papers reported horror stories about drug addiction, political upheaval, racial violence and intermarriage. Thousands of Western teen-agers, volunteers and students, streamed into the country, and they appeared to be the vanguard of the long-awaited wave of immigration. Young Americans like me were in great demand, both as symbols of the new *aliyah* and as witnesses to the decline of life in the United States. Our stories about hippies, race riots and the generally alienated climate in America were lapped up with satisfaction by Israelis who were suddenly presented with confirmation that they had made the right decision and were now in a position to gloat. Thousands of letters were dispatched to relatives abroad, admonishing them to come live in Israel before it was too late; and more than a few distraught parents wrote back to say they were seriously considering the idea.

Of course, no such mass immigration ever took place. The American and European Jewish communities rode out the upheavals of the sixties and early seventies, unwilling or unable to leave. Neither the glorious victory of the Six Day War nor the equally impressive, if far more traumatic, military success of Yom Kippur could bring Jews to Israel, and Israelis began to understand for the first time that, if such dramatic events had proven inadequate, the odds were that the dream of reuniting the bulk of Western Jewry in the homeland was apt to remain just that—a dream. The militant insistence of David Ben Gurion that the diaspora was an illegitimate and temporary condition gave way to the tacit admission that the Jewish world would, for the foreseeable future, be a bipolar one, with an axis in New York as well as one in Jerusalem.

The Six Day War and Yom Kippur did, however, have a major impact on the diaspora, which became far more Israeli-oriented than it had been before 1967. Foreign Jews felt a pride in the accomplishments of their Israeli cousins of a kind that had once been expressed in Leon Uris's *Exodus*. In the book, perhaps the single most influential work ever written on modern Israel, the American-Jewish sea captain Bill Fry tells Kitty, the Gentile nurse, about his feelings for the young country. "All my life I've heard I'm supposed to be a coward because I'm a Jew. Let me tell you, kid. Every time the Palmach blows up a British depot or knocks the hell out of some Arabs he's winning respect for me. He's making a liar out of everyone who tells me Jews are yellow. The guys over here are fighting my battle for respect . . . understand that?" In the years after the Six Day War this attitude deepened and spread in the diaspora, and became a kind of substitute for actually living in Israel. Inevitably, it also created an unequal balance, a kind of player-fan relationship that casts Israel as the home team and Israelis as Jewish superjocks.

It is, in many ways, an uncomfortable and unnatural relationship on both sides. The Jewish fans have an enormous emotional investment in their team and support it loyally by buying season tickets (in the form of UJA contributions), attending off-season banquets with the stars (usually Israeli generals or government leaders) and, of course, by following the team's fortunes in the press and on television. Some even send their children to local summer camps that serve as a kind of Jewish Little League, where youngsters are taught the rudiments of Hebrew, Israeli history and culture. But it is generally understood that this training is aimed at making children well-rounded American Jews; the average parent no more expects them to become Israelis than professional baseball players.

The serious work of the Jewish people in this century is left to the Israelis themselves, who are often perceived as muscular and crude. Every day, hundreds of red and white air-conditioned tour buses crisscross the country with visitors who have come to marvel at the strenuous exertions of the Israelis, and they are greeted by a combination of gratitude for their support and disappointment at their continued unwillingness to get out on the field and do their part for the team.

Sometimes Israelis react with harsher emotions. About ten years ago I visited a poverty area on the outskirts of Tel Aviv, where I found a group of Israeli teen-agers hanging around a corner. They were delighted to talk about life in their neighborhood, regaling me with stories through a hail of sunflower-seed husks which they spit on the ground like little Hebrew vowels. In the course of the conversation one of them astonished me by saying that their houses still had no running water. "It's worse than a refugee camp," he said bitterly. Naturally I wondered why, in the shadow of Tel Aviv's sky-scrapers, the neighborhood remained in such a run-down condition. "Listen, *habibi*," he said, with a worldly cynicism, "almost every day the government brings tourists here. They stare out the windows at us, and the guides tell them how poor we are. 'These Jews are your family' they tell them, 'and they don't even have any water at home.' Then they ask them for contributions. This isn't a neighborhood—it's a business. You ever hear of anybody shutting down a profitable business?"

I was thinking about that conversation when, one night in 1982, I gave a speech for Israel Bonds at a fund-raising event at a Philadelphia country club. It was an opulent affair, the men sleek in their evening clothes, the women dazzling in an array of fashions and jewelry that probably represented more money than the average Israeli earns in a year, and as I spoke about the current political situation, I found myself growing frustrated and angry at the smugness and comfort of these fans. I felt resentment at being a part of what amounted to a plea for help, and only a certainty that it would do no good kept me from telling them why. I sat down to mild applause, disgusted with myself for participating in the whole thing.

Following my speech, a local doctor who was in charge of the fund raising got up. "The other day," he told his audience, "I was rummaging through my attic, and I found this." He held up a dog-eared, yellowed pamphlet, which he said was the yearbook of the Philadelphia Jewish community from 1916. He opened it at random. "Al Stein (or some such name)," he called out, "did you ever live at 1511 Spring Street?"

"My grandfather Max lived there," said the surprised Stein.

"Well, in 1916 your grandfather gave two dollars and eleven cents to the community. Harry Gottleib, did you ever live at 603 Pine?"

One by one the doctor read off names and addresses and the contributions of fathers and grandfathers. The sums sounded ridiculous—ninety-two cents, three dollars and six cents, a dollar nineteen—and the audience laughed and joshed each other about them. People began calling out names, asking to hear what their own families had given. After a few minutes, the doctor paused.

"Do you know what these sums mean? Just think back on how poor your folks were in those days. And then, one day someone came to them and said, 'We need a contribution for other Jews, who are even poorer than you are.' And what did your grandfather do? He didn't ask about a tax exemption, or demand a plaque. He reached into his pockets and took out all the money he had and put it on the table. Ninety-two cents, if that was what he had, or a dollar nineteen."

There was a hush in the room, and the doctor paused dramatically. "I'm not going to tell you what to give here tonight," he said, "but I can tell you one thing. Fifty years from now someone will be standing on this dais with a book of the community from 1982. Your grandchildren will be sitting in the audience. And what you do now will determine how they feel then."

There was a long silence, and then the room broke into a frenzy of shouted contributions. I sat at the dais, as moved as anyone in the room by the picture of communal solidarity that the doctor had evoked. It was a rare glimpse of the inner dynamic of Jewish continuity, and one that most Israelis would never see.

A few months later I was visiting Rachel's Tomb, near Bethlehem, when a tour bus full of American Jews arrived. They were straight out of Central Casting, dressed in bermudas and sports shirts with little alligators over the pockets, weighted down by expensive cameras and souvenirs of the Holy Land. As they crowded into the tiny building that houses the tomb, an old Yemenite Jew dressed in a dirty robe and wearing long side curls hung on the fringe of the group. He held out his hand, palm up, in the universal posture of supplication, mumbling Hebrew psalms as he approached one of the tourists. "Beat it," the American said roughly. "I'm not giving any money to an Arab."

"He's not an Arab," the tour guide explained. "He's a Jew."

"What?" the American said in disbelief. "What kind of a Jew?"

"A Yemenite," said the guide. "He's asking for a contribution to charity."

"Come 'ere, you old *shnorrer*," the tourist said, suddenly expansive. He pulled a dollar bill out of his wallet and put it in the ancient's hand. "Keep the change, you old *gonif*," he said with a wink, in the tone of a man paying off a gin rummy debt in a country-club locker room. The Yemenite mumbled a blessing and walked away, uncomprehending.

As time goes by, the diaspora and Israeli Jews understand each other less and less. Thirty years ago they spoke a common language—Yiddish—and shared Eastern European origins. Today, when Sephardic Jews make up more than half of Israel's population and Jews in the United States and Europe have become increasingly assimilated, the gulf is wide and getting wider. Even sabras from European backgrounds find the connection with the diaspora mysterious. Recently two American Jewish activists came to visit, and we sat in my living room discussing the prospects for *aliyah* from the United States. My wife Miri, whose parents emigrated from Germany in the thirties, listened silently to the conversation. Finally, one of the Americans turned to her. "What do you think Israel should do to attract immigrants?" he asked.

Miri looked surprised, and with typical Israeli directness she replied, "Nothing."

"Nothing?" said the American. "If you don't do anything, people will never come."

"So what?" said Miri, closing the discussion.

Miri's attitude is not atypical of the young generation of Israelis, who have long since given up hope of large-scale immigration from the West. To them, Israel is a country, not a concept, and although she has nothing against American immigrants (she married one, after all), she has no special interest in recruiting them.

The failure of Israel to attract the bulk of Western Jewry, and the slowly dwindling common ground between Israelis and the diaspora, are an outgrowth of the development of both communities, reflecting the fact that in the last twenty years a new generation of Israelis, born and raised in the country, has become a majority. It is no longer unusual to find army units or high school classes where virtually everyone is a sabra, and although sabras are not the heroic figures of Leon Uris's fantasies, nor the New Jewish Men and Women of the pioneer blueprint, they form an increasingly distinct and separate group. Often, despite ethnic, religious and cultural differences, they have more in common with one another than with their cousins in the diaspora, and, barring some unforeseen development, this gap will continue to grow in the future.

Israelis are still too diverse, and Israeli society still too complex, for easy generalizations about the nature of the country and its people. But one thing is clear: Israelis are in the process of becoming an identifiably different kind of Jew, one that reflects the special circumstances of their lives. Some of these influences are obvious: the lingering traces of Labor Zionist ideology, the pressures of an endless war with the Arab world, the cross-fertilization of the various tribes who have regrouped in the homeland, and the constraints of life in a small, crowded country. But beyond anything else, Israelis are the first Jews in two thousand years to live their lives without the dominating influence of Gentile society. It is this fact, far more than any utopian master plan, that makes Israel such an experimental and exciting place. Almost forty years after its birth, it is still in the process of becoming, of evolving into a true expression of the fears and hopes and capacities of its people; an expression of what Jews are like when Jews are on their own.

PART IV

A GOOD COUNTRY IN A BAD NEIGHBORHOOD

12

"A Light Unto the Nations"

On a chilly April afternoon in 1979, I flew down to Um Hashiba, in the Sinai, to attend an historic ceremony—the exchange of the Articles of Peace between Egypt and Israel. Um Hashiba is a desolate desert mountaintop. Once a secret Israeli military installation, it was converted into an American base for monitoring the Egyptian-Israeli deployment in the Sinai after the Yom Kippur War, and like all U.S. installations, it took on something of the Midwest, even in this distant setting. The compound consisted of prefab buildings which, on close inspection, turned out to be copies—in design and interior decoration—of a Holiday Inn. There were even soda machines in the halls, and Magic Fingers compatible beds in the spacious living quarters. All that was missing was a marquee: WELCOME ISRAELI AND EGYPTIAN DELEGATES—TRY OUR WEDNESDAY TURKEY SPECIAL, ALL YOU CAN EAT FOR $2.99.

The ceremony itself featured the first joint parade by Israeli and Egyptian troops, and the soldiers of the two erstwhile enemies lined up shoulder to shoulder on the compound's parade ground while the delegates huddled in one of the rooms for a last-minute conference. The Egyptian soldiers belonged to a special ceremonial unit, and they were magnificent: tall, bronze-colored men dressed in spotless black uniforms and white gloves, standing at rigid and seemingly endless attention.

At the end of their line came the Israeli contingent. The Israeli Army places an extremely low priority on military ceremony, and it chooses its representatives on such occasions the same way it selects the armored corps male glee club—at random. Juxtaposed, the two units made a striking contrast. The Israelis were, almost without exception, nearly a head shorter than the Egyptians, and their uniforms were dusty and mismatched, baggy around the knee and drooping in the crotch.

As the delay lengthened, the Israelis became fidgety, shifting rifles for comfort, pushing back glasses with a middle finger, whispering to each other out of the sides of their mouths. The overall impression was of a group of schoolboys playing soldier next to a row of statues.

After a few minutes one of the Israeli officers came over to where I was standing with the assembled journalists. "When are we going to get started here?" he asked. I couldn't tell him, and the two of us stood gazing at the assembled troops. Suddenly the young captain turned to me with a smile on his face. "How did we ever beat these guys?" he said softly. "How do we do it?"

There is probably no society on the face of the earth that asks as many questions about itself as Israel does. More than one hundred years after the first pioneers set foot in Palestine, almost four decades into statehood, Israelis remain unable to take their country or themselves for granted. The debate rages in the press, in classrooms, in army tents and at Friday night get-togethers—who are we and what are we doing here? What kind of country are we building? Should we build? In many ways, in its late thirties Israel is still a nation that doesn't know what it wants to be when it grows up.

Alongside the confusion about what should be is a deep dissatisfaction with what is. The early Zionists, with their utopianism or messianism, set inaccessible goals—goals that a great many Israelis took seriously. And who could blame them, after all, given Israel's almost mythological biography? For two thousand years Jews dreamed sweet dreams of life under their own rule in the ancestral homeland. And suddenly, in a breathtaking rush of history, that dream came true. Not merely a state, but a Hebrew nation in the Land of the Bible. Not just a society, but a workers' paradise in which human dust from a hundred diasporas would come together to be rehabilitated and made healthy and whole. Not simply another democracy, but a veritable Light Unto the Nations. At its inception, and for years afterward, Israelis lived in the present tense, but they thought and dreamed in future perfect.

Of course this kind of idealism is a prescription for eventual disillusionment. For years it blinded people to the imperfections of Israel, which were lost in clouds of euphoria and patriotism. During the Era of High Certitude, which reached its apogee during the Six Day War, many believed that the dream might actually come true, that Israel was on the way to becoming a heroic, model society.

And then came the Yom Kippur War, and suddenly Israel was plunged into a dark depression, a mood that has stayed with the country to one degree or another ever since. Self-doubt replaced certitude; criticism, long muted, became strident and harsh. The Glorious Fathers and their Golden Sons were revealed as simply Jews, some competent and wise, others foolish and weak and even corrupt. Almost overnight, Israel was transformed from a land of answers to one of anguished questions.

Ironically, the sense of unfulfilled promise at the heart of that anguish has been sharpened by the very successes of Jewish nationalism. Hebrew has been revitalized, and there are millions who speak it—and now know that it is possible to be as banal in that language as in any other. Jews have become farmers and factory workers—and in the process have discovered that farm work means manure and marketing, and industry involves strikes and dirty fingernails. The exiles have been brought together, but the romance of reunion has given way to the strain of accommodating so many different outlooks and cultures in a tiny land. Jews have learned to be soldiers, but they have also learned that soldiering can be a dreary and sometimes ugly endeavor. There is, after two millennia, a national parliament in Jerusalem—filled with mediocrities who cut deals in smoke-filled rooms. A Jewish state has come into being, an ancient dream come true, but no one really anticipated the hostile Arabs who surround it, or the enemies, from Khomeini to the Soviet Union, who continue to harass it. The Yom Kippur War was many things to many people, but most of all it was the moment when Israel began to grow up and to realize that it was a real country with the flaws and weaknesses of real countries everywhere.

This realization has been a shattering one for many Israelis, particularly opinion makers on the left and right. Day by day they fill the papers and the airwaves with the most alarming assessments of the national character and future. Once upon a time, their lament goes, Israel was a beautiful place, a shining city on a hill, full of ideals and self-sacrifice. Today, it has degenerated into a selfish and immoral society on the brink of catastrophe or collapse. Rabbis decry its "Hellenism" and lack of Jewish values; secularists warn of messianism and theocracy. Hawks deplore the lack of pioneer spirit and the defeatism of the doves; doves warn of the dangers of militarism. Polls are published showing that a large number of young people have little commitment to democracy, and these polls are used to prove that Israel is on the brink of becoming a dictatorship. Commentators point to Israelis living abroad, or foreign Jews who decline to come, as evidence that Israel is an unattractive and repulsive place. Professors criticize the erosion of the work ethic, and sound alarms about the imminent disintegration of the national economy. The only debate seems to be which of these disasters will overtake Israel first. It is treated as axiomatic by many critics that Israel is in decline, that it has changed for the worse over the past decade and a half.

A few years ago Arik Einstein, one of Israel's leading singers, recorded a song that perfectly expressed a gloomy dissatisfaction about an Israel where everything was better before he arrived. The song is at once bitter and wistful, a paean to the great era of pioneering when things were simple, before the idealism of the early Zionists crashed on the rocks of reality. It is a gentle song with a harsh message—that somehow things have gone wrong; the great promise has been betrayed.

What is most striking about this view is the discrepancy between what it assumes and what has actually happened in Israel over the past twenty years or so. The country I came to in

1967 was in many ways an admirable place, and certainly one with a command of admirable rhetoric, but it was hardly the Eden many Israelis recall it as having been. And if it has changed a great deal from its early period, many of those changes seem to me to be for the good, at least in terms of the Western secular, liberal values I brought with me from Pontiac, Michigan.

To begin with the obvious, Israel has gone from an essentially one-party state, in which elections were simply a process of ratification, to a genuine multiparty system in which politics is a vehicle for change. Democracy in Israel got its first serious test in 1977, when Labor handed over the government to the Likud; and again in 1984, when the Likud returned control to Labor. Both parties now know that there is an electoral price for incompetence, and just as important, the public has shown that it will not hesitate to impose it.

Over the past decade, power in Israel has passed from a small, centralized elite to what can fairly be called, in that grand old sixties phrase, "the people." Naturally there are members of the old elite, including journalists and intellectuals, who feel that the people aren't quite ready to get along without their leadership; but the fact is that they are now unable to impose this leadership on others—an index of how far Israel has come since the days of Mapai's Great Israeli-Making Machine.

With the decline of the elite, Israel has become not only more democratic but also more pluralistic. The definition of who is an Israeli has expanded from one type to many, and there is a great deal more tolerance of cultures and customs that don't come from within a fifty-mile radius of Minsk. During the past decade the Oriental Jews have made almost unbelievable progress in becoming an integral part of society. In 1971 the Black Panthers shocked the establishment with their inflammatory rhetoric. Today, Sephardim make up a large part of that establishment: two Deputy Prime Ministers, half a dozen Cabinet ministers, the chief of staff of the army, the head of the Histadrut Labor Federation, and a great many senior civil servants, diplomats and wealthy businessmen.

Even more important, an increasingly large number of ordinary Oriental Jews feel they are no longer outsiders.

There are still ethnic divisions in Israel, of course, and there will be for some time. On the Sephardi side there are activists who fan the embers of old resentments, just as on the Ashkenazi side there are Ethnic Purity diehards who see the rise of the Sephardim as synonymous with social decay. But in truth, the tensions that have accompanied the integration of Sephardim into Israeli life have been remarkably mild. More important, such tensions are a sign of national health, the inevitable by-product of any successful struggle for acceptance and equality.

In recent years Israel has become a far more open society than it was during its first two decades. There was a time when David Ben Gurion used the Shin Bet—the Israeli secret service—to spy on his political opponents, including his fellow Labor Zionists. For a long period senior civil service and army posts were available only to those with the right party affiliations and voting records, and a large part of the population was excluded from positions of authority and responsibility on political grounds. Those days are long gone, however; and if abuses of power and patronage still exist, they are no longer built into the system.

Over the years, freedom of the press has also flourished. Until 1965 the government ran the national radio directly out of the Prime Minister's Office, and the establishment refused to allow the introduction of television until 1968. Today, both TV and radio are run by a public, BBC-type authority, and while they are not completely free of government efforts to influence them, they are usually critical and reliable in their news coverage. The onetime steady diet of morale-building broadcasts, pioneer music and public-service announcements has been replaced by adversarial interview programs and talk shows on which politicians are no longer accorded the kid-gloves treatment they received in the fifties and sixties.

Newspapers have become more reliable too. On the eve of the 1973 war, a number of military correspondents, aware of the possibility of an Arab sneak attack, censored themselves at the request of the army. Many of these reporters never forgave themselves for this dereliction of duty, and the tone of reporting in Israel since the war has been far more skeptical and aggressive. Moreover, in recent years the number of newspapers and magazines has grown in Israel, and they provide the public with a more critical and honest view of the country than was available before the mid-seventies.

This view often creates the impression that Israel is less ethical or enlightened than it once was. In fact, "bad news" is simply more available today, and Israelis more aware of it. In 1953, for example, the government ordered a reprisal raid on the Jordanian village of Kibiyah. The raid, which was in retaliation for Arab terrorism, ended in tragedy when dozens of Arab civilians were killed in what Arik Sharon, the commander of the operation, later called a mistake. But at the time, Prime Minister David Ben Gurion simply lied to the country and the Knesset, claiming that the raid had been carried out not by the army but by a group of enraged Israeli villagers. This transparent nonsense was accepted by the parliamentary opposition as well as by the press, and most of the country had no idea what had actually happened.

An incident like Kibiyah could happen again today. Israel is, as it was then, in a state of war with much of the Arab world, and in wartime such things occasionally take place. But it is wholly impossible that an Israeli Prime Minister could get away with lying about it to the country, and it is doubtful that one would try. The massacre at the Sabra and Shatilla refugee camps, which was carried out by Lebanese Christians, and for which Israel bore only an indirect and unintended responsibility, resulted in mass demonstrations and a commission of inquiry. More recently, the killing of two captured terrorists by the Israeli Army was exposed by the local press, despite government efforts to hush up the affair. Many Israelis, recalling the absence of such reports in earlier times, mistakenly conclude that incidents of this kind didn't take place in the good old days; but those who were involved in security affairs know better. In the Israel of the eighties, information is no longer the province of a few trusted insiders.

One of the main arguments for Israel's presumed decline is the growth of orthodox influence—and religious coercion— that is supposed to have taken place in recent years. To make this point, however, means to ignore history. The central elements of orthodoxy in Israeli life were all put into place in the late forties and early fifties. The Chief Rabbinate and its control of personal status through religious courts; the separate orthodox school system; military exemptions for yeshiva students and religious girls; sabbath and holiday blue laws; the tradition of buying off religious parties; and rabbinical involvement in Israeli citizenship laws have all been features of Israeli life from the very beginning. The gains that the orthodox agenda has made in recent years have, in fact, been marginal and largely symbolic. The law against El Al flights on the sabbath, for example, is now enforced, but a number of other airlines still fly in and out of Israel on Saturdays and holidays. It is more difficult to get an abortion than it once was, but still not very hard. For the average Israeli, the degree of outside religious interference in daily life is no more or less than it was twenty-five or thirty years ago.

What has changed is the public perception. Orthodox Jews, like Sephardim and others outside the pioneer orbit, are more visible today and more self-confident. In Jerusalem, this self-assurance is sometimes translated into acts of ultra-orthodox extremism; but it is equally true that in Tel Aviv, the country's largest city, an opposite trend toward secularization has been in evidence for a decade or more.

Many oldtime Israelis deplore the decline in the quality of life, but I must admit that I don't share this view. As Israel has become a modern, industrialized country—and its population has risen from 650,000 to 4 million in less than forty years—a good deal of intimacy has been lost. Moreover, the elite no longer controls the nation's culture, entertainment and tastes. This is, of course, a great loss for the veterans, but not necessarily for the rest of us.

Naturally, modernization has not been an unmixed blessing. There is, for example, more crime in Israel today than there once was (although cities remain, by American standards, extremely safe).

But there are also better restaurants, newer films, bigger and more comfortable apartments, far more automobiles, a greater variety of music, theater and art, more universities, better sports facilities, more efficient public services—and more tolerance of nonconformity. In short, Israel has made the same trade-off that other modern societies have made. Many Israelis deplore the materialism, fast-buck mentality and selfishness that have replaced the old pioneer austerity, but not many would want to go back to the good old days.

Few would deny that Israel is more democratic, open, sophisticated, efficient and, for all its economic difficulties, prosperous than it once was. But despite these changes, many Israelis remain depressed about its loss of innocence. Their attitude is reminiscent of the nostalgia that many white middle-class Americans feel for the *Ozzie and Harriet* days of the mid-fifties. These were the good old days in suburbia, but the problem was that most Americans didn't live there. In a similar way, the Israeli elite—which is that articulate, sophisticated segment of society to which foreigners listen—longs for the happy days of the fifties and sixties, forgetting that they were far from happy for a majority of their fellow citizens, or for the country as a whole.

To admit that Israel is, in most ways, a better, more mature country than it once was in no way denigrates the achievements of the founding fathers. They confronted an almost impossible set of challenges, and if they made mistakes, the mistakes were, by and large, made for commendable reasons. The regime Ben Gurion established was highly centralized, paternalistic and intolerant, but it was, at bottom, democratic—a claim that few other postwar nation-builders can make.

Nor is it fair to attribute the liberalization of Israeli society primarily to Menachem Begin. Many of the abuses of the early years—such as the misuse of the secret service and state broadcasting media, the military government that controlled Israel's Arabs until the mid-sixties or the Mapai vendetta against Herut and its supporters—were corrected by Ben Gurion's successor, Levi Eshkol, a vastly underrated Prime Minister. Other excesses simply disappeared with time, as Israel developed and matured. It is likely, for example, that the absorption of the Sephardi masses into the national mainstream would have occurred, out of sheer demographic weight, sooner or later. Similarly, the growth of the Israeli middle class, the rapid rise in the standard of living and the trend toward decentralization of state power would all have come whether or not Menachem Begin had been elected in 1977. It is unfair to attribute these changes to the Likud, but it is idle to deny that they have taken place and that, on the whole, they have made Israel a better place to live for most of its citizens.

And yet, despite all of the achievements and progress of recent years, Israelis continue to regard their country and themselves with disappointment, even suspicion. What about the *spirit* of the country, its ideals and sense of mission? This question arises in various contexts, but it is most frequently directed to the single most pervasive question of Israel's public life: the generations-long confrontation with the Arab world, and especially the Palestinians.

When I arrived in Israel, during the Era of High Certitude, everything was clear. Israel was a peace-loving David whose victory over the Arab Goliath was a triumph of right over might. The war left Israel in control of large areas previously under Arab rule—the West Bank, Gaza, the Sinai and Golan Heights—which were to be returned shortly (with certain territorial adjustments) in exchange for peace.

Few doubted that peace was at hand. Moshe Dayan announced that he was "waiting for a phone call" from Jordan's King Hussein. The implication was clear—Israel could afford to be gracious and generous; time was on its side.

It didn't quite work out that way. Following the Six Day War the Arab Summit meeting in Khartoum issued its famous "three no's": no negotiations, no recognition and no peace. The PLO established a terror base in Jordan, the Egyptians opened a war of attrition across the Suez Canal, and the Arabs in the occupied territories carried out acts of violence against Israeli civilians. But despite these disappointments it was widely believed that the Arabs would eventually come to their senses and that when they did, Israel should trade occupied territories for peace.

In fact, many thought that the temporary occupation of the West Bank and Gaza would have a positive impact on Arab-Jewish relations. Shortly after joining the army in 1970, I was assigned to the staff of the military government of the West Bank. My commanding officer was Major Rafi, an almost stereotypical sabra son. Jerusalem-born, he served in the elite Palmach during the War of Independence and was one of the Israelis taken prisoner by the Jordanians at the fall of Gush Etzion in 1948.

Rafi spent a year in a Jordanian prison camp, and later he fought in the 1956 and 1967 wars. Like most Real Israelis he had a casual contempt for the "Arab mentality" and a hard-line view of Israel's security interests. But he was also a man of uncommon good nature and he tended to like Arabs as individuals. It was through him that I first saw the conflicts inherent in the Real Israeli's view of our neighbors.

In those days official Israeli doctrine declared that no such thing as "Palestinians" existed. The people in the West Bank were simply Arabs, and as such they were perceived as backward, prone to incitement and violence, incompetent (bad craftsmanship was always called "Arab work") and primitive. At the same time, they had a charming folklore and a warm-hearted hospitality that made them picturesque and almost attractive.

After the Six Day War, tens of thousands of West Bank Arabs were caught outside the area—students who had been away at school, fathers who had been working in other Arab countries and so forth. Israeli policy was to allow them to return, and it was our unit's task to administer this program, known as Family Reunion. Every week we received dozens of applications for repatriation which were discussed at a weekly interministerial meeting. There, Rafi was transformed from an Israeli military man and Arab fighter into an advocate of Arab rights. He presented each case as if it involved a member of his own family, often reminding his fellow committee members of the conventional wisdom of the day—Israel did not intend to stay in the West Bank, and a humane occupation was our chance to forge links with the people there. Israelis believed that to know them would be to love them. Arab hatred of Israel was supposedly a function of simple ignorance; exposure to Israel would correct it. Rafi put the goal succinctly: Israeli behavior toward the Arabs should be aimed at winning us "the Nobel Prize for military occupation."

Of course there were other approaches, even then. A small group of Israelis, mostly orthodox, demanded the right to live in the West Bank city of Hebron, the burial site of the Biblical patriarchs; and in 1970 they were allowed to establish a settlement nearby known as Kiriat Arba. The sons and daughters of the settlers who had been massacred at Gush Etzion in 1948 were allowed to return to the area, also near Hebron, to reestablish their family homes. And Israel began putting up border villages along the Jordan River. But none of this gave any great cause for concern. After all, any peace agreement with Jordan would mean territorial compromise, and the Jordanians, it was generally believed, would be willing to show flexibility on the question of Hebron, the Jordan Valley and, of course, Jerusalem, which was annexed to Israel only a couple of weeks after the Six Day War.

The 1973 war, which changed so much in Israel, permanently altered the Israeli attitude toward the Arabs in general—and the Palestinians of the West Bank in particular. Suddenly the Arab world was no longer a collection of laughable tin-pot dictators and cowardly soldiers who, according to legend, were afraid of the dark and kicked their boots off to escape through the sand at the merest approach of the Israeli Army. Moreover, the Arabs now appeared to be a formidable political and economic power by virtue of their dreaded "oil weapon." For the first time, Israel began to question whether time was indeed on its side.

The Yom Kippur War also put the Palestinian issue at the top of the Middle East agenda. The 1974 Arab Summit meeting in Rabat declared the PLO—a terrorist organization with a charter calling for Israel's destruction—to be the sole representative of the Palestinian people. This meant that the million Arabs of the West Bank and Gaza, whom Israel had hoped to impress with its liberality and humane generosity, were now "supporters" of an organization dedicated to its destruction.

This assumption was confirmed by the 1976 municipal elections in the West Bank. Four years earlier, Israel had proudly permitted the area's residents to elect their own mayors and city councils, as an exercise in democracy; and most of the winners had been members of the old-line, pro-Jordanian aristocracy. Now, in 1976, the royalists were defeated by a new generation of pro-PLO candidates who made no secret of their allegiance. They opposed a return of the West Bank to Jordan, were ungrateful for the prosperity that Israeli occupation had brought to the region and unimpressed by Israel's efforts to "win the Nobel Prize." As Palestinian nationalists they wanted a state in the West Bank, a state their leaders in Beirut openly declared would be the first step in the eventual replacement of Israel by a "democratic, secular Arab Palestine."

The 1973 war also unleashed Gush Emunim, a Jewish movement that was, in many ways, a mirror image of the new Palestinian leadership. Like the Palestinians the supporters of Gush Emunim believed that the entire area—from the Mediterranean to the Jordan River—was a single territorial and political unit. They, too, opposed redividing it; instead, they demanded that Israel annex the West Bank and Gaza.

The Gush Emunim activists were modern orthodox men and women who had grown up in the fifties and early sixties on the periphery of the Real Israel. During the Era of High Certitude their views hadn't counted, but in the general breakdown of confidence that followed the war, they were able to exploit the weakness and hesitation of the Rabin government to begin "establishing facts" in the West Bank. They set up settlements without government approval, dragging the irresolute politicians of the Labor party behind them.

One of Prime Minister-elect Menachem Begin's first acts was to visit one of the Gush settlements, where he danced with the pioneers, holding a Torah scroll aloft, and proclaimed that, under his government, such settlements would receive government support. And during the next seven years Begin encouraged Jews to move to the area. At Camp David he agreed to autonomy for the Arab residents, an agreement that foreclosed, at least temporarily, his ultimate goal of formal annexation; but he sought to create conditions under which the West Bank and Gaza could never fall under Arab control.

It was this resolve, more than any other single issue, that split the Israeli public, and continues to do so until today. Supporters of the Begin view come not only from the zealots of Gush Emunim—never a mass movement—but from an increasingly large proportion of the general population. Some have been convinced by ideology and logic. Begin argued that since Zionism's original claim on Palestine was based on the Jews' right to return to their Biblical homeland, any decision to surrender Hebron, Jericho or Bethlehem would ultimately undermine the logic and legitimacy of Israeli sovereignty over Tel Aviv, the Negev or the Galilee.

There are also those who favor keeping the West Bank and Gaza for economic reasons. Thousands of young Israeli families have bought subsidized government apartments—"only fifteen minutes from downtown Tel Aviv," as the ads proclaim. And many businesses in Israel are dependent on Arab labor. These factors have created a powerful nonideological lobby for the status quo.

By far the largest number of hawks are convinced by the security argument. The West Bank is, after all, not geographically separated from the rest of Israel. During the days of Jordanian control it was frequently the staging ground for sniping or terrorist raids into Israel—and from its hills, Jerusalem and Tel Aviv are within artillery or even rifle range. What, many wonder, would happen if the West Bank became a radical, Soviet-armed Palestinian State.

Opponents of annexation have questions of their own. How, they demand, can Israel continue to be a Jewish state if it absorbs the million Arabs of the West Bank and Gaza? What impact will prolonged military occupation have on the democratic nature of the state and on the morality of the young soldiers sent to occupy the area? And, at an even deeper level, what will the consequences be for peace? The Arabs, these Israeli doves maintain, can never agree to an Israeli annexation of the region, and keeping it would ensure a state of permanent war with the Palestinians.

Throughout the late seventies and early eighties, political and emotional battle lines were drawn over the question of the future of the West Bank. Typically, the debate is rich in paradox and overlaid with the emotional and temperamental contradictions of the Israeli experience.

The Israeli left, for example, represented most eloquently by the Peace Now movement, finds itself in the anomalous position of arguing a classic rightist position—that Israel must be a Jewish state, without a significant non-Jewish minority;

while the right, most vocally represented by Gush Emunim, insists that Jews and Arabs can live in peaceful coexistence and that a significant Arab minority would not endanger the Jewish nature of the country.

There is paradox, too, in the right's adoption of the settlement techniques of the labor movement, and its frequent invocation of the Labor Zionist past—when the displacing of Arabs through peaceful means was considered not only necessary but morally justifiable. Today's West Bank activists are far more likely to quote Ben Gurion or Berl Katznelson than Menachem Begin's mentor, Ze'ev Jabotinsky.

Naturally, the debate does not take place in a vacuum. For eighty years Zionists have been torn between two conflicting impulses in the face of Arab hostility: to seek to accommodate it through compromise, as Ben Gurion did when he accepted the 1947 UN Partition Plan (a plan whose rejection by the Arabs brought on the War of Independence), or to outlast it by erecting what Jabotinsky called "a wall of steel." In the self-confident years before the Yom Kippur War, the nation's mood was inclined toward the former; but since 1973, Israelis have been increasingly dubious about Arab intentions and less willing to take risks.

Another paradox is that peace with Egypt seemingly strengthened the logic of both camps. Optimistic "rationalists" point out that Sadat's initiative demonstrates that peace is possible, and that territorial concessions (in the Sinai) brought it about. But the pessimists are quick to answer that the settlement with Egypt is a disappointment. Not only has it made the radical Arabs even more radical, but it has failed to lead to anything more than a cold and suspicious relationship.

At the deepest level, the dividing line is a temperamental one. Optimists like Ezer Weizman argue that the *Israelis* are destined to remain in the Middle East permanently, and that theirs is a powerful nation fully capable of taking care of itself in the rough-and-tumble of Middle Eastern diplomacy. On the other side, pessimists, like Ariel Sharon, have maintained that the *Jews* are not like other nations and that, quite apart from the Arab character, Jews must learn history's lesson: that they can expect the worst and can depend only on their own military strength.

Over the past decade Israel has become, paradoxically, both more hawkish and more dovish. Gush Emunim has emerged, but so has Peace Now. Israel has built settlements in the West Bank, and torn them down in Sinai. The almost constant battle with the Arab world has left people exhausted and frustrated, and it is not surprising that a great many have retreated into inflexible positions that make further thought unnecessary. But an even larger number of Israelis remain torn by the dilemma of the West Bank's future and, in broader terms, about the appropriate response to the continued hostility of the Arabs. The Sadat initiative demonstrated that this middle group can be galvanized by dramatic evidence of Arab moderation; the initial enthusiasm that greeted the war in Lebanon showed that it can be mobilized to support hard-line policies aimed at combating Arab hostility. And the widespread disappointment with the results of both—the peace with Egypt and the war in Lebanon—have only added to the confusion. The truth is that most Israelis are two people, capable of believing both that "the whole world is against us" and that "we're just like everyone else," i.e., that we are both "Jews" and "Israelis."

This dichotomy is not new, of course; back in the sixties, Prime Minister Levi Eshkol used to refer to it as the *"Shimshon der nebedicher"* complex—poor little Samson. But in those days, when the government and the party thought for everyone, the problem wasn't nearly so acute. Today, with no founding fathers left, people are forced to think for themselves.

For most Israelis—even nonpolitical ones—it is a confusing and highly personal problem. It surfaces not only in the national debate but in the course of daily decisions—where to buy an apartment, what to tell your children, how to approach your annual reserve duty. At these moments, many Israelis conduct internal dialogues that go something like this:

Should we keep the West Bank?
Damn right. It's right outside the window here. Imagine what life would be like if the Arabs had an army within spitting distance of this living room.
In other words, you are against a Palestinian State?

A Palestinian State in the West Bank? Of course I'm against it. And I don't want the Jordanian Army there, either.

Then we are going to wind up ruling a million Arabs permanently. Is that what you want?

Certainly not. We didn't establish Israel in order to turn it into a binational state, or to rule people against their will.

Well, do you imagine that the Arabs out there will ask to remain under Israeli control?

No, I know they won't.

So how will you rule them? Under a permanent military government?

No, if we keep the West Bank, we'll have to offer them citizenship and give them the vote.

At which point they'll begin undermining the Jewish nature of the state. Won't they?

Not necessarily. Maybe they'll decide they don't want Israeli citizenship. Or maybe a million Jews will move to Israel from the USSR, and maintain the balance. Stranger things have happened.

Wishful thinking! Are you willing to risk the future on mysticism?

I'm not a mystic; I'm a Zionist. To be a realist here, you have to believe in miracles—remember?

Save that for the UJA. And stick to the point. You know damn well that a Jewish State can't absorb more Arabs, by definition. Besides, do you know of any example of Arabs living in a democracy? Majorities repress minorities, or minorities seize power, like in Syria, and repress the majority. And every border between two Arab states turns into a battle zone.

Wait a minute. I thought you were supposed to be the liberal. Besides, if every border turns into a battle zone, I'd be crazy to put a Palestinian border within spitting distance of my living room, wouldn't I?

Not if the alternative is turning the country into a police state to keep disenfranchised Arabs in line. Why not try peace for a change?

Because I'm afraid to, that's why.

What, afraid of peace?

No, afraid that after we return territory, the Arab world will use it to launch new attacks on us. Do you really believe that all the Palestinians want is the West Bank? The real problem is that the Arab world doesn't want us here.

Maybe that's true. But if you don't take chances, there will never be peace. And taking chances means making concessions. If you keep the territory, the Arabs won't launch attacks?

They probably will. They always have. But at least this way, the attacks don't start within spitting distance of my living room.

Then why not annex the West Bank and be done with it?

Because I don't want all those Arabs living in Israel, damn it. And even if we do it, no one will accept the annexation, anyway.

So, in other words, you are against annexation?

Right.

But you're also against giving the territory to the PLO?

Right.

And you don't want to go on ruling the area under a military government?

Right again.

So what's the best thing to do?

Damned if I know.

Well, what about a territorial compromise with Jordan?

Forget it. King Hussein has rejected that for the past twenty years.

How about autonomy?

You mean, like the United States and Puerto Rico? That would be all right with me. But the Palestinians will never accept it.

So Jordan won't accept a compromise, and the Palestinians won't accept autonomy. And you don't want to annex it, and you're afraid to give it all back. What's left?

Let's watch the basketball game on television.

There are thousands of Israelis who replay this scene in their heads every day, although they are more likely to be people my age, in their late thirties or early forties, than those under thirty. An entire generation has grown up since the Six Day War, and for them the West Bank has always been a part of the country, and the Palestinians have always been the enemy.

Few of these young Israelis understand, much less speak, the high-flown ideological Beginese, or the mystical language of Gush Emunim. But a lifetime of conflict, the pressures of Arab animosity and the lessons of modern Jewish history have toughened and hardened them. Their attitude tends to be straightforward—fear and distrust and, increasingly, hatred of the enemy.

Militancy is nothing new to Israelis. But most people make a distinction—at least in public—between "the Arabs" and Arab individuals. "The Arabs" means the Arab states (or the PLO), Israel's declared enemies, and it is respectable, even popular to take a hard line against them. But it has been traditionally considered loutish to express hatred of Arabs as individuals, and the educational system has long tried to impress this on the country's youth.

Recently, however, there have been signs that this distinction is no longer completely clear. Polls taken in 1985, after a long series of terrorist murders, showed a growing, if still marginal, degree of support for Rabbi Meir Kahane, the Brooklyn-born racist who favors forced expulsion of the Arabs. Kahane was especially popular among people under twenty-one. Israeli public-opinion surveys are notoriously unreliable, and it is likely that they exaggerated the support for "Kahane-ism," as the rabbi's doctrine is known. But concern about its spread was sufficient to inspire the army's radio station to stage a marathon broadcast in mid-October 1985 on the dangers of racism.

The broadcast was probably unprecedented in the history of modern communications. For sixteen straight hours the radio station, which is run by the army but enjoys a mass audience, brought together politicians from every major party, mayors and members of Knesset, generals and labor leaders, football heroes and university professors, rabbis, movie stars and intellectuals to deliver a mass denunciation of Kahane and his program. Speaker after speaker emphasized a single message—the Arab governments and terror organizations are the enemy, not the Arabs of Israel or the West Bank. These Arabs, the participants all agreed, are our neighbors, and ways must be found to live together with them in peace and mutual respect.

It was a poignant program, made all the more so by the news bulletins broadcast at the top of every hour. There were reports on the funerals of Israeli campers, most of them children, who had been shot by an Egyptian soldier in the Sinai and left to bleed to death; on the hijacking of an Italian cruise ship by PLO terrorists (who later killed an American Jewish tourist and threw his body overboard); on the aftermath of the apprehension of five local Arabs who had murdered five Israelis and wounded twenty others because they wanted "to kill Jews"; on the casualty figures from Tunisia, where a policeman opened fire on a crowd of Jewish worshipers, killing four; and on two Israeli seamen who were tortured to death by Palestinians in Barcelona the previous evening. These frightening bulletins were a bizarre counterpoint to the message of moderation and tolerance of the marathon, a reminder of how hard it is to be a good country in a bad neighborhood.

Perhaps the most striking aspect of the army radio's broadcast was the fact that it approached the question of racism from a pragmatic point of view. Few of the participants spent much time denouncing Kahane-ism as sinful; they concentrated instead on its dangers for Israeli society. Some talked about Kahane's desire to abolish democracy and replace it with a Jewish theocracy; others concentrated on the threat of creating an Arab backlash and widespread civil disobedience. For a program of its kind, there was a notable lack of moralizing.

Many foreigners, who know Jews primarily through their diaspora neighbors, are accustomed to thinking of the country in religious, even spiritual terms, as if it were a gigantic synagogue. Israel does have a spiritual side, and the public can occasionally show a surprising moral sensitivity—as it did in the aftermath of the Sabra and Shatilla massacre in 1982. But on the whole, Israeli policy and behavior have been, and continue to be, determined primarily by the imperatives of national security, perceived self-interest, domestic politics and other pragmatic considerations—just as they are in every normal democratic society.

Which, despite its tortured collective biography, is precisely what Israel is in the process of becoming. In the course of writing this book I asked my daughter, Michal, now thirteen years old, to invite some of her friends over to talk about Israel. The kids, all eighth-graders in a nonreligious junior high school, were much amused by the notion that their opinions were worth putting into a book, but once the conversation began, they went at it with the usual Israeli competitiveness and intensity. We talked about relations between Sephardim and Ashkenazim (both groups were represented), and between orthodox and secular Jews with unsurprising results, the kids' ideas clearly reflecting the opinions of their parents.

I was mildly surprised to find that the kids' dominant attitude toward Arabs was fear, not hatred, but when it came to suggesting a solution to the conflict, their notions were no more original than those of their elders. We sat on my porch, looking over the Judaean Desert, eating chocolate chip cookies and drinking lemonade, and I had just about given up on eliciting any fascinating new insights. For no special reason I asked them what the phrase "A Light Unto the Nations" meant to them.

Suddenly the stream of articulate adolescent wisdom stopped, and all of them, including Michal, looked at me blankly. "I think it's something from the Bible," one of them ventured, and the others nodded.

"Okay," I said, "but what does it mean? What does it mean for you, personally?"

The kids looked at each other, embarrassed at not knowing the right answer. Clearly they had no idea of what I was getting at.

"You mean you never heard of the phrase 'A Light Unto the Nations'?" I said in exaggerated wonder. "Ben Gurion used it all the time."

"Oh, Ben Gurion," one of the boys said in relief. "We haven't got to him in school yet."

David Ben Gurion, who arrived in Palestine in 1906 along with other pioneers of the Second Aliyah, dreamed of creating a model society, a paradigm of social justice, Jewish unity and universal brotherhood. Those dreams have given way to something quite different—a modern, industrialized democracy; a state in which only a minority of the world's Jews have chosen to live; a nation haunted by demons that Ben Gurion, in 1906, could never have imagined; a society of long-separated tribes struggling toward cultural, religious and social equilibrium; a people at war with its neighbors and unsure, after two millennia of dependence on others, of how to conduct its own affairs.

But Ben Gurion and his comrades had a second dream, as well. They hoped to normalize the condition of the Jews, to turn them into *am k'chol ha'amim*, "a nation like any other." And in this they may well prove successful. Israelis are not the giants of contemporary fiction, nor the devils of Arab propaganda; neither Biblical heroes nor ethereal saints. Israelis are dock workers and labor leaders, like Yehoshua Peretz of Ashdod. They are insurance executives like Shimshi Cohen, the middle-class revolutionary with his shattered eardrum and Danish furniture. They are Avi Zaguri, the proprietor of La Belle, and Danny Sanderson, the rock star in a flak jacket. They are the lady on the bus in Haifa with the red toenails and the blue tattoo, Shaul Evron in search of satisfaction for his mouth, my wife Miri, who doesn't really care if the Jews move to Israel or not.

Israel is Menachem Begin in Oslo receiving the Nobel Prize for Peace—and Menachem Begin in Lebanon, lashing out at ghosts. It is the Jewish terrorists who attacked Arab civilians and the hard-eyed security men who caught them, the zealots of Gush Emunim and the rationalists of Peace Now. Israel is a country of idealists and clubhouse pols, of heroes and hustlers, hard hats and holy men.

Mostly, Israel is a country of ordinary people who get their kids off to school every morning and go to work, people who want security and prosperity and a little fun. Like everyone else they are confused by confusing situations, fear and dislike their enemies, have fine impulses and dark ones.

Today, more than ever, Israel is the sum of these people. For two thousand years, religion and communal solidarity and the world's hostility held the Jews together in the diaspora and shaped their national character, but in this century, Zionism has rendered a country out of prayers and poetry. Both religion and Zionist ideology worked from a blueprint, depended on leadership and authority, dreamed grandiose dreams for the Jewish people. These influences—religion and ideology—are still potent forces in Israel, but they no longer determine the shape of society or the direction of the country. They brought the Jews to the Land of Israel to rebuild an independent state; but in recent years that state has been increasingly taken over by its own people, and it is they who will determine what Israel will be when it finally grows up.